IMAGES
of America

AROUND TILTON

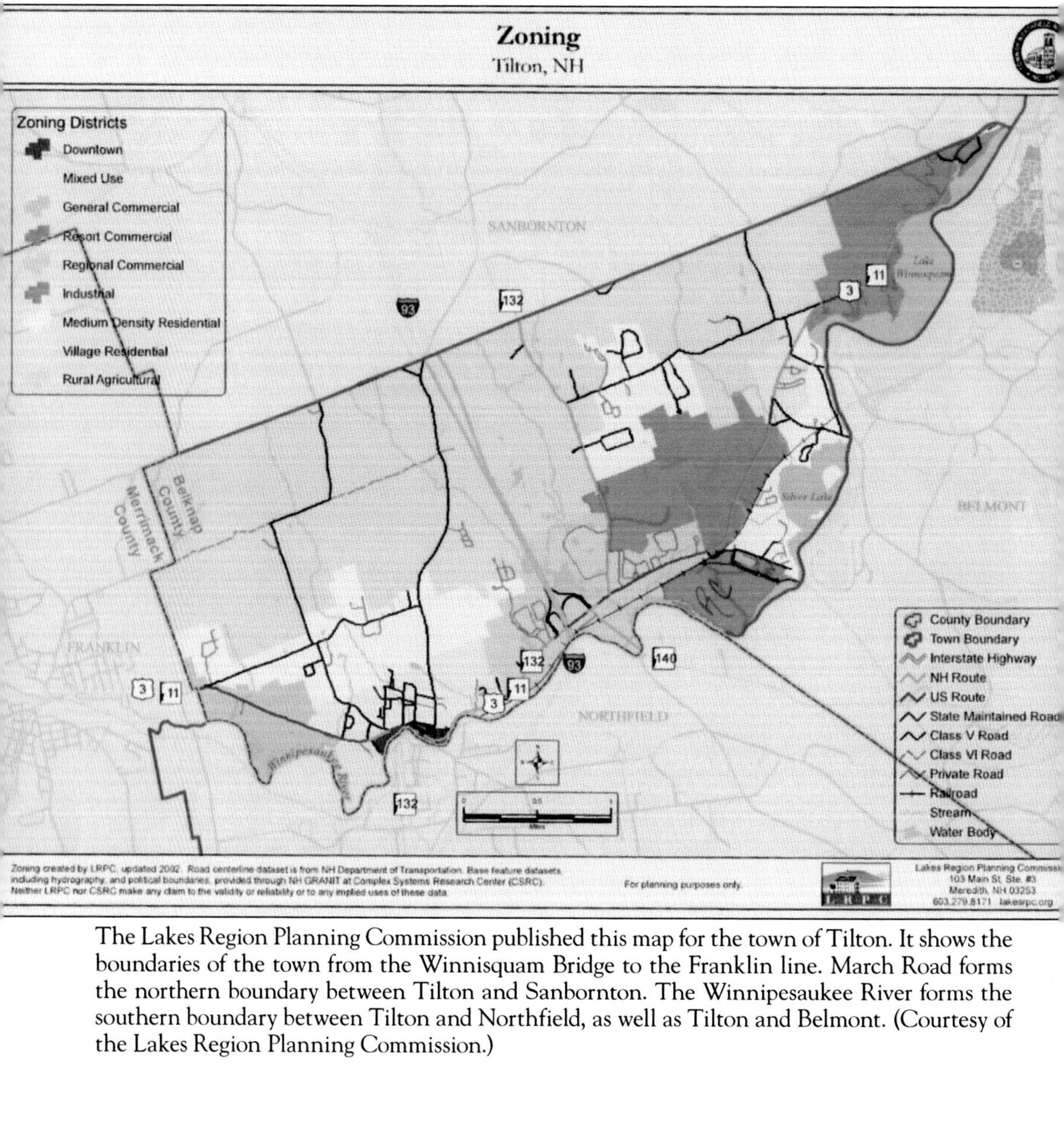

The Lakes Region Planning Commission published this map for the town of Tilton. It shows the boundaries of the town from the Winnisquam Bridge to the Franklin line. March Road forms the northern boundary between Tilton and Sanbornton. The Winnipesaukee River forms the southern boundary between Tilton and Northfield, as well as Tilton and Belmont. (Courtesy of the Lakes Region Planning Commission.)

On the Cover: Members of the Wyatt family gather hay on this Lancaster Hill farm around 1915. With wagons pulled by horses or mules, haying by hand was a long and tedious chore on hot, dry summer days. This family farm, then owned by Harry Clark Wyatt, the maternal grandfather of Karl Barnard, remains in the family today. (Courtesy of the Karl Barnard family.)

IMAGES
of America

AROUND TILTON

Bonnie Randall, Carol Stone,
and Dennis Evans

ARCADIA
PUBLISHING

ISBN 978-0-7385-9237-4

Published by Arcadia Publishing
Charleston, South Carolina

Printed in the United States of America

Library of Congress Control Number: 2011941927

For all general information, please contact Arcadia Publishing:
Telephone 843-853-2070
Fax 843-853-0044
E-mail sales@arcadiapublishing.com
For customer service and orders:
Toll-Free 1-888-313-2665

Visit us on the Internet at www.arcadiapublishing.com

To the people of Tilton,
past, present, and future

Contents

Acknowledgments		6
Introduction		7
1.	Our Tilton Legacy	9
2.	Agriculture and Early Times	27
3.	Business and Industry	47
4.	Community Life	79
5.	Learning and Faith	107

ACKNOWLEDGMENTS

We would like to give special thanks to director Mary Ahlgren and her staff at Hall Memorial Library for their assistance and access to the local history room where many of the enclosed photographs are archived. We also give thanks to the staff of Tilton Town Hall for their support, encouragement, and access to materials. We are very grateful to our proofreader, George Mansfield of Mansfield's Books and More, and to Ronald P. Mills Sr., EdD, for his expertise in antique automobile identification. Because this publication required the use of only high-resolution, archival photographs, and because the selection of available pictures was limited, many individuals and organizations worthy of inclusion in a history of Tilton will not be found in these pages. We wish to extend our sincere appreciation to all who have assisted us by loaning personal photographs, postcards, information, and memories. Space prevents us from mentioning all of you by name, so we offer a heartfelt thank-you. We could not have done this without you.

Introduction

Around Tilton will cover the years from 1850 to 1950, starting with the attempt to separate from Sanbornton, when Tilton was known as Sanbornton Bridge. Lochmere was sometimes called East Tilton, and a small area of land on Lake Winnisquam belonging to the town of Tilton was called Winnisquam.

The first action to form the town of Tilton was a petition presented to the New Hampshire General Court in 1850. Ten years later, two special town meetings were held in Sanbornton to act on the division of the two communities, but nothing came of it. A special town meeting was held on May 18, 1869, to act on an article to divide the two towns. A total of 150 voters approved the article, while 105 voters dismissed it. The division was approved by Gov. Onslow Stearns on June 30, 1869.

Tilton is united industrially, commercially, and residentially with Northfield, which is located to the south across the Winnipesaukee River. At 12 square miles, Tilton is the smallest town in total area in Belknap County—necessitating shared civic, educational, recreational, and religious responsibilities.

Some of the things Tilton shares with Northfield are the fire department and EMS services; the police department until 1960; district nurse services; the aqueduct company; the school district, which became the Winnisquam Regional School District; Hall Memorial Library; the *Memorial Arch*; the Pines Community Center; the Charles Dwinall Field; the Maj. Charles E. Tilton Field on Sargent Street, previously called the Tilton Fairgrounds; parades; Old Home Day; and churches of all denominations. Residents of both Tilton and Northfield were actively involved in our nation's military history. Located in the community are memorials recognizing those who served our country in conflicts between 1850 and 1950.

There are some little-known facts about Tilton that should be noted in this history. Alfred Tilton, son of Charles E. Tilton, was infatuated with trains. His greatest desire was to be a railroad engineer. To satisfy Alfred's desire, his father persuaded the railroad to go between Franklin and Belmont through Tilton and provided the means for the railroad station to be built. Alexander Hamilton Tilton, the uncle of Charles, gifted the town and Park Cemetery with a granite building just inside the gates for securing the remains through the winter season. Considering the extent of the mills in the community, it is interesting to note that the economies of the northern part of Tilton and the hamlet of Lochmere were primarily agricultural, providing half of the town's annual income.

Lochmere and Winnisquam, as part of Tilton, also offer us some little-known facts. Winnisquam's Mosquito Bridge, at one time, had an enforced speed limit of five miles per hour. In his two-volume work *The History of Sanbornton, New Hampshire,* Rev. M.T. Runnels quoted a paper published in 1822 titled "An Indian Fort, Situated on the Right Bank of the Winnipeseogee River near the Head of Little Bay in Sanbornton." On or near this spot, in present-day Lochmere, was a Colonial fort that has been investigated by members of the Archeological Society of New Hampshire.

Remnants of both sets of occupants have been cataloged and preserved. The Amoskeag Mills of Manchester first tried to buy this piece of property from the Bamfords to establish their mills in Lochmere, but the two parties were not able to reach a mutual agreement.

Places of special interest include Tilton School, formerly New Hampshire Conference Seminary and Female College; Riverfront Place, formerly the Arthur S. Brown Manufacturing Company, the New Hampshire Veterans' Home; Lochmere Post Office and Country Store; and the Winnisquam House, now the Shalimar Resort.

Some of the more notable citizens of Tilton were Charles E. Tilton, businessman and philanthropist; Maude Bickford, businesswoman and woman of interest; Myron Meserve, a businessman on Main Street for over 60 years; Arthur S. Brown, owner of the A.S. Brown Manufacturing Company, more commonly known as Tilton Endless Belts; Dr. Archie Grevior, general medical practitioner; Mary Baker Eddy, the founder of the Christian Science religion; Roscoe Wright, photographer; and F. Marjorie Cross, longtime teacher in the Tilton–Northfield School District.

This book includes outstanding images of the statuary gifts of Charles E. Tilton; the Union School; the Tilton–Northfield High School under construction; and five local churches—Lochmere Baptist, Northfield-Tilton Congregational, Trinity Episcopalian, Tilton–Northfield United Methodist, and the Church of the Assumption, Roman Catholic. Some of the larger farms, such as those owned by the Abbott, Stone, and Wadleigh families, have also been included.

A few of the mills that were so important to the growth of this community (but were not singled out) include the Burleigh Optical Company and Lord Brothers' Manufacturing Company, both of which produced eyeglasses; Dodge's Mill, which manufactured hosiery in downtown Tilton; and the Tilton Machine Shop. Also not mentioned in detail are the following: the excelsior factory, the Lake Company which was also called the Water Power Company, the Burleigh Clothing Mill, and various other trade shops such as blacksmiths, shoe repair shops, wheelwrights, and a clock repair shop (all in the Lochmere area).

Since the focus of this publication is 1850 to 1950, the authors have not ventured into the extensive changes that have taken place since 1950. One of the most notable changes is the disappearance of many local farms. The local economy is now based largely on the tourist industry and retail sales; thus, large retail stores, restaurants, and overnight accommodations have consumed open areas of land.

One of the subjects not discussed in this text is the number and size of local cemeteries. There are at least 10, not counting the family burial grounds that can be found on many of the older farms. Many of these cemeteries are passed every day and little notice is given; yet, they have given so much to so many of us, and we honor and praise them by these words and images.

To date, *Around Tilton* is the only pictorial history about this unique town. Many in the community have private libraries of documents, photographs, and memories that show the growth of the area and introduce families who have been instrumental in the formation of Tilton, Lochmere, and Winnisquam. Many of the photographs included in this volume are being published or shared for the first time.

One

Our Tilton Legacy

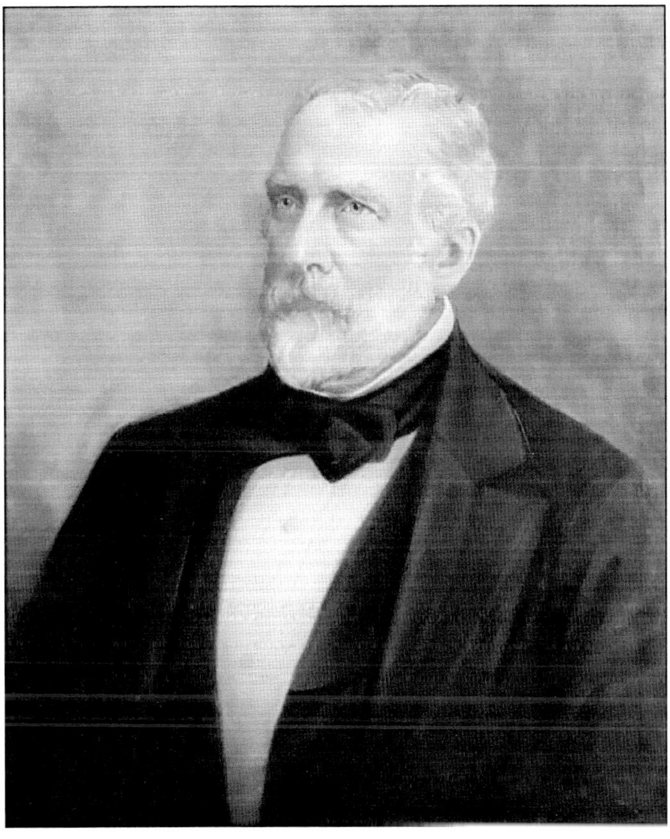

Charles Elliott Tilton, born on September 18, 1827, was one member of a distinguished family that shaped the culture of the town now called Tilton. Beginning in 1849 as a supply merchant to gold miners in California, Tilton acquired extraordinary wealth through land development, banking, and railroad businesses in the American West. In 1880, Charles retired to Tilton and bestowed upon it a legacy still seen and felt today. (Portrait courtesy of the Tilton School.)

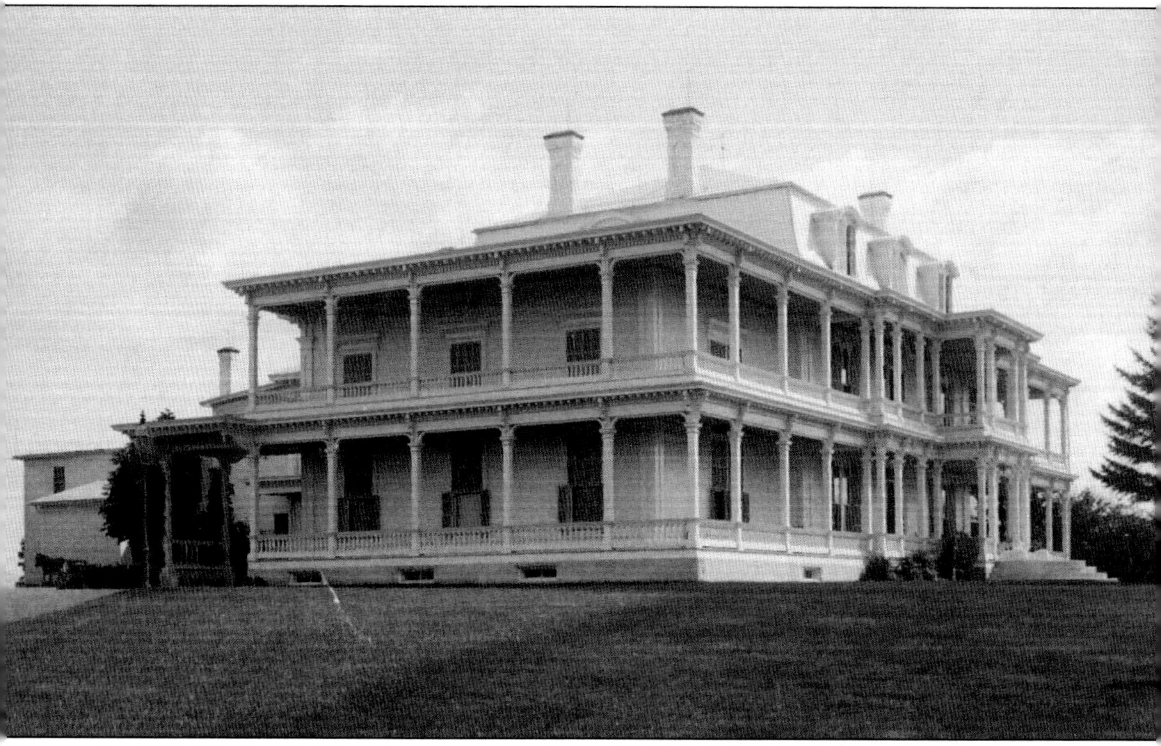

In 1861, Charles E. Tilton began construction of his home on a hill that overlooked the town. Completed in 1864, the home was a mansard-roofed, three-story main block with a one-story front porch. In the late 1870s, east and west wings were added, with a two-story drawing room to the west and a two-story aviary/conservatory to the east. By 1884, a second story was added to the porch, the verandah was extended to include the wings and stone terraces were built beyond the front steps. From this time on, the home became known as "The Terraces." Overall, the mansion is eclectic—influenced by Italianate and Victorian architectural styles. It was the site of receptions for many of the day's celebrities, including Civil War generals William Tecumseh Sherman and Philip Sheridan, and even Pres. Benjamin Harrison in 1891. (Photograph by T.C. Moon; courtesy of Joy Tilton.)

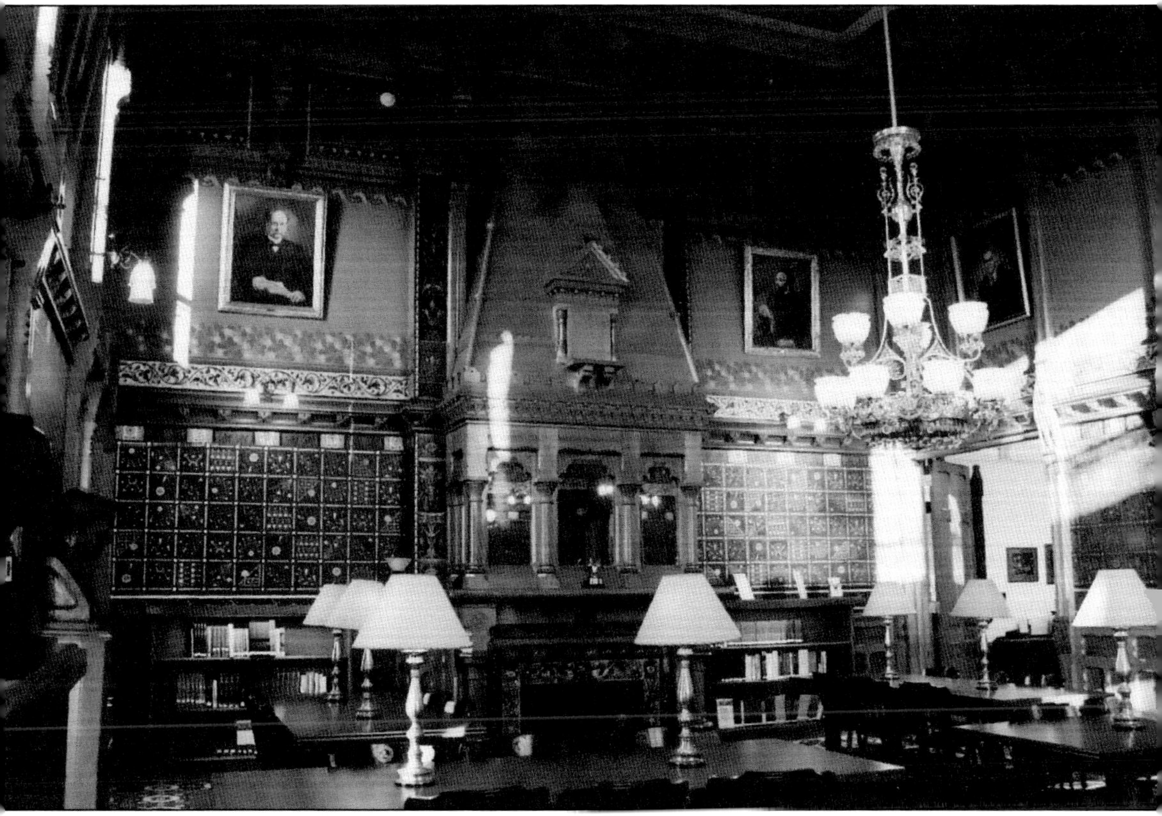

The west wing of the Tilton Mansion served as a massive, two-story drawing room. Tilton personally selected 7,500 feet of South American mahogany for the room's elaborate wainscoting. The wood divides the room into rectangular panels—decorated with gold-leafed geometric designs and hand painted by an Italian artist. The focal points of the room are the large, 22-foot Tudor fireplace and the gold, silver, and crystal chandelier. Flowers, griffins, vines, cherubs, inlays, and relief carvings vie for attention on the frescoed ceiling. Tilton's second wife, Genevieve, added this room to the main house in 1882. (Photograph by Dennis Evans.)

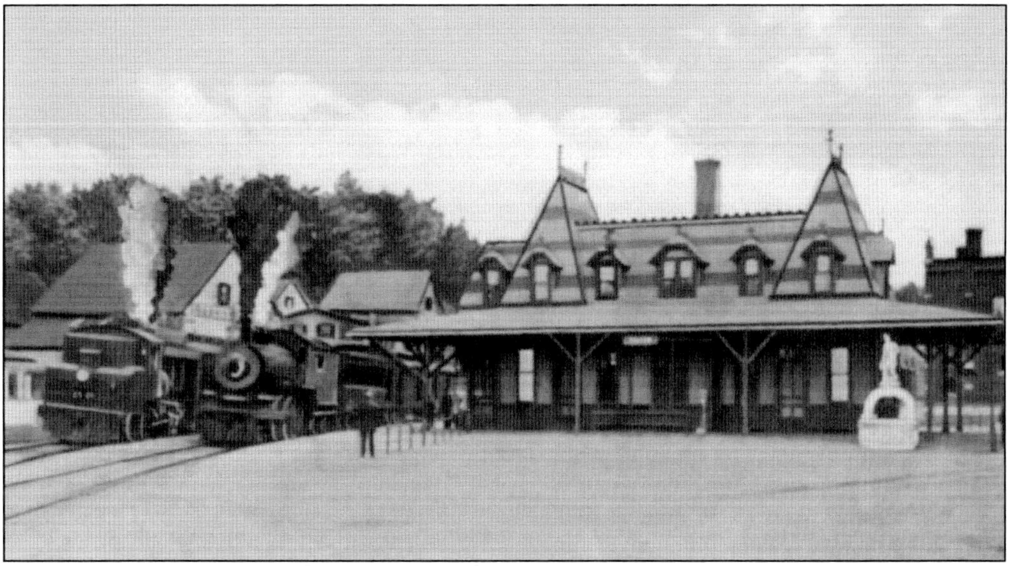

Charles E. Tilton built the Victorian-style railroad station around 1879 as an adjunct to the Franklin–Belmont rail line. He did this for his son Alfred, whose ambition was to be a railroad engineer. When Alfred's interest waned, his father deeded the station to the town. The livery stables (seen beyond the two engines) belonged to the Loverin Hotel. (Courtesy of the Hall Memorial Library.)

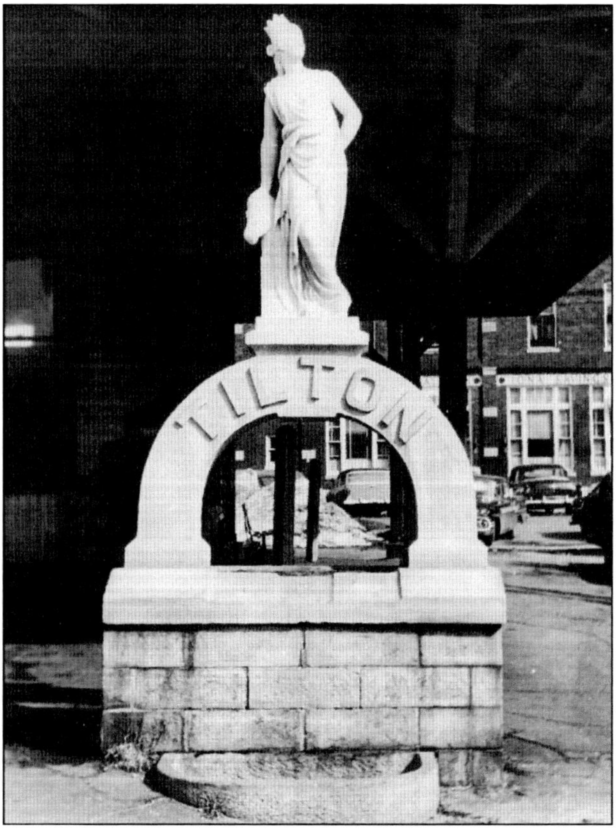

After 1879, Charles E. Tilton returned from his very successful enterprises in the West and continued to make a showplace of his hometown. This marble sculpture, *Europa*, stands on a high granite arch. Placed near the railroad station in 1882, she is affectionately called "Timetable Mabel" as she seems to be watching for the next train. She was later moved closer to the Tilton Island Park. (Courtesy of Tilton Town Hall.)

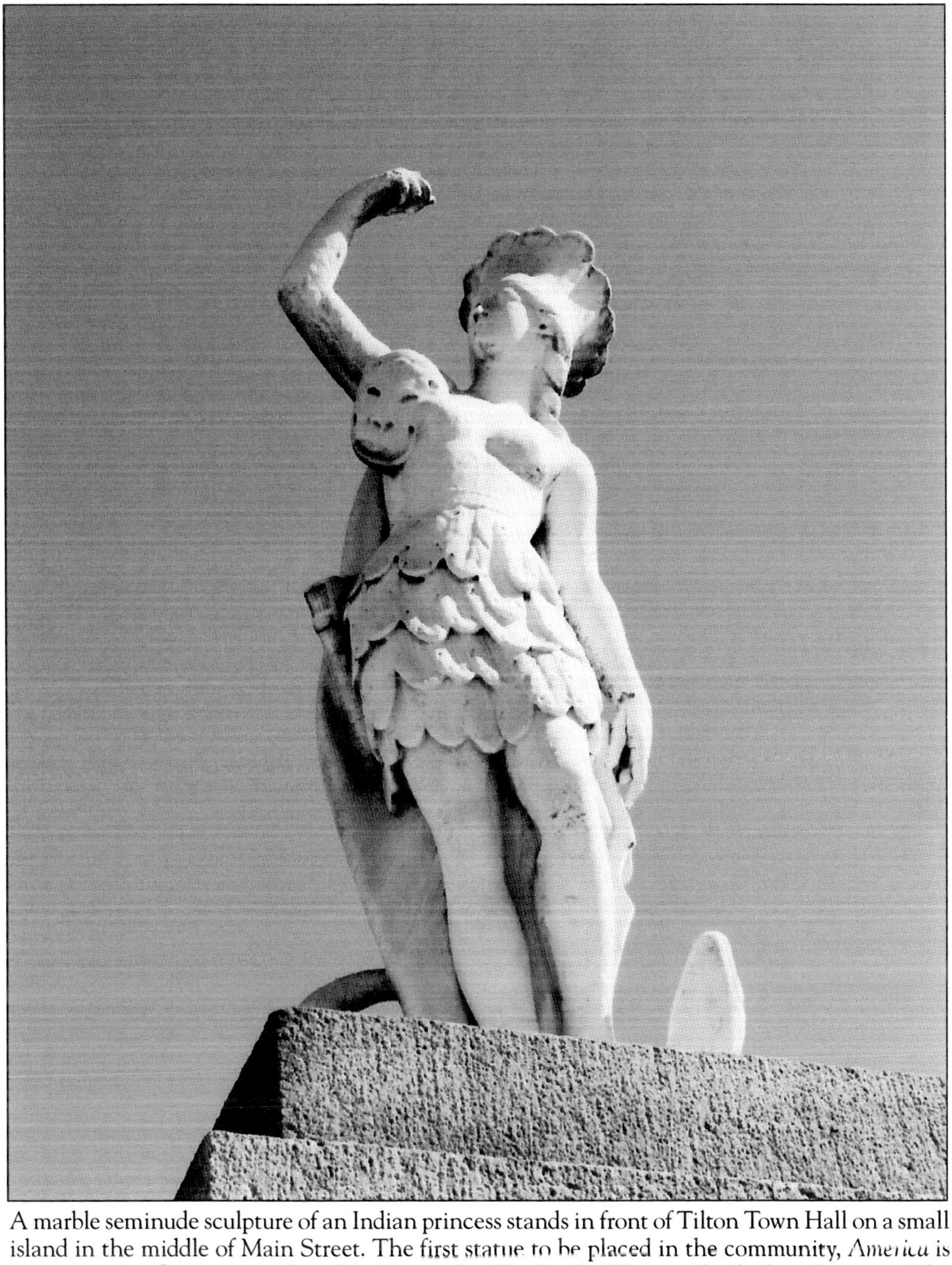

A marble seminude sculpture of an Indian princess stands in front of Tilton Town Hall on a small island in the middle of Main Street. The first statue to be placed in the community, *America* is part of a trio of statues purchased in Europe by Charles E. Tilton and gifted to the town. The statues are named *America*, *Europa*, and *Asia*. *America* arrived in town in 1873, rather than in 1872, as it says on the pedestal. The head of a serpent, whose tail rests on the pedestal, can be seen over her right shoulder. The sculptor (unknown) was said to have been of great reputation. In September 1881, a watering trough was built on the east side of the small island for the animals coming and going through town. Many publications have mistakenly referred to this leaf-skirted figure as "Miss America." (Photograph by Dennis Evans.)

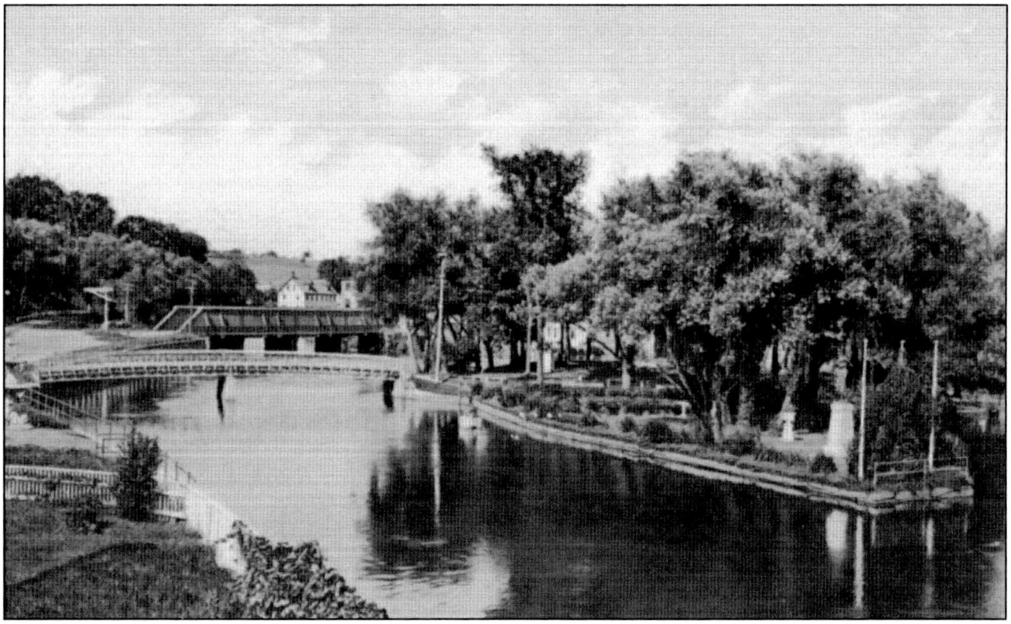

The above photograph shows Tilton Island Park, purchased for the use and enjoyment of the community by Charles E. Tilton. A cast-iron bridge, constructed in 1881 by A.D. Briggs and Company of Springfield, Massachusetts, provides access to the island. Unusual Truesdell trusses support the bridge. The extraordinary photograph below shows the extent of Tilton's statuary gifts, which included delicate cherubs, dolphins, and seahorses spouting water, as well as a giant fountain. Tilton Island Park was a continuation of the beneficence bestowed in honor of some of the earliest settlers of the town. (Above, courtesy of the Hall Memorial Library; below, courtesy of Tilton Town Hall.)

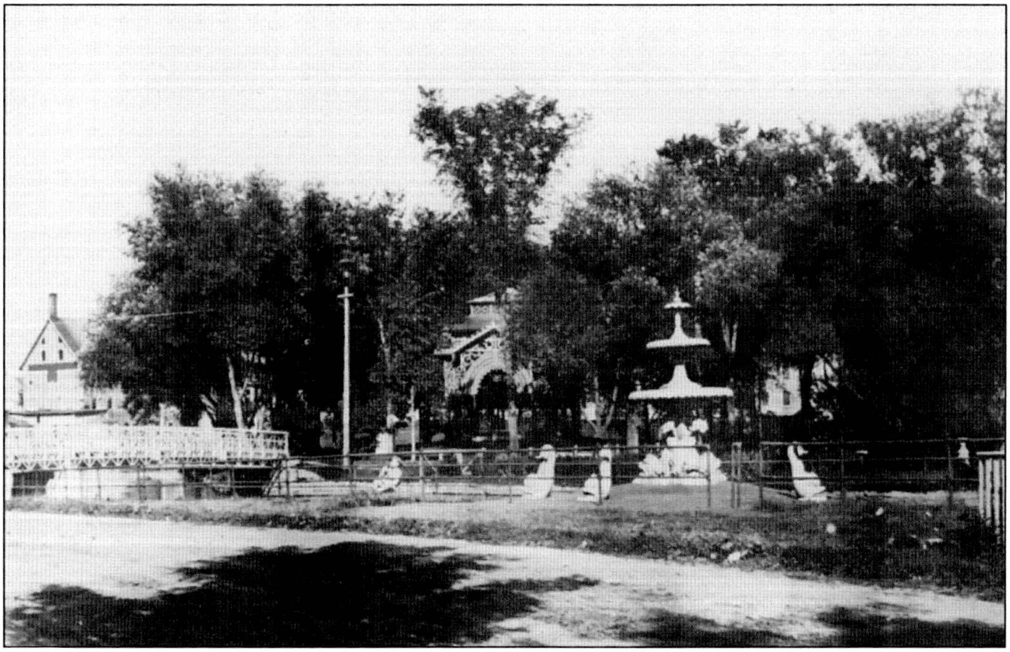

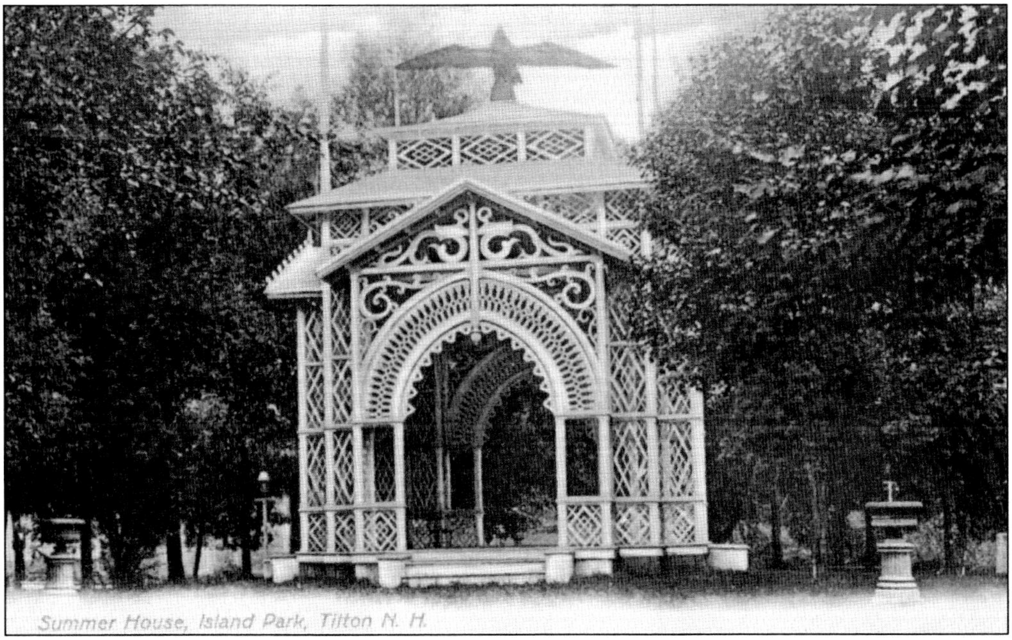

In 1873, the *Merrimack Journal* reported, "Charles E. Tilton is erecting his summerhouse on the island near his residence. It is a wire structure, which he purchased in England." The design of the gazebo or "summerhouse" was taken from one at the Vienna Exposition. The large bronze eagle on the roof is now in a museum in Vermont. Reading a newspaper and resting on the steps of the gazebo, two women enjoy the peace and quiet of the park. Another statue gifted by Tilton can be seen near the trees on the far left side of the photograph. (Above, courtesy of the Hall Memorial Library; below, courtesy of Tilton Town Hall.)

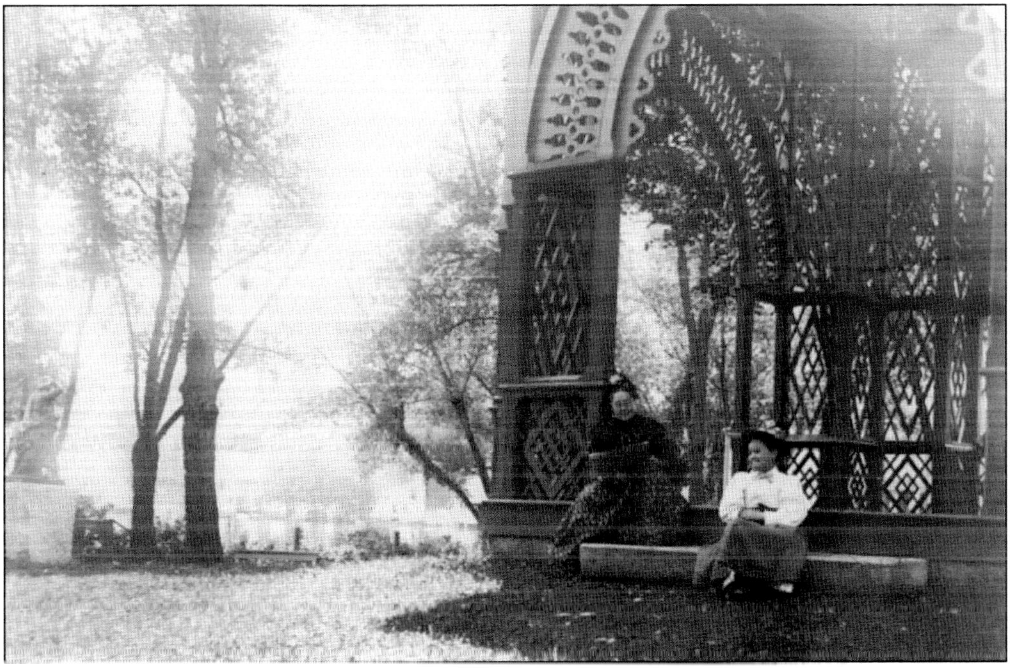

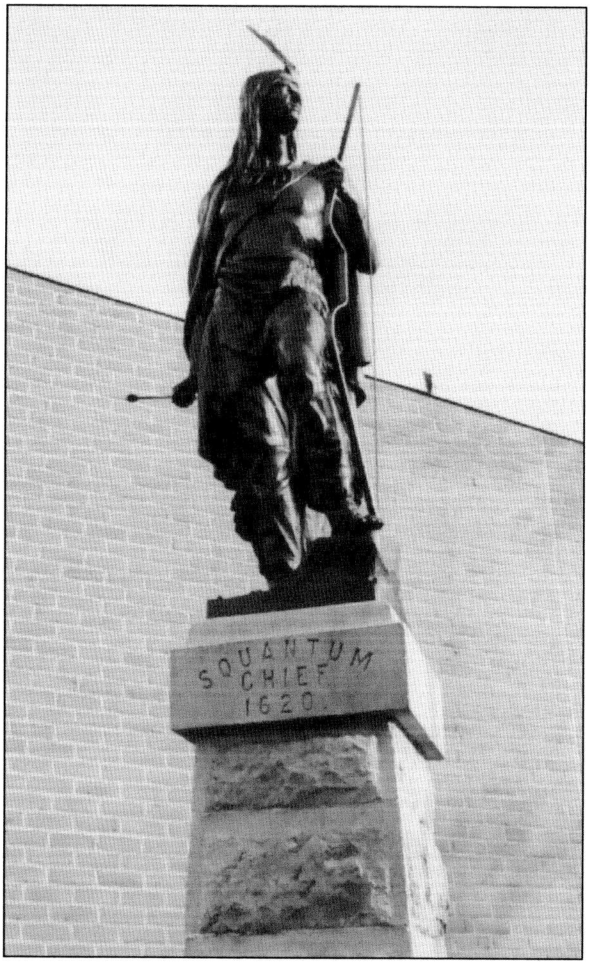

Made of zinc by the J.I. Mott Ironworks in New York and standing on a marble pedestal, *Squantum* was another gift of Charles E. Tilton. This distinguished Native American chief was very important to the pilgrims in Massachusetts. For many years, *Squantum* stood guard in the parking lot next to the railroad station. (Photograph by Dennis Evans.)

This statue that overlooks the Winnipesaukee River was placed in Tilton Island Park. The three houses shown on the left are actually in Northfield, and the *Memorial Arch* is just visible above the tree line. The larger house on the right is in Tilton. (Courtesy of Carolyn Sylvia and Barbara Hemingway.)

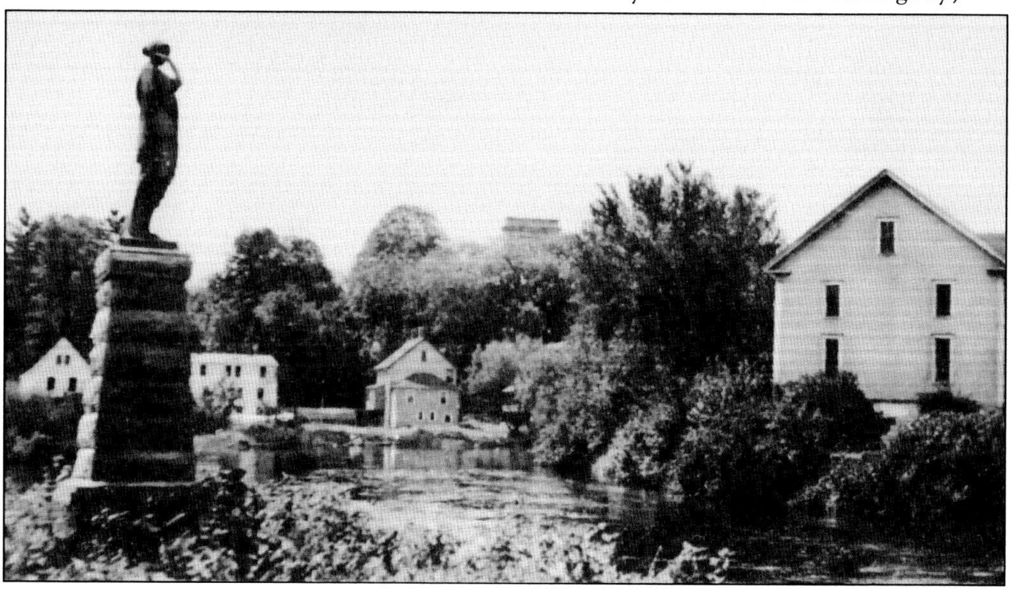

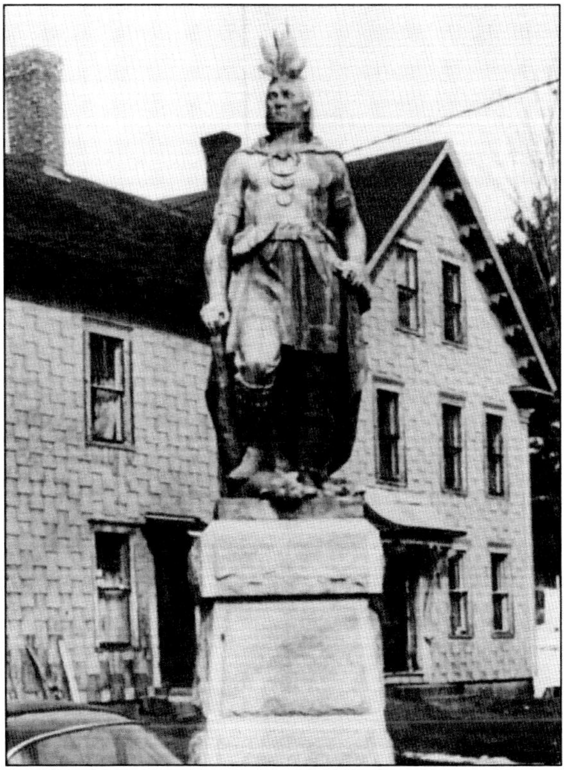

This is one of the two statues that stood on opposite sides of the entrance to Driving Park, across the street from Park Cemetery. This statue of a Native American warrior was cast in bronze. (Courtesy of Tilton Town Hall.)

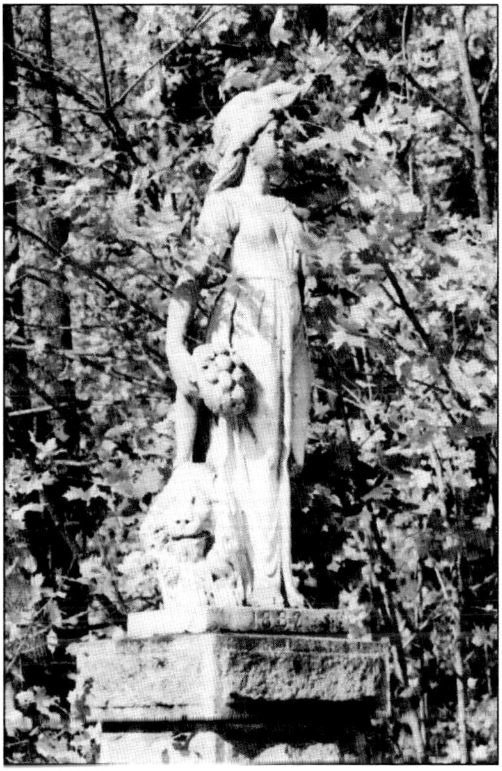

There is some speculation that this statue at the Driving Park is *Asia*, one of the trio of marble statues purchased by Charles E. Tilton and named after three of the world's continents: America, Asia, and Europe. *Asia* holds a bird and a cornucopia, and a lion rests beside her. The only marking on this piece of statuary is the date: 1882. The 7.5 acre Driving Park was also called "Deer Park." (Photograph by Dennis Evans.)

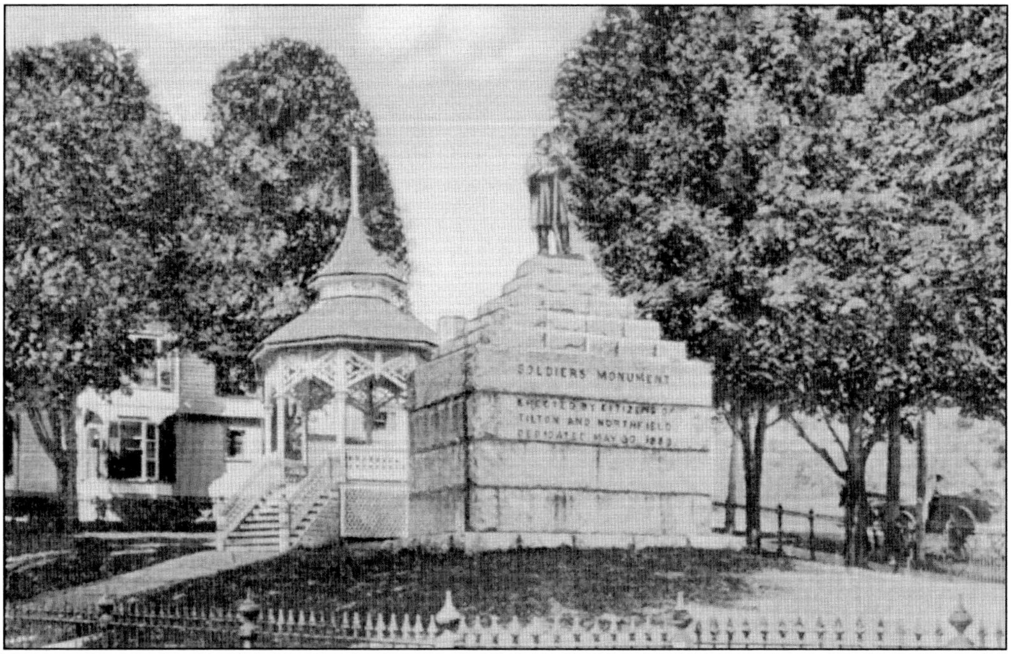

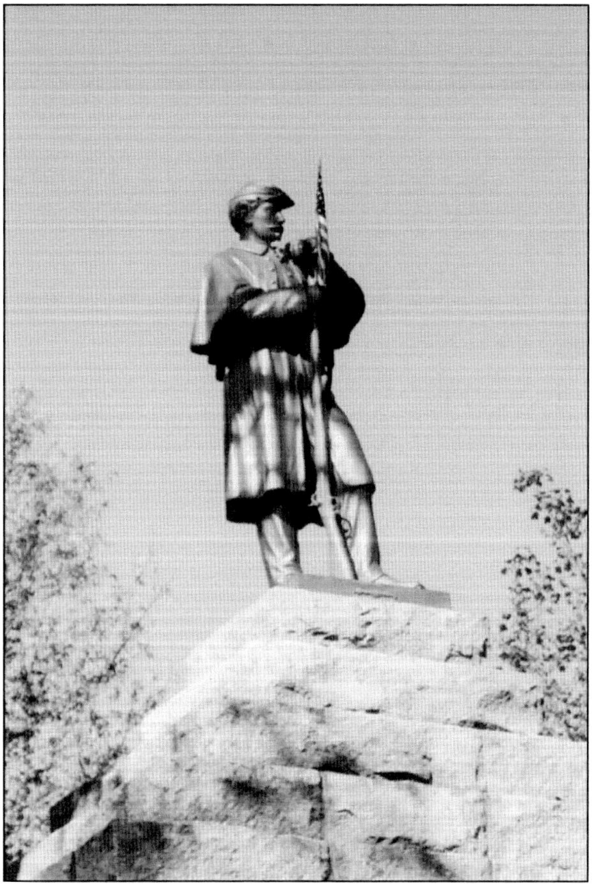

Charles E. Tilton donated the granite base of this monument. The inscription reads, "Erected by citizens of Tilton and Northfield, dedicated May 30, 1889." Summer concerts were held at the bandstand for many years. Some of the stately Victorian homes of Tilton are visible in the background. (Courtesy of the Hall Memorial Library.)

The *Soldiers Monument* is located in the small park at the intersection of Main and Winter Streets. The local Grand Army of the Republic post raised funds through public subscription for the bronze statue, which was cast by J.L. Mott Iron Works in New York. (Photograph by Dennis Evans.)

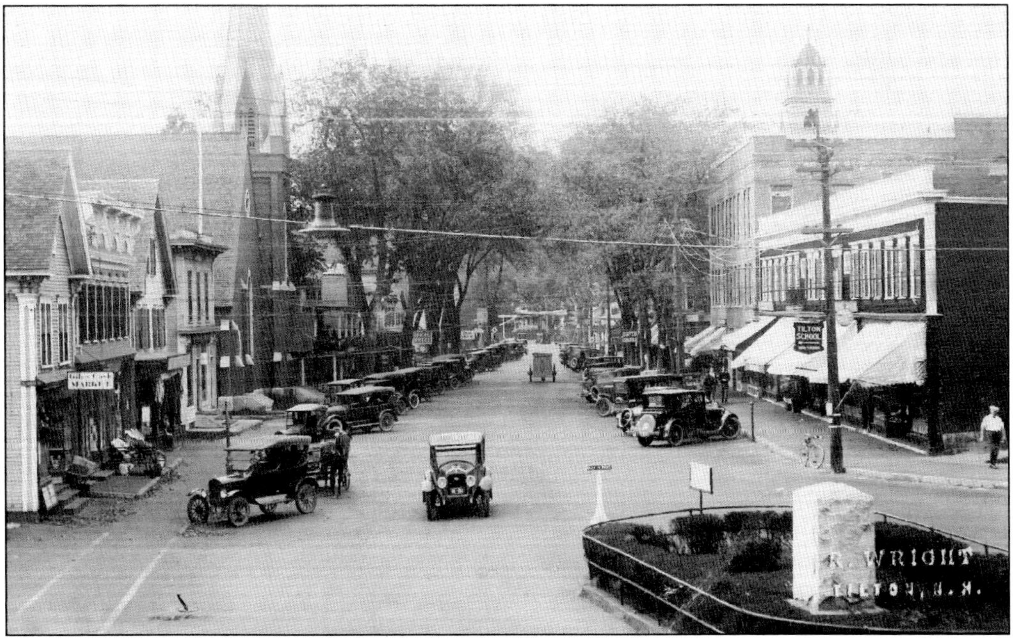

Erected by the town in 1919, the *World War I Memorial Monument* is a rough, rectangular stone standing in the intersection of School, Main, and Bridge Streets. In the earlier photograph above, the fenced-in area around the memorial was larger than in the later photograph (below). The late-1940s photograph shows the town hall and the Tilton Inn on the left. *America* stands between the monument, the tree, and the Hill Block on the right. The bronze plaque on the face of the monument reads, "In honor of those from the town of Tilton who devoted themselves to the cause of freedom in the service of our country, 1914–1919." (Both photographs courtesy of the Randall family.)

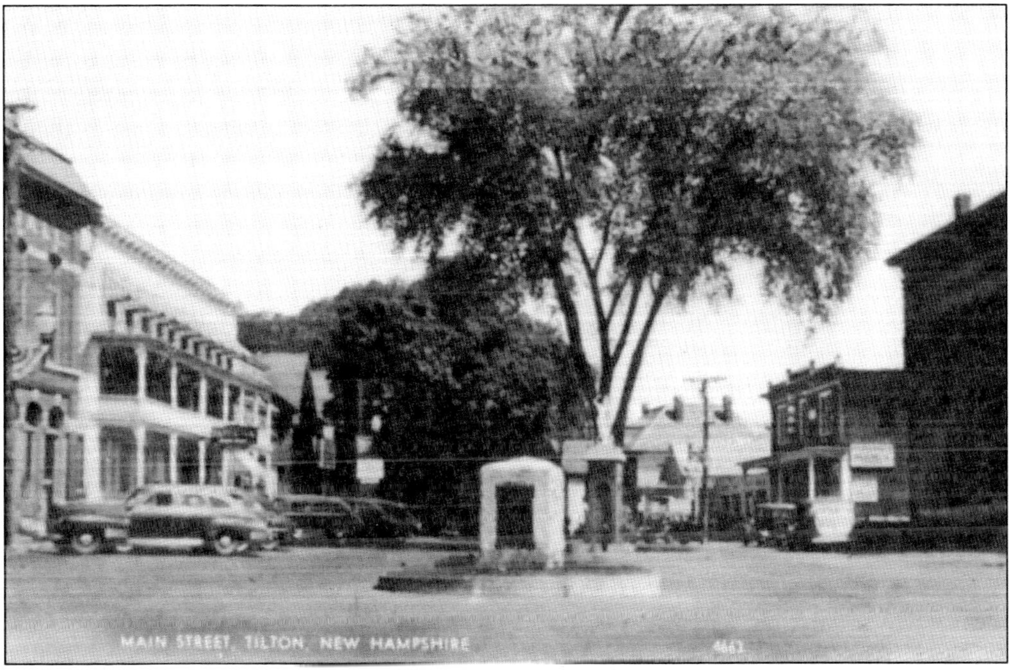

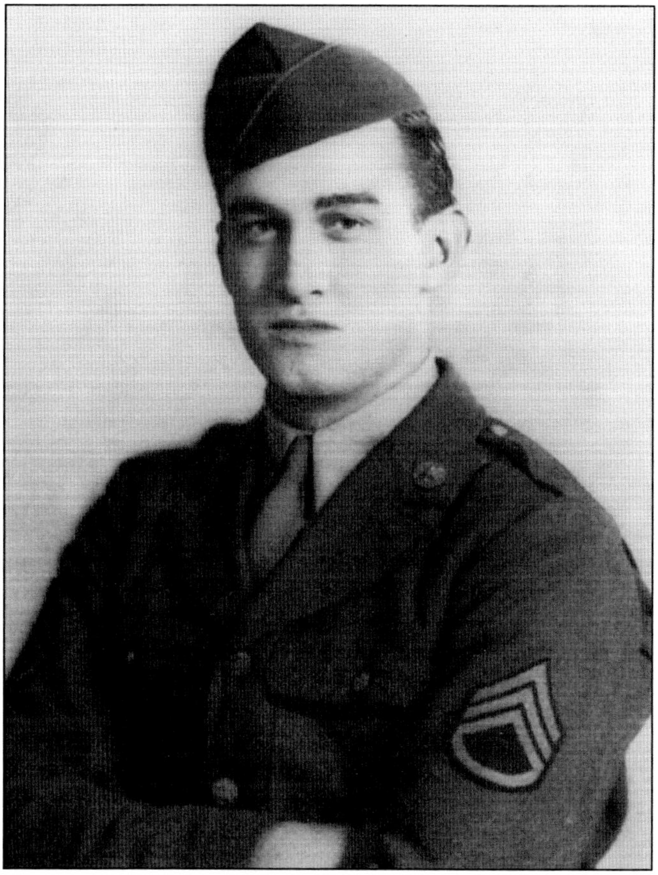

S.Sgt. Roy Jordan Jr., pictured above, represents the Tilton residents who were on active duty during World War II. He served in Australia, the Philippines, and New Guinea. He was a member of the first graduating class of Tilton–Northfield High School in 1940 and pursued a career as an electrical contractor after the war. Shown below is the monument dedicated by the citizens of Tilton and Northfield that reads, "In grateful tribute to the men and women who served in the Armed Forces of our country in World War II." This monument stands on the front lawn of the Tilton–Northfield High School. (Above, courtesy of the Roy Jordan family; below, photograph by Dennis Evans.)

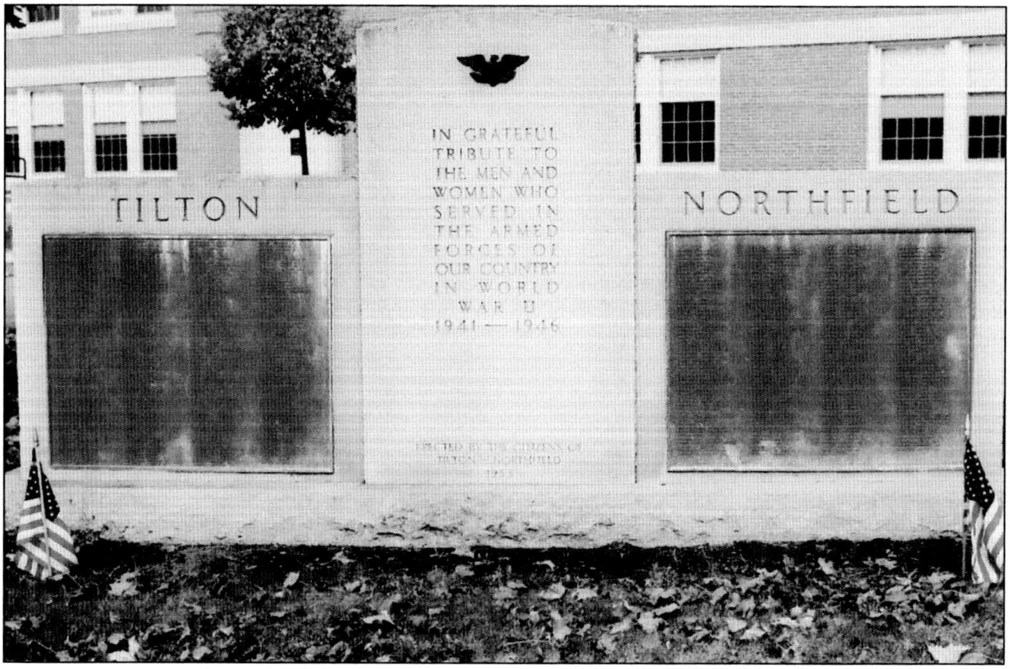

The *Memorial Arch*, to the right, is located on a hill in Northfield above the Winnipesaukee River. It was constructed of Concord granite in 1882 on land purchased by Charles E. Tilton. The contractor was Leonard Conant. The dimensions of 55 feet by 40 feet were suggested to Conant in keeping with arches seen by Tilton in Italy; however, the *Memorial Arch* is not an exact replica of its Italian counterparts. Gas lamps were placed on each corner of the monument. The gas for the lights—a mixture of calcium carbide and water—was provided by a small gas plant on the northern side of Arch Hill. *Memorial Arch* was a tribute to the memory of the Tilton family. (Above, courtesy of Tilton Town Hall; below, courtesy of the Hall Memorial Library.)

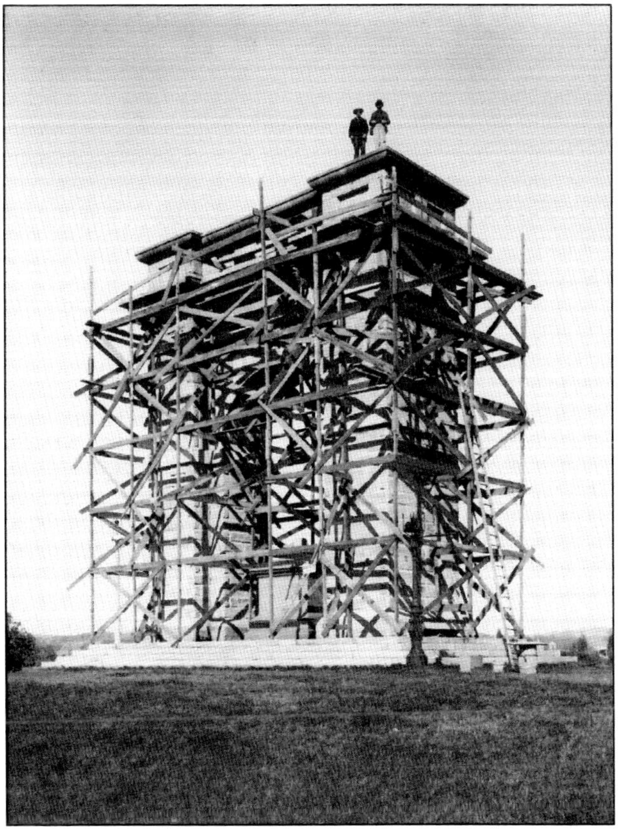

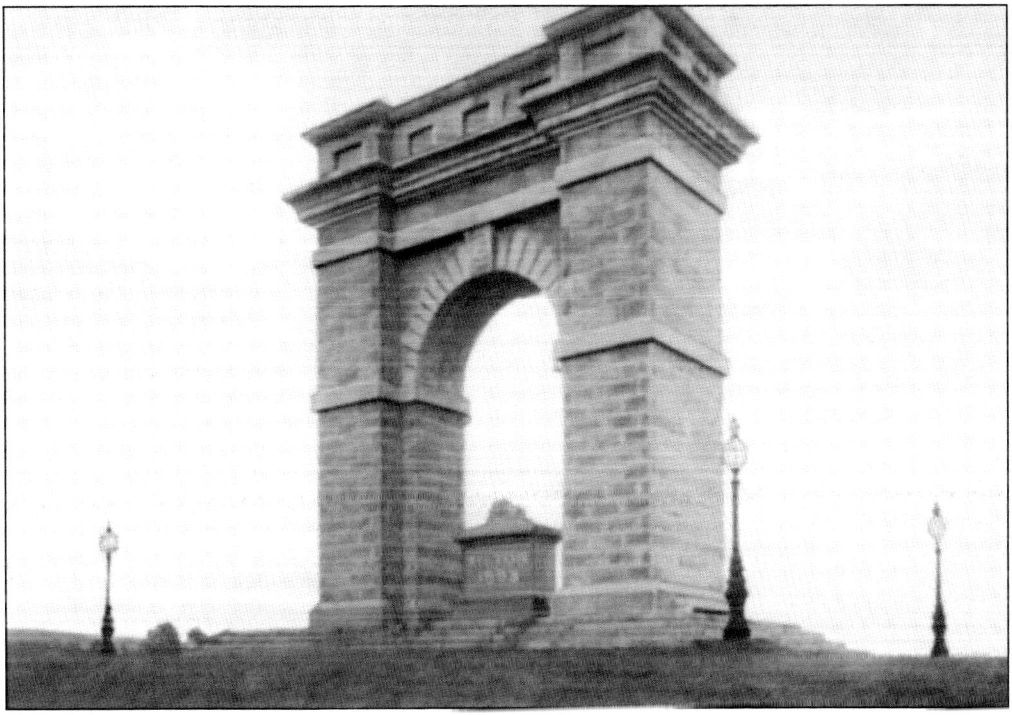

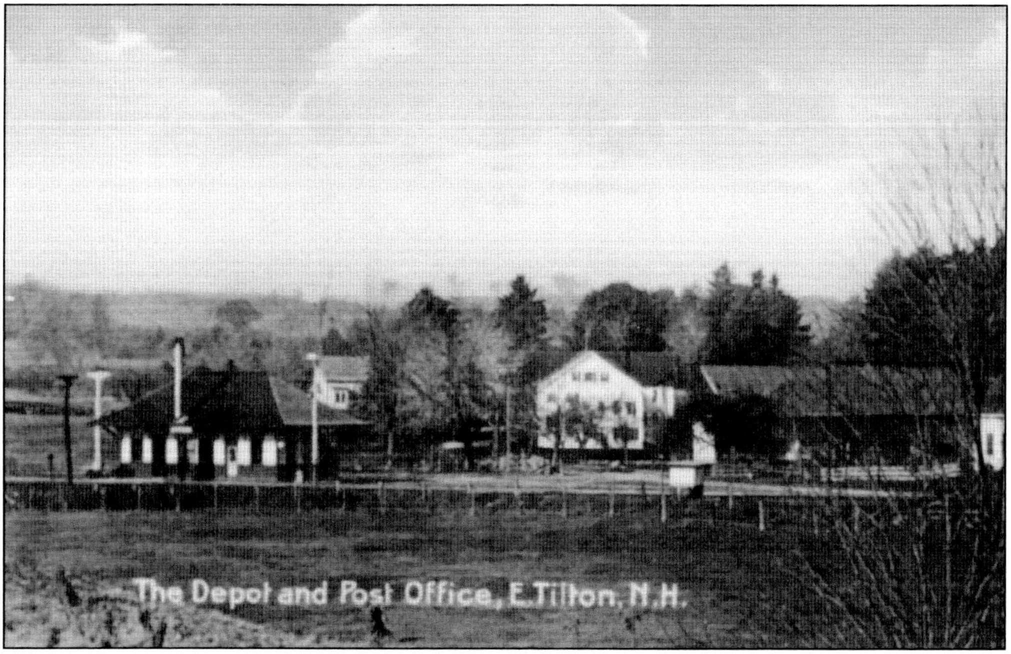

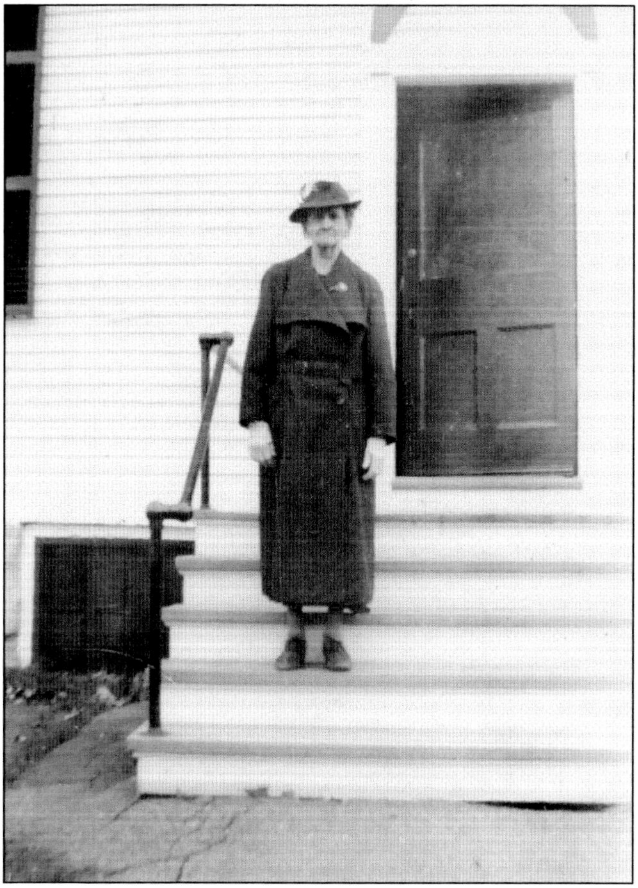

The first settlers of Lochmere (also known as "East Tilton") were the Bamfords. The deed for the property was issued to Anna Bamford in 1769. This information is from *A History of Lochmere, New Hampshire*, by the Lochmere Woman's Club, 1974–1975. When the railroad arrived around 1845, more settlers came to the area. Lochmere became a hamlet of Tilton (formerly Sanbornton Bridge) in 1869. Lillias M. Bamford (a descendant of Anna Bamford) is pictured here in 1942. She was a teacher and a Tilton Town District School Board member in the 1920s. She was the third generation of Bamfords to live in the house next to the railroad tracks, not far from the Lochmere station. (Above, courtesy of the Randall family; left, courtesy of the Karl Barnard family.)

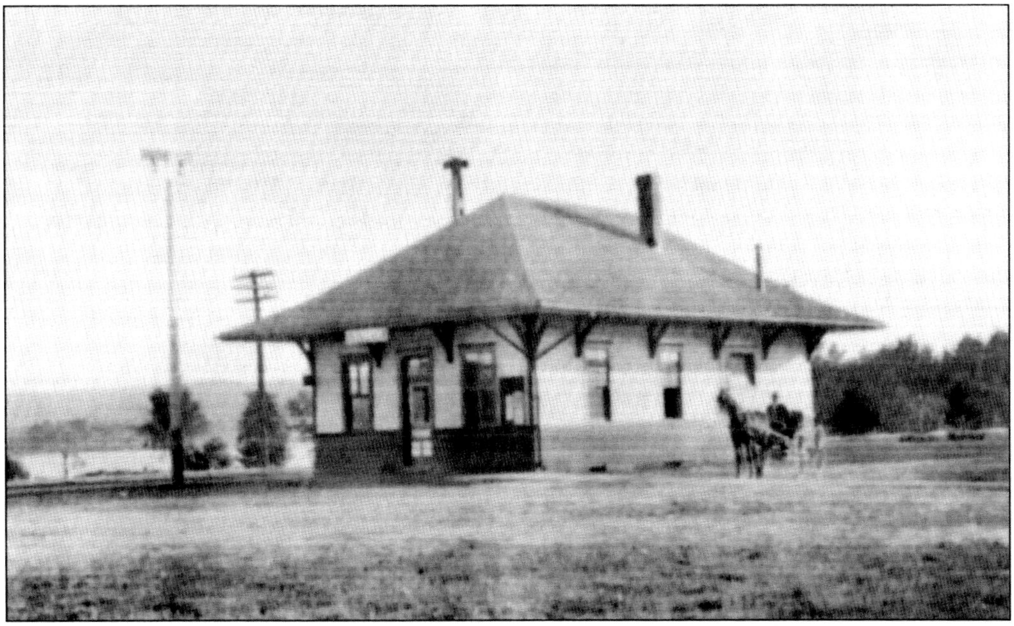

The "East Tilton" railroad stop was renamed Lochmere to avoid confusion with the Tilton station. The first station agent in this building was Jacob Bamford. The name "Lochmere" came from the Scottish word for "lake" and the Old English word for "sea." Lochmere developed as a hamlet of Tilton because it was located on the railroad route. In the 1916 image below, four well-dressed passengers wait for their train to arrive. (Above, courtesy of the Shaw family; below, courtesy of Jim and Elaine Lamanuzzi.)

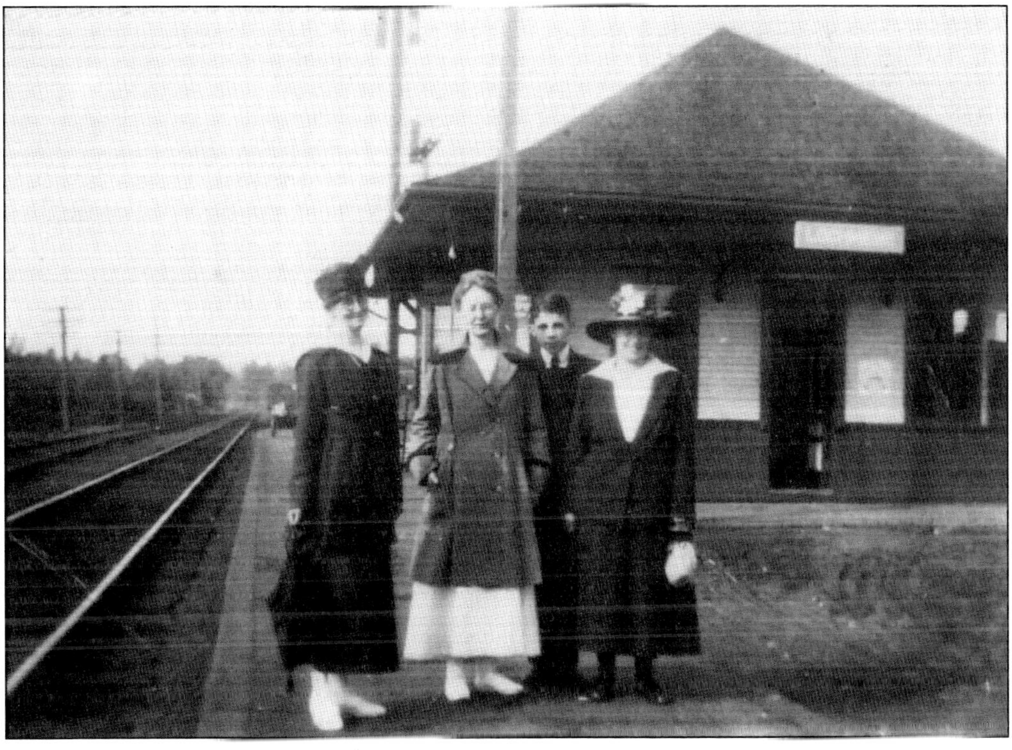

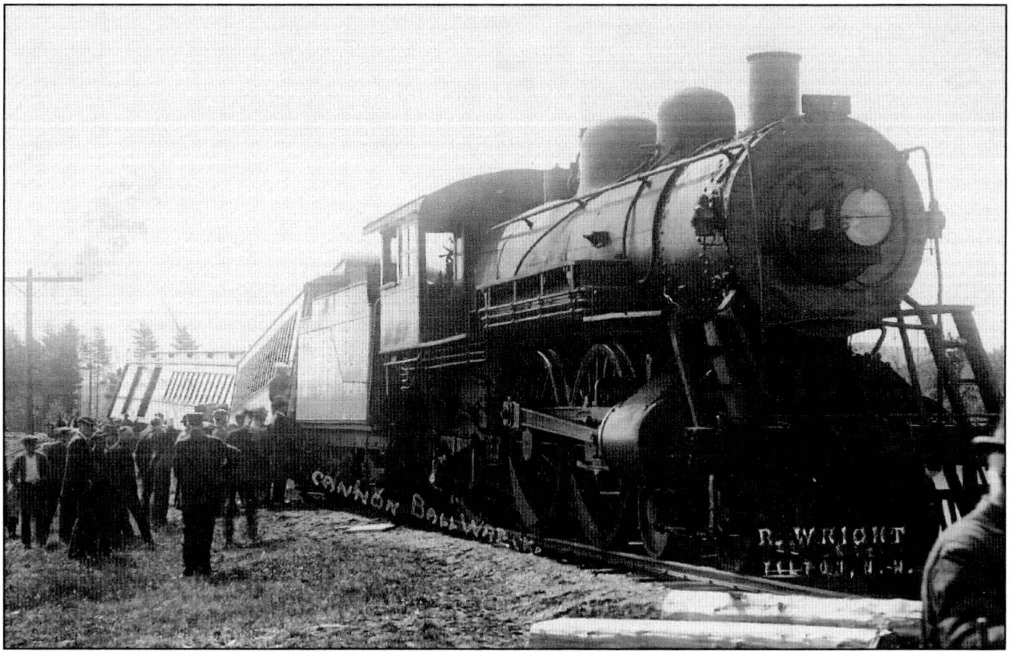

Local photographer Roscoe Wright captured the *Allouette 522*—a passenger train from Montreal, Canada—as it came through Tilton around 1937. The train struck a truck carrying a very large log from Knapp's sawmill as it tried to turn around near the crossing on Knapp Road. Frank Swain and Mr. Batchelder and his son were killed in this accident, and only the Batchelders' dog survived. Taken by T.C. Moon, the photograph below shows a freight train derailed on the trestle in downtown Tilton. The workmen are not looking forward to the massive task facing them. (Above, courtesy of the Randall family; below, courtesy of the Moulton family.)

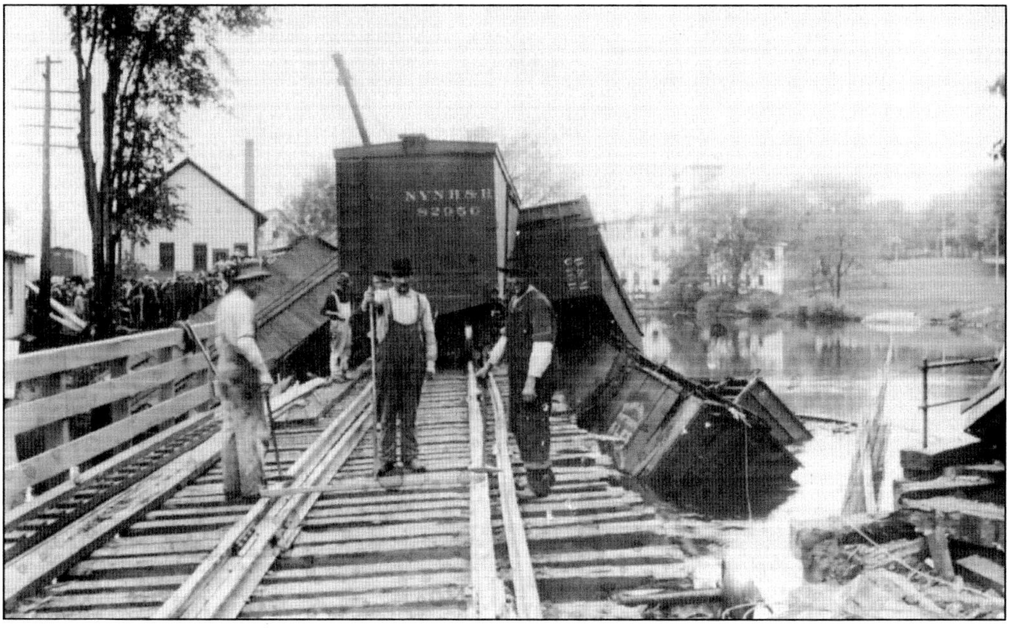

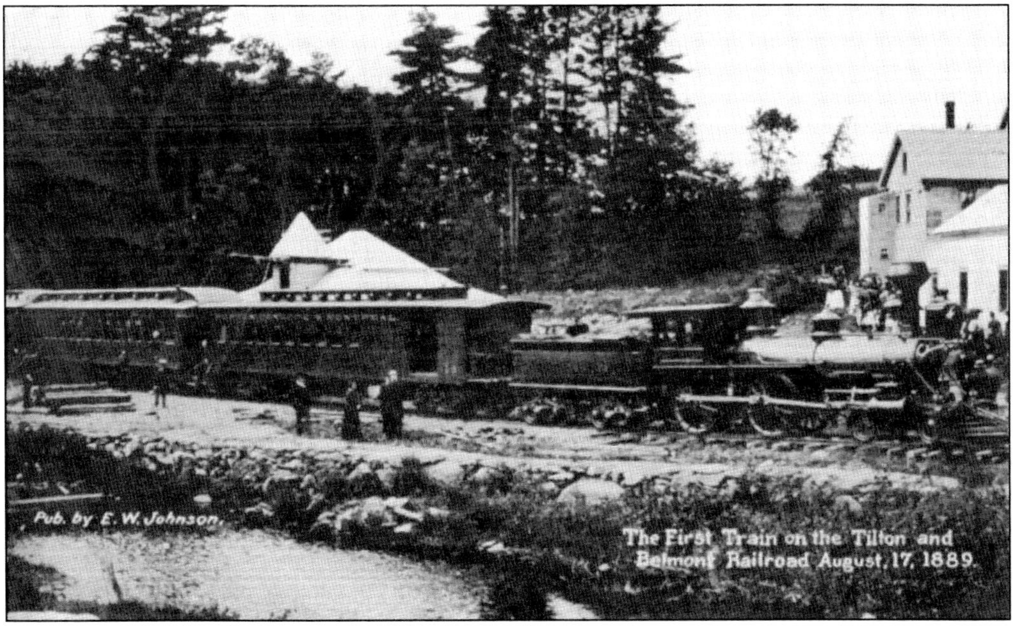

Charles E. Tilton's influence on the Boston Concord and Montreal Railroads in New Hampshire played a significant role in the location of the Franklin–Tilton line, as well as the Tilton–Belmont line. The photograph above shows the first train on the Tilton—Belmont line in August 17, 1889. It was a day of great rejoicing in those towns for the advantages of closer access and communication. The photograph below shows one of the local railroad section crews. Paul Stinson, second from left in the back row, was the section boss. Others identified include Earl Lockwood, Clarence Pike, and Lian Haywood. (Above, courtesy of the Moulton family; below, courtesy of Pauli's Restaurant in Tilton.)

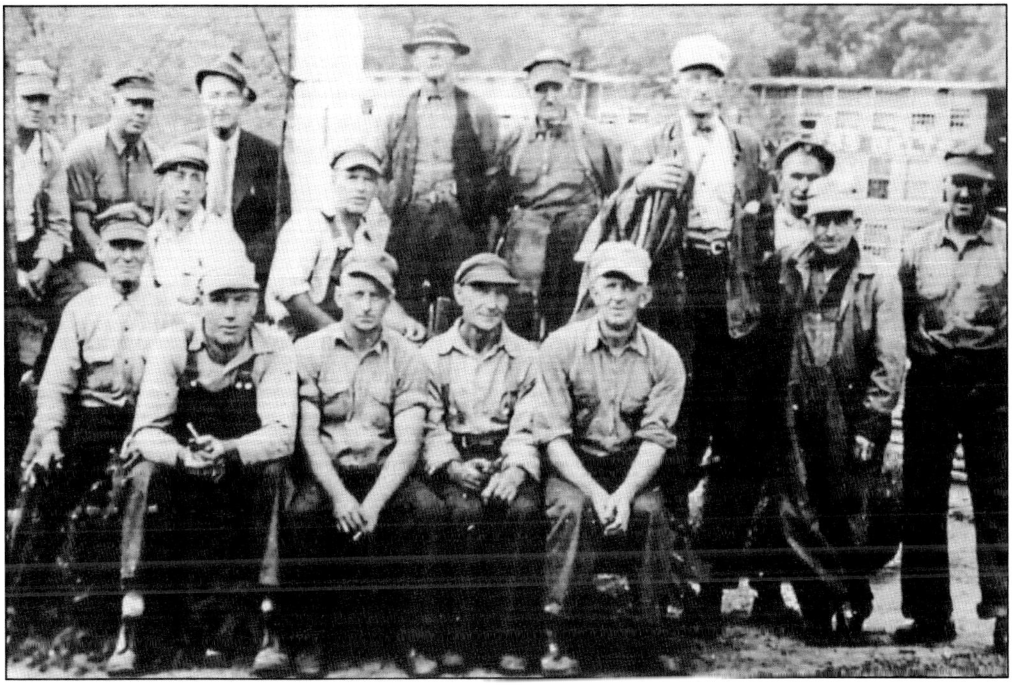

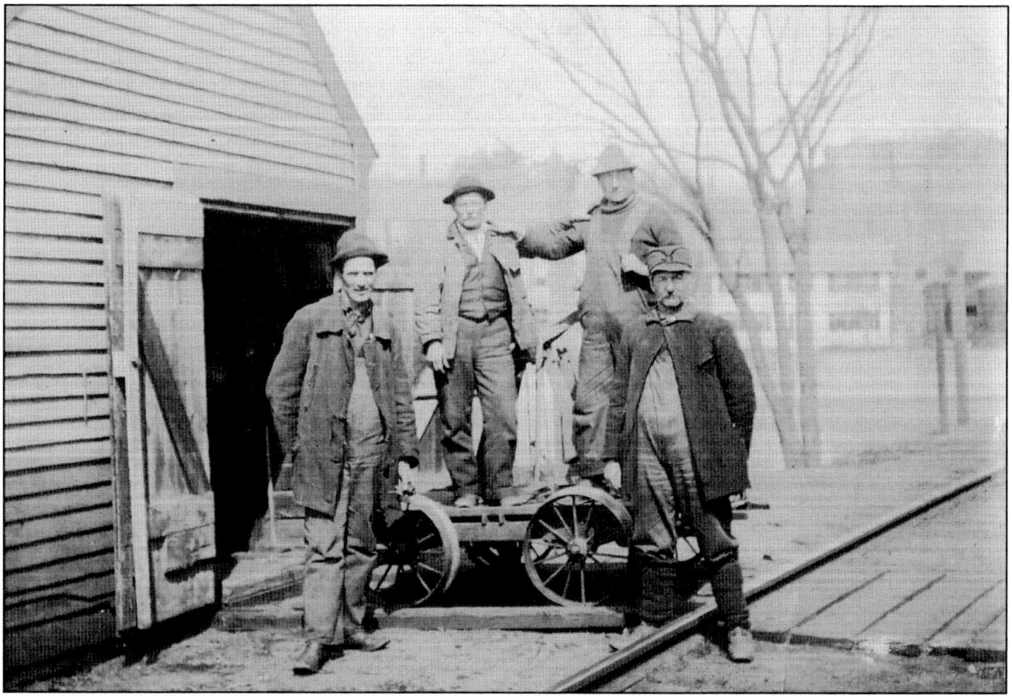

At the end of the Tilton–Belmont rail spur—a section of the Boston and Maine Railroad—this handcar crew poses with their special mode of transportation. The camaraderie between the men is obvious. The second man from the right is Henry Shaw, and the others are unidentified. (Courtesy of Helen Hollister Holbrook.)

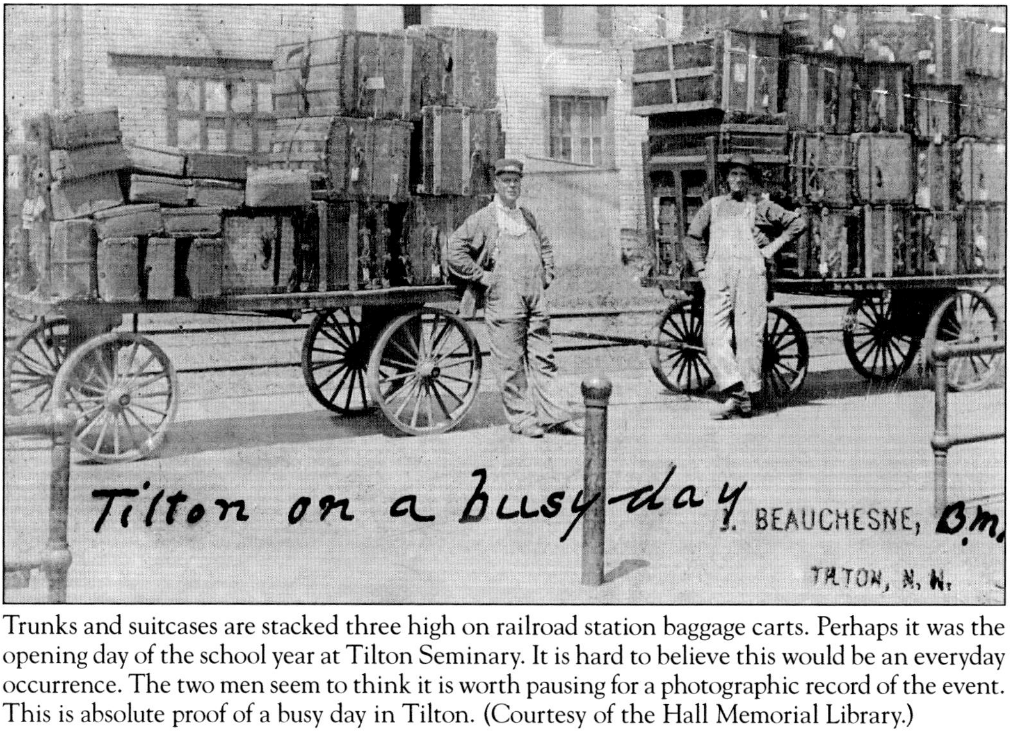

Trunks and suitcases are stacked three high on railroad station baggage carts. Perhaps it was the opening day of the school year at Tilton Seminary. It is hard to believe this would be an everyday occurrence. The two men seem to think it is worth pausing for a photographic record of the event. This is absolute proof of a busy day in Tilton. (Courtesy of the Hall Memorial Library.)

Two

Agriculture and Early Times

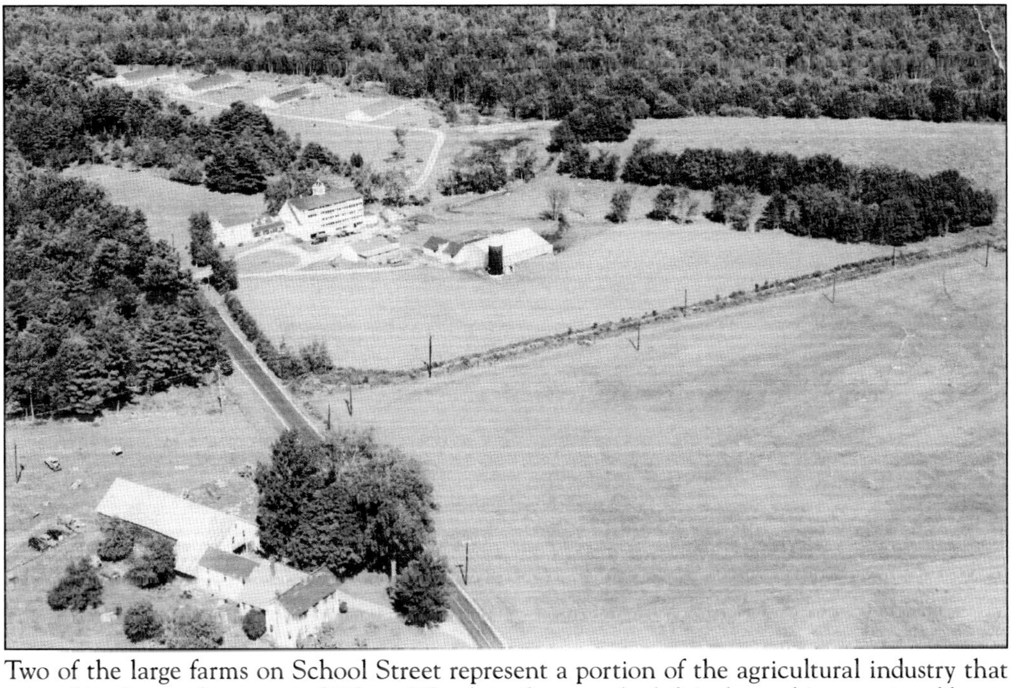

Two of the large farms on School Street represent a portion of the agricultural industry that existed in the northern part of Tilton. The dairy farm on the left is the multigenerational home of the Wadleigh family. The property on the right was purchased by the Hamilton family and operated as a very large chicken farm for many years. (Photograph by H.C. Ballard; courtesy of Phyllis Hamilton.)

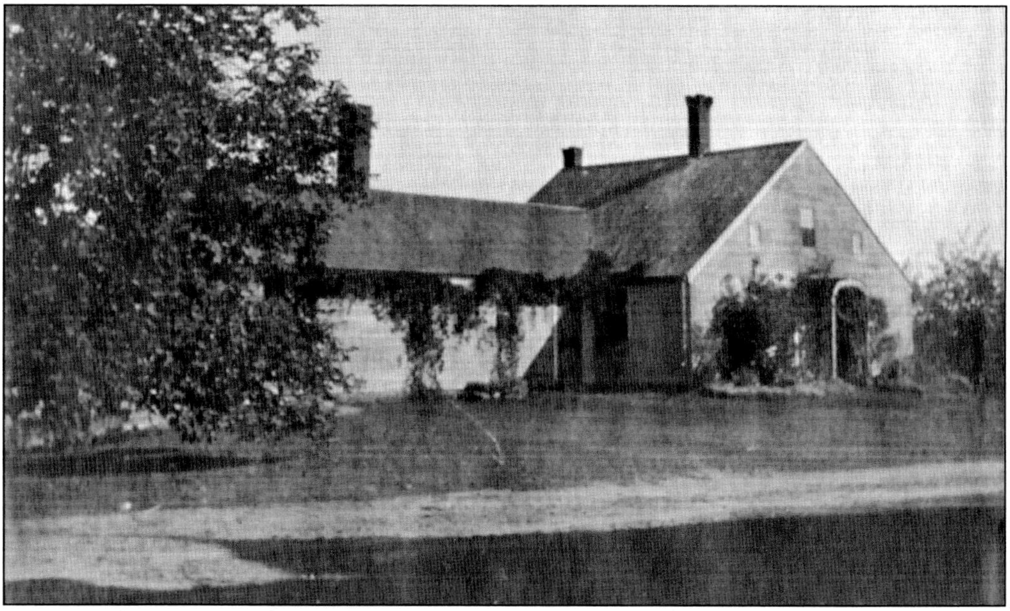

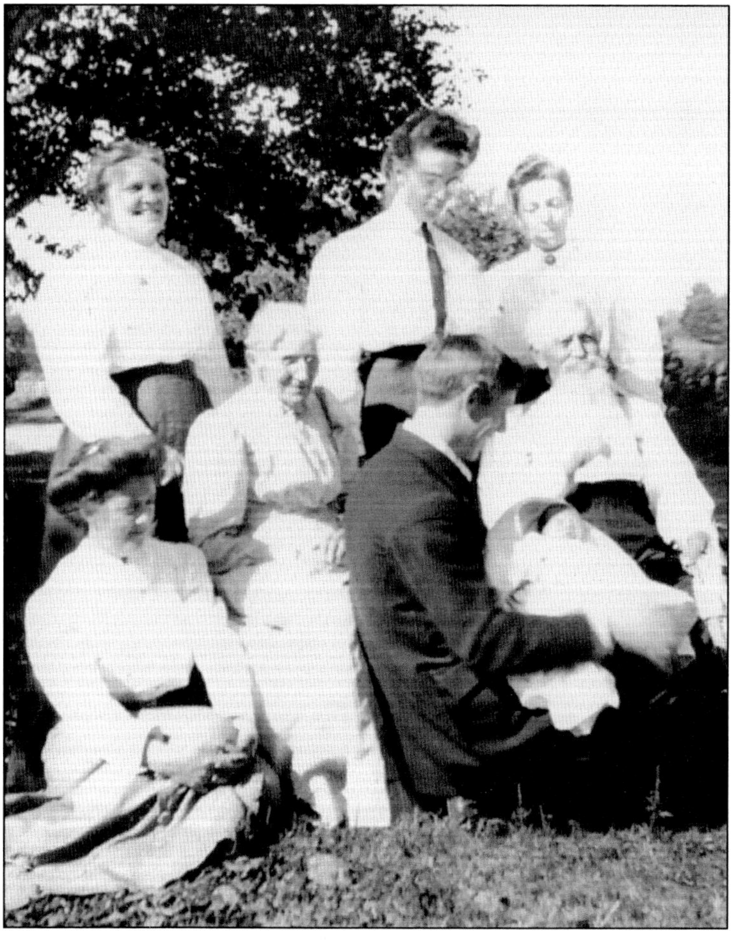

Shown above, the Abbott family homestead was built in 1800. This multigenerational home and farm is located on the Sanborn Road. Some of the products of this diversified farm were hay, lumber, maple products, produce, and flowers. The photograph below shows four generations of the Abbot family gathered in 1909. Family members are, from left to right, (first row) Gladys Abbott, Laura Bell Sanborn, Burt Abbott, holding his first son, Arthur, and Horace Sanborn; (second row) Luthera Sanborn Abbott, Carrie Mae Ward Abbott, and her mother, Mrs. Ward. (Both photographs courtesy of the Abbott family.)

Milton Dean Stone, son of George S. and Alice (Dean) Stone, was born on August 15, 1897, in the family home on March Road. Stone, a 1917 graduate of Tilton Seminary, was the second-generation owner and operator of Brook Hill Farm. Well known for introducing Ayrshire cattle to the local dairy industry, he was an active participant in community and agricultural organizations. (Courtesy of the Stone family.)

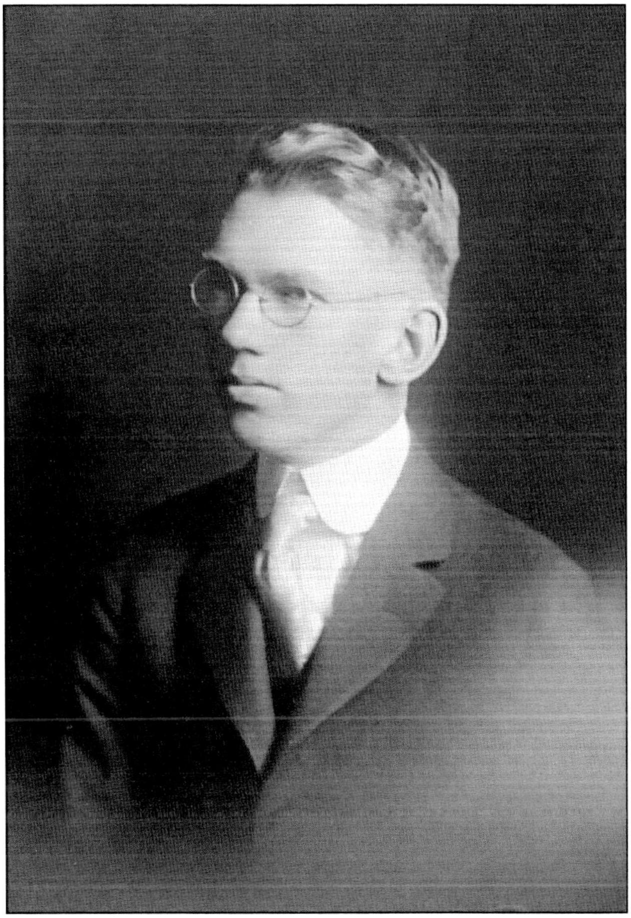

This Colonial home, built in 1790 on March Road in Tilton, was purchased by George S. Stone in 1890. Known as Brook Hill Farm, this 250-acre dairy farm consisted of two homes, a large barn, and several out buildings. Interestingly, the side-by-side homes were located in different towns. The larger home pictured here was in Tilton, and the smaller home, not shown, was to the left in Sanbornton. (Courtesy of the Stone family.)

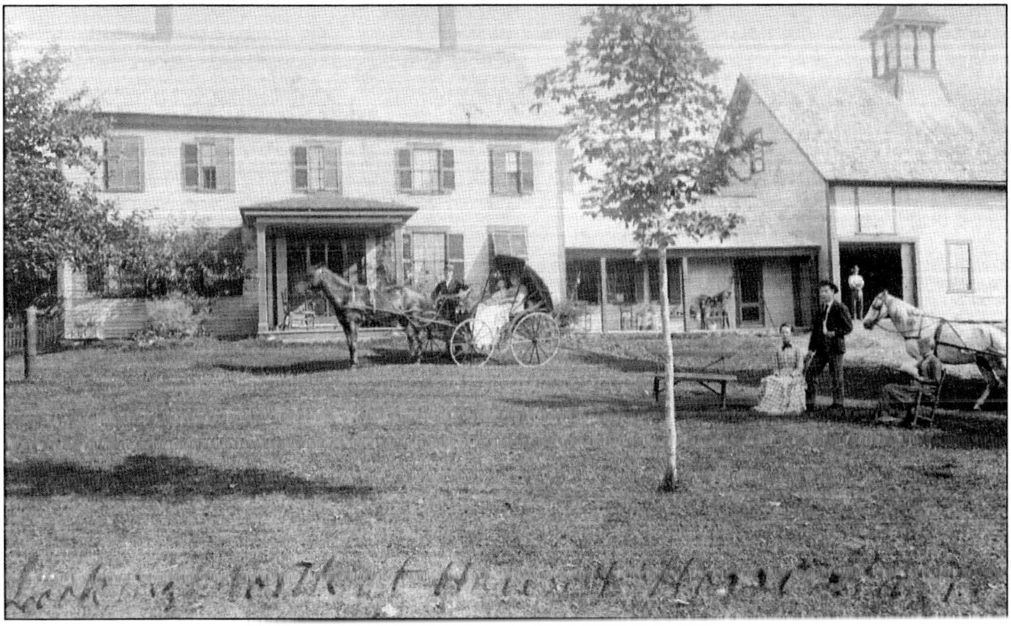

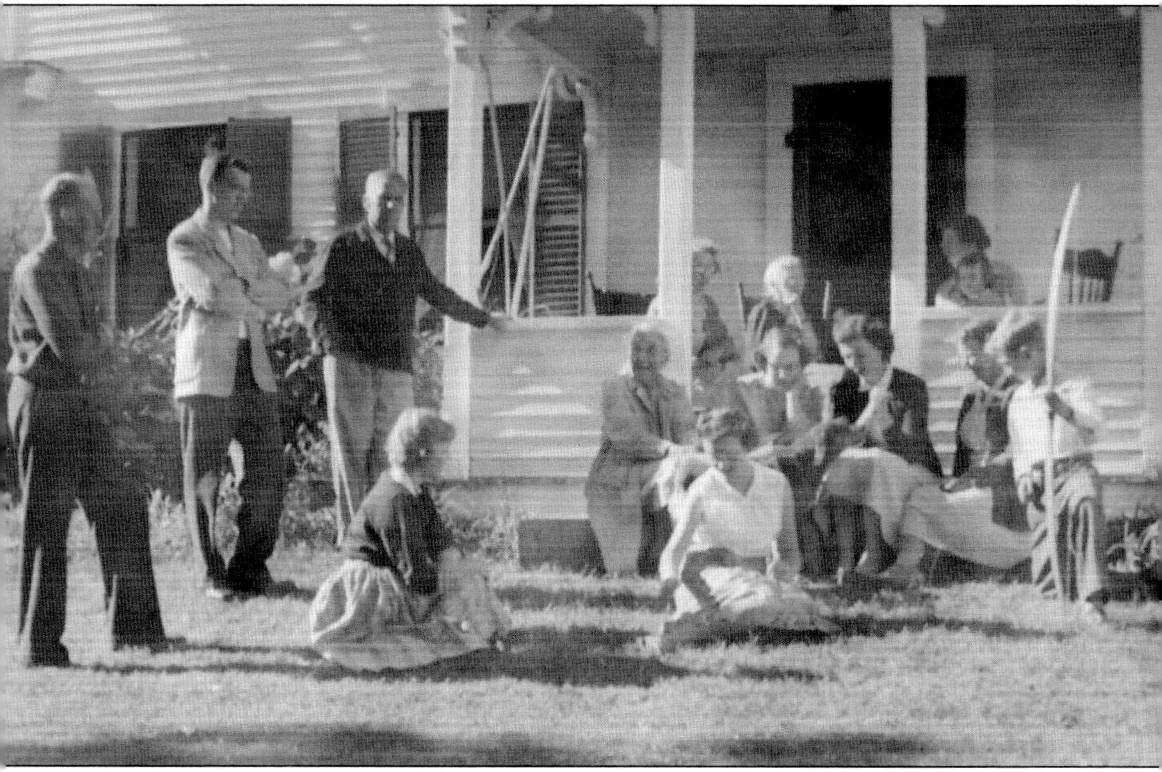

Brook Hill Farm is the scene for a gathering of the Stone and Woodman families. Standing on the left are, from left to right, Milton D. Stone, Arthur Woodman, and Clarence Woodman. On the porch are, from left to right, Elizabeth K. Nystrom, Alice Stone, and Marion Stone Woodman with Ellen Woodman on her grandmother's lap. On the steps of the porch are, from left to right, Bessie Kelley, Rosemary J. Woodman, Harriet Stone, and Eleanor Kelley Stone. On the ground are, from left to right, Jean Stone, Elizabeth Stone, and George Milton Stone, who is holding a handmade bow. Elizabeth Nystrom's husband, Gus, took this photograph. These two families had a lineal connection through the sister-brother relationship of Marion and Milton and worked the Brook Hill Farm in partnership from 1914 to 1935. (Courtesy of the Stone family.)

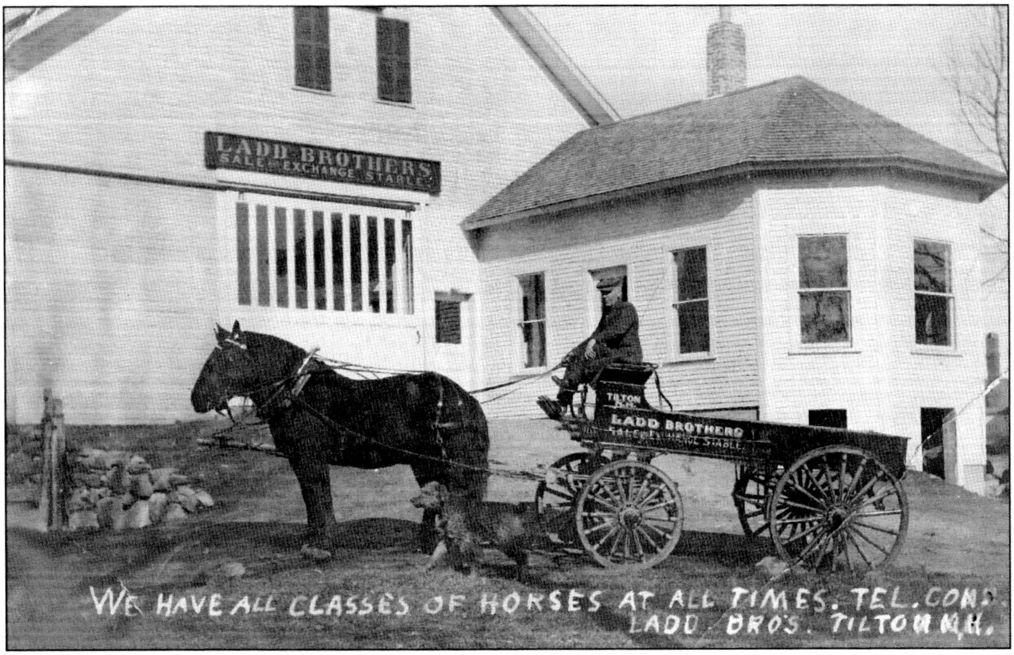

Ladd Brothers Sale and Exchange Stables was located on Tilton's East Main Street near the eastern end of Morrison Avenue. The high wagon advertised the stables as it traveled the local area carrying goods to their customers. According to advertisements, Ladd Brothers had all classes of horses at all times. In the photograph below, we see the results of an early-morning winter fire, which destroyed the unusual and beautiful barn. The large family home can be seen intact in the background on the left. Records do not indicate whether this structure was rebuilt. (Both photographs courtesy of the Moulton family.)

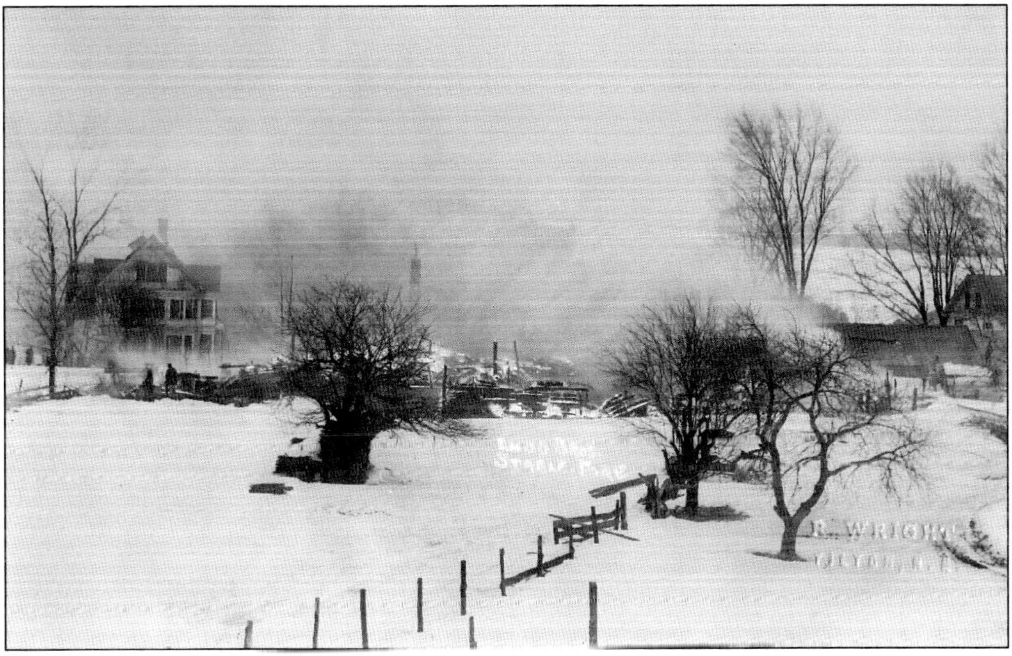

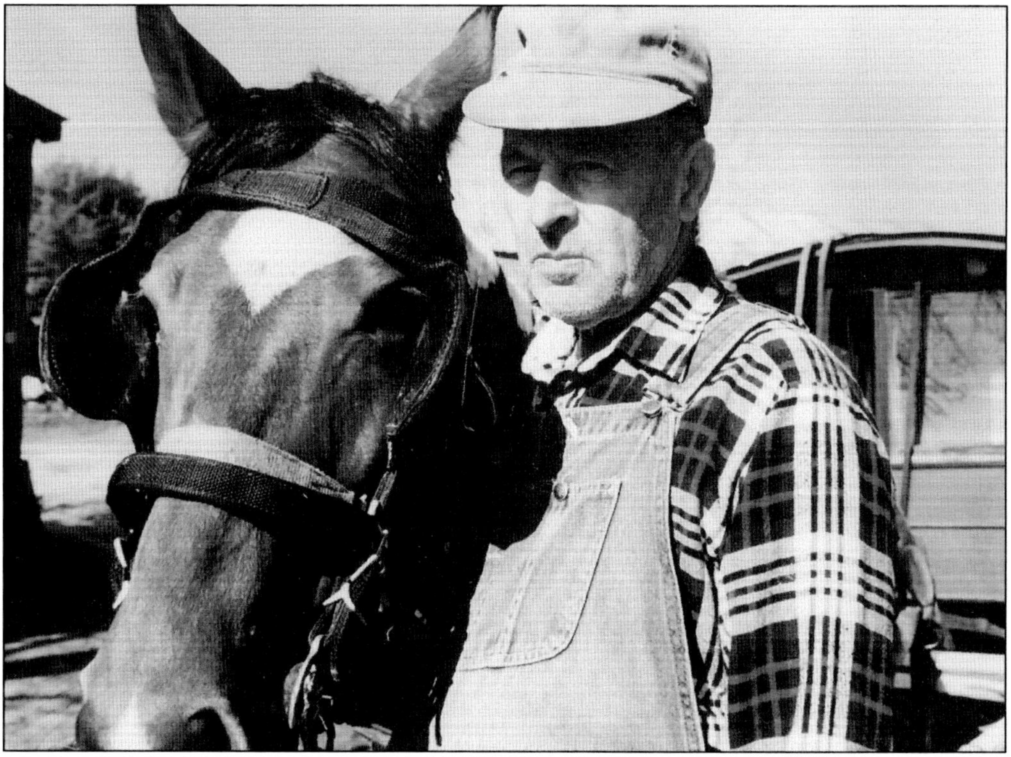

Bert Southwick, a lifelong resident of Northfield and longtime Tilton and Northfield businessman, is seen above with one of his beloved horses. Southwick began delivering eggs, milk, and vegetables in the two towns when he was 14 years old—first by bicycle, and later by the horse-drawn milk wagon shown below. He is one of the last old-time peddlers. A hardworking, quiet man, he was often seen along the roads of the two communities with local children following him. His horse knew where to stop for deliveries, and quite often, a young pony was taken along to learn the route. Southwick was a local legend in his time and our own. (Courtesy of the Hall Memorial Library.)

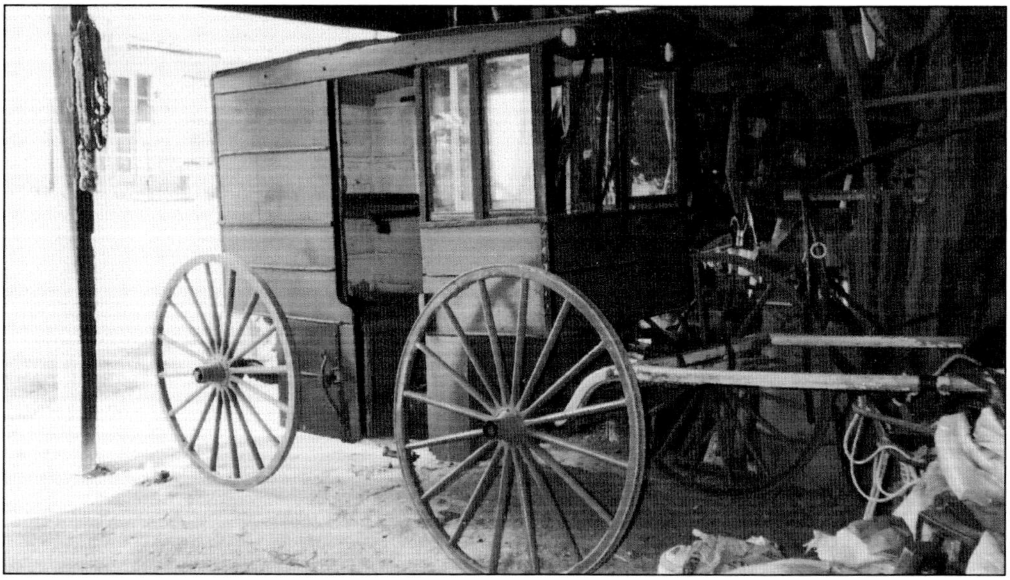

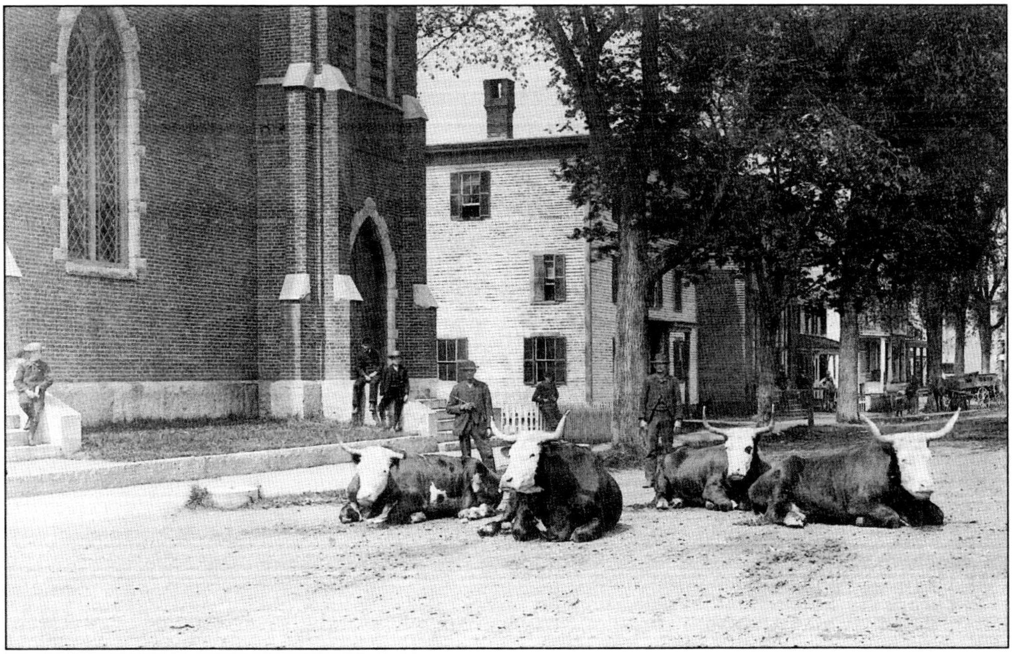

A small herd of Hereford Cross cattle was an unusual sight on Main Street in front of the Trinity Episcopal Church. The young man closest to the animals is holding a switch, which he probably needed to move them to their destination. The other people in the area do not seem unduly concerned or surprised. (Courtesy of the William Lawrence family.)

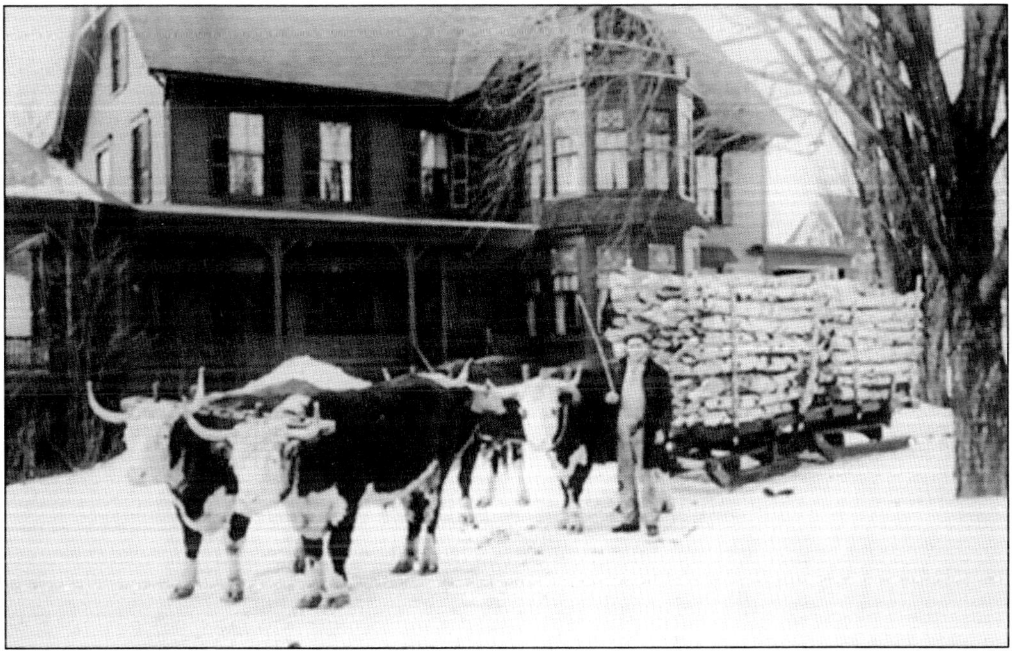

Two yoke of cattle, which appear to be the same breed as seen in the previous photograph, are shown in work mode rather than at rest. The wood is being hauled into the Peabody–Brown estate on West Main Street. The gentleman in the photograph is guiding the animals and the wood-laden sled. (Courtesy of the Peabody-Brown estate.)

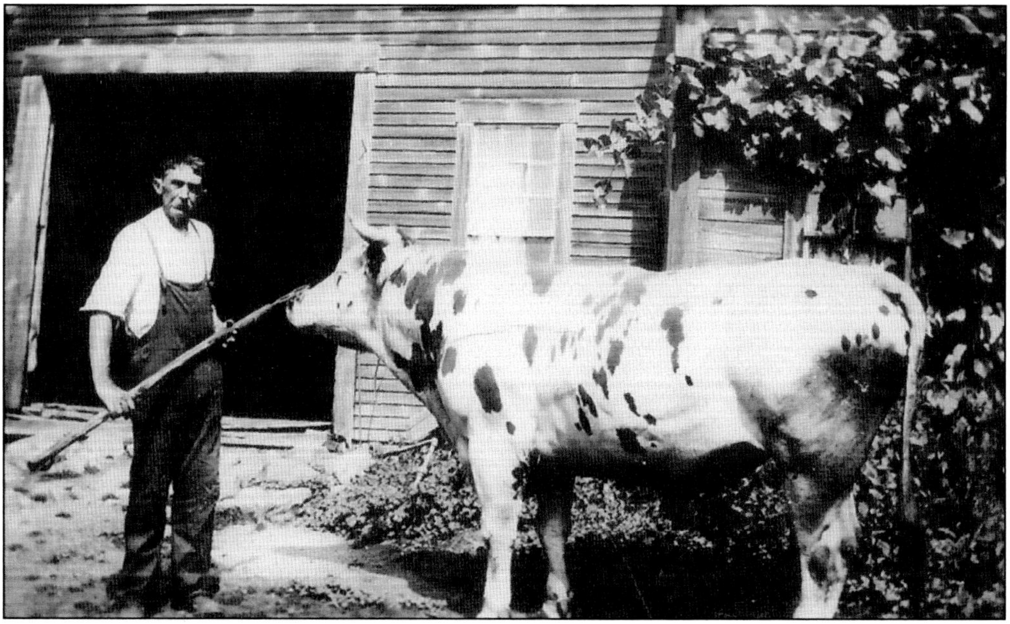

George Colby Wyatt (1851–1930) stands with his prize bull on the family farm on Sanborn Road. In his hands is a rod used to grab the ring in the bull's nose, which was the easiest way to control such a large animal. Wyatt's son Arthur continued the farm on the death of his father. (Courtesy of the Wyatt family.)

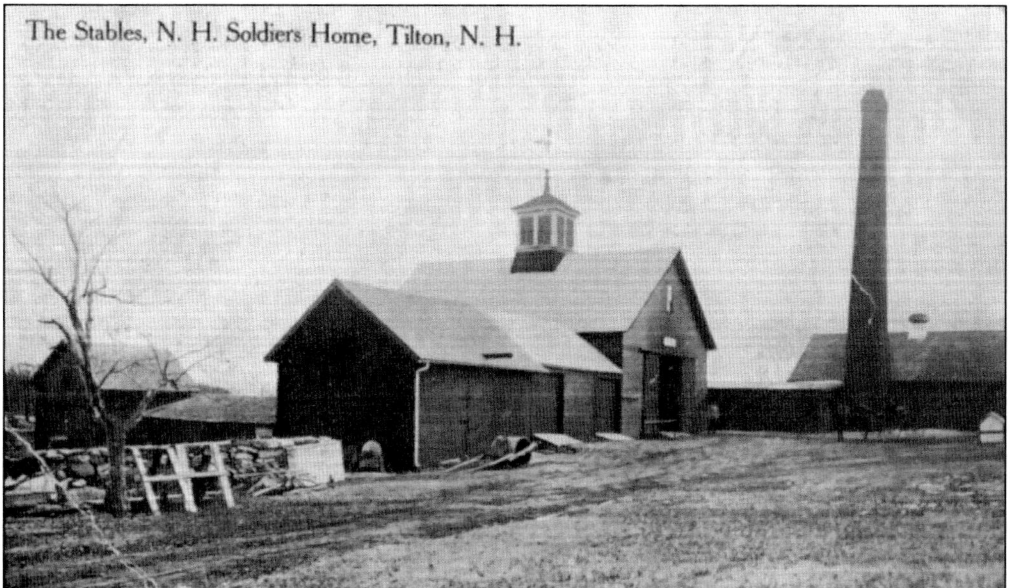

Two of the buildings on the property of the New Hampshire Soldiers' Home are pictured here. The larger building housed stables where they kept horses used for parades and wagon transportation. The building with the smokestack was the heating plant for the large facility. (Courtesy of the Moulton family.)

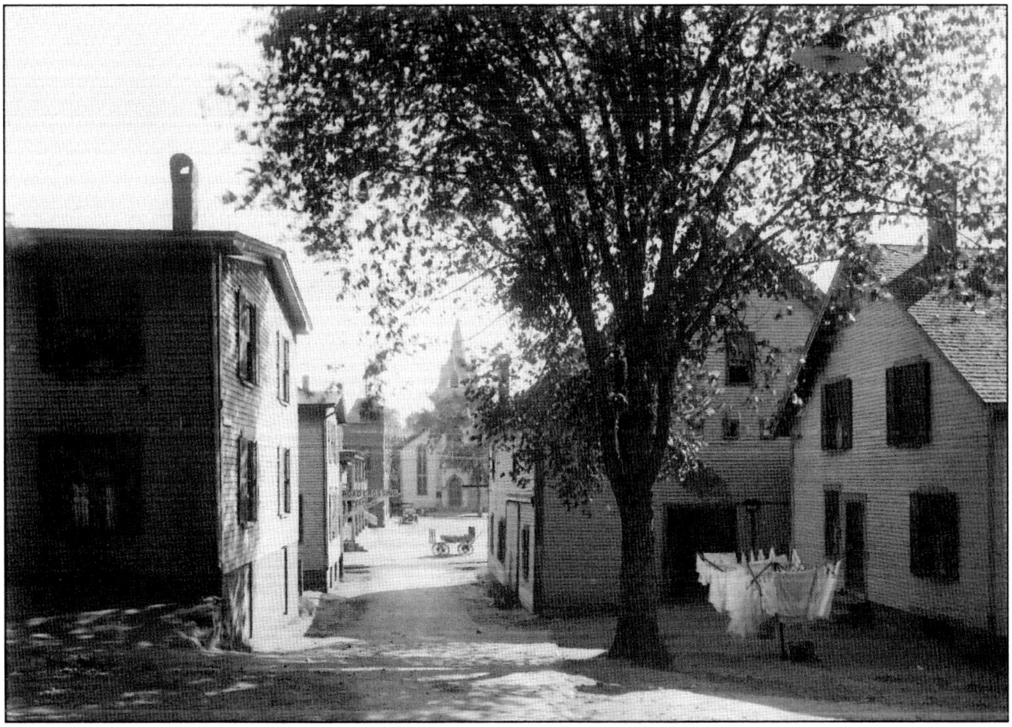

On a peaceful and picturesque afternoon on Central Street in the middle of Tilton, clothes are hung out to dry. At the far end of this lane is the Tilton–Northfield Methodist Church. A railroad baggage cart waits next to the tracks for the train to arrive. Central Street, shown on the map below, actually crossed Pleasant Street and led to Knowles Hall at Tilton School. The map also shows the streets as they were originally named, as well as the historically significant buildings. (Photograph courtesy of Tilton Town Hall; map drawn by Kelsey Stone.)

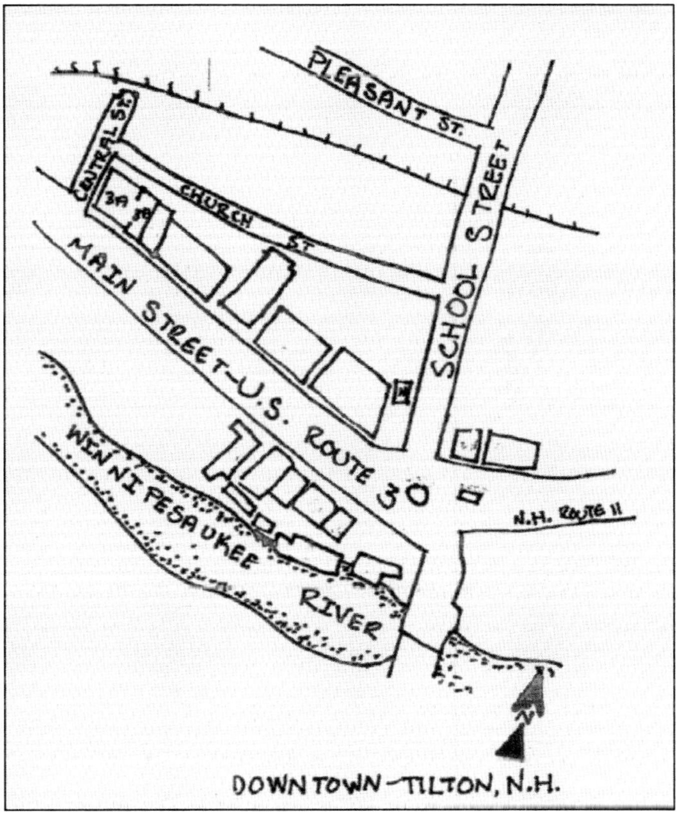

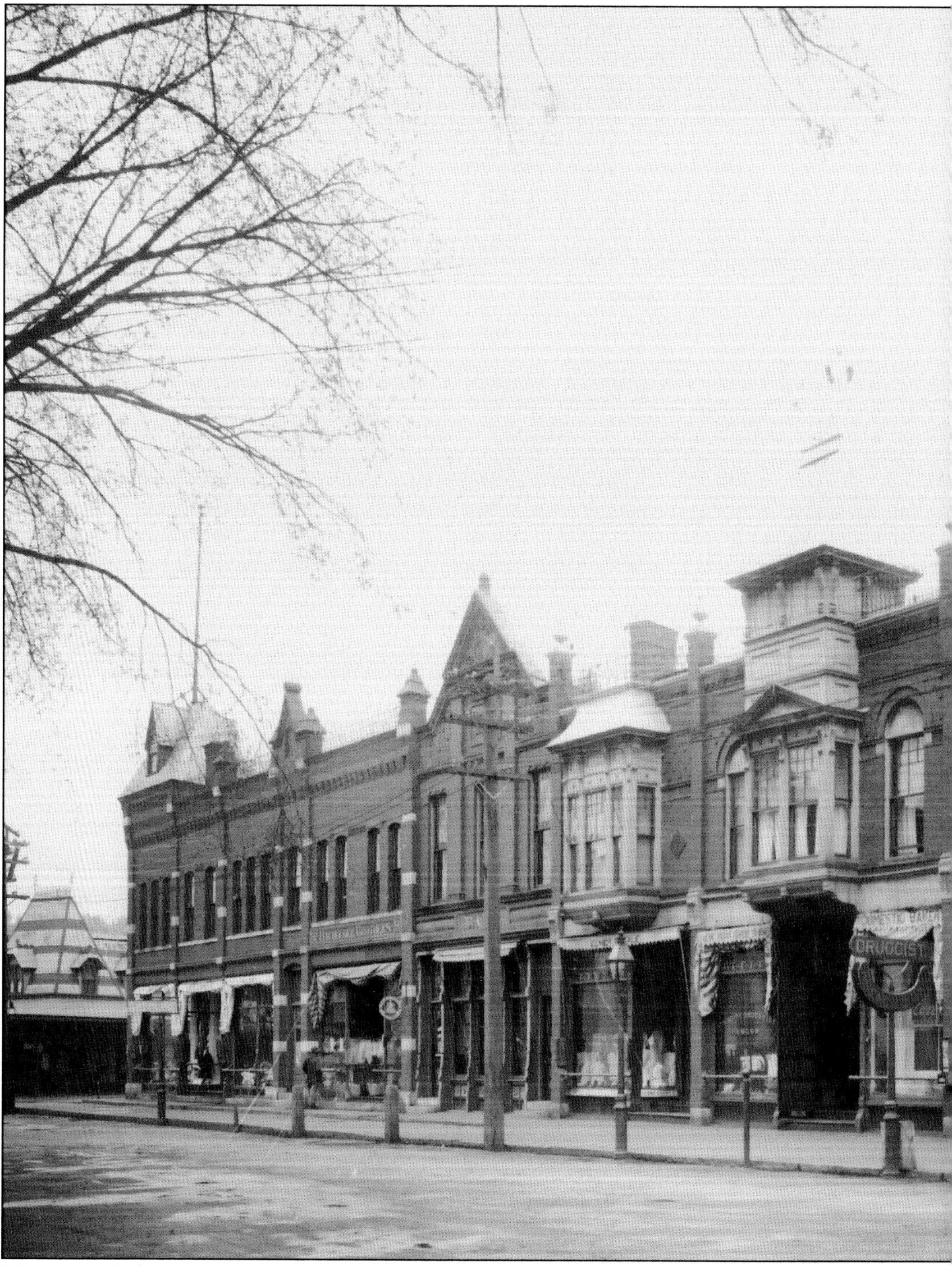

This view of a business section of Main Street starts with the railroad station on the left. To the right of the station is a Victorian brick structure—the first of three commercial blocks. Charles E. Tilton commissioned the building in 1886 and named it after himself. Next is a narrow, brick building constructed around 1887 for the Citizens National Bank and the Iona Savings Bank. These banks moved to the Charles E. Tilton Block in 1926. In 1887, Tilton commissioned the

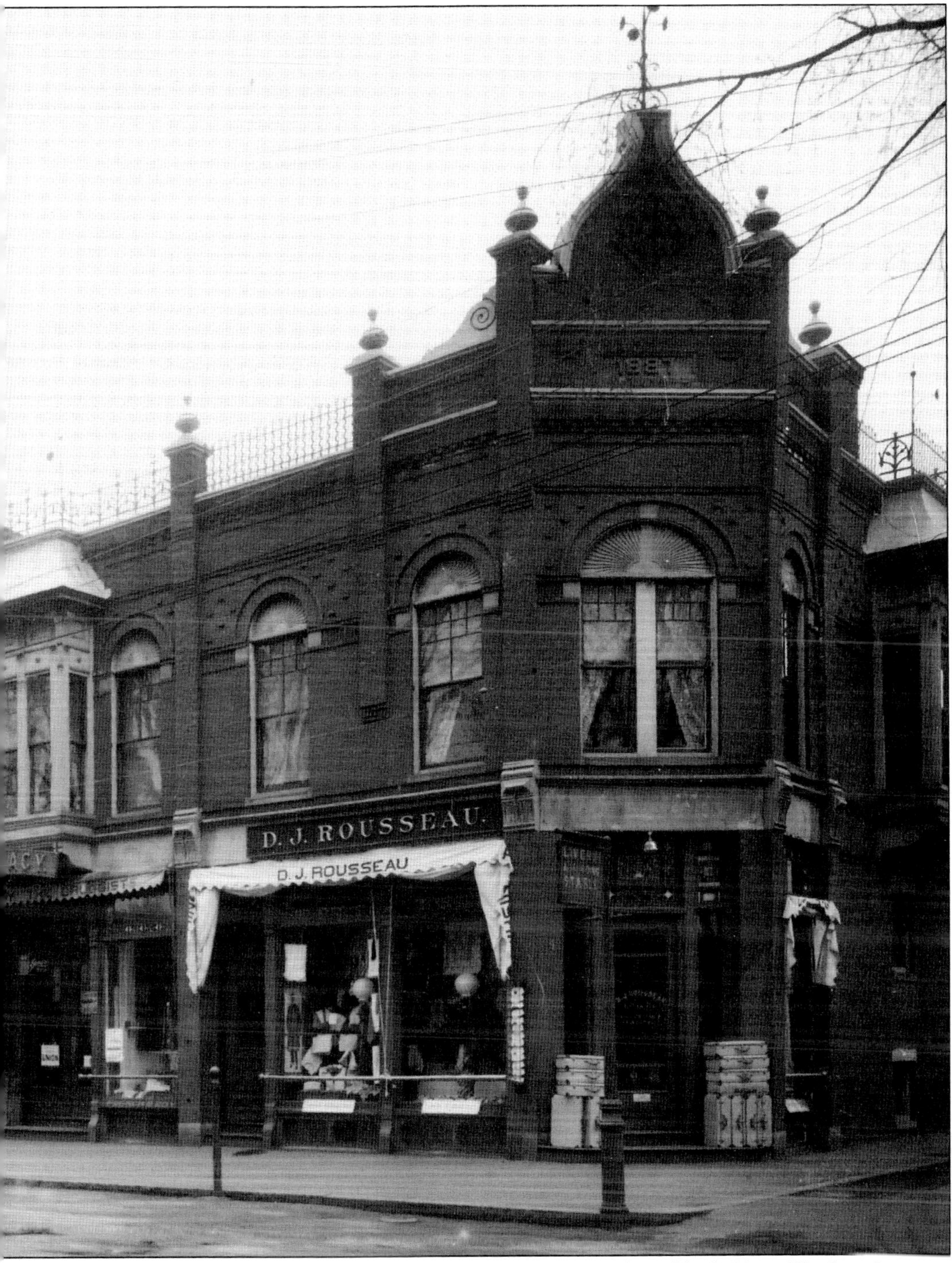

next block, which he gave to his son Alfred Edwin Tilton. The Alfred Tilton Block is the most elaborate building on Main Street, and has the unusual feature of a "corner store with a corner door." Queen Anne, Tudor Revival, Italianate, and Second French Empire architecture can be seen in the photograph. (Courtesy of Tilton Town Hall.)

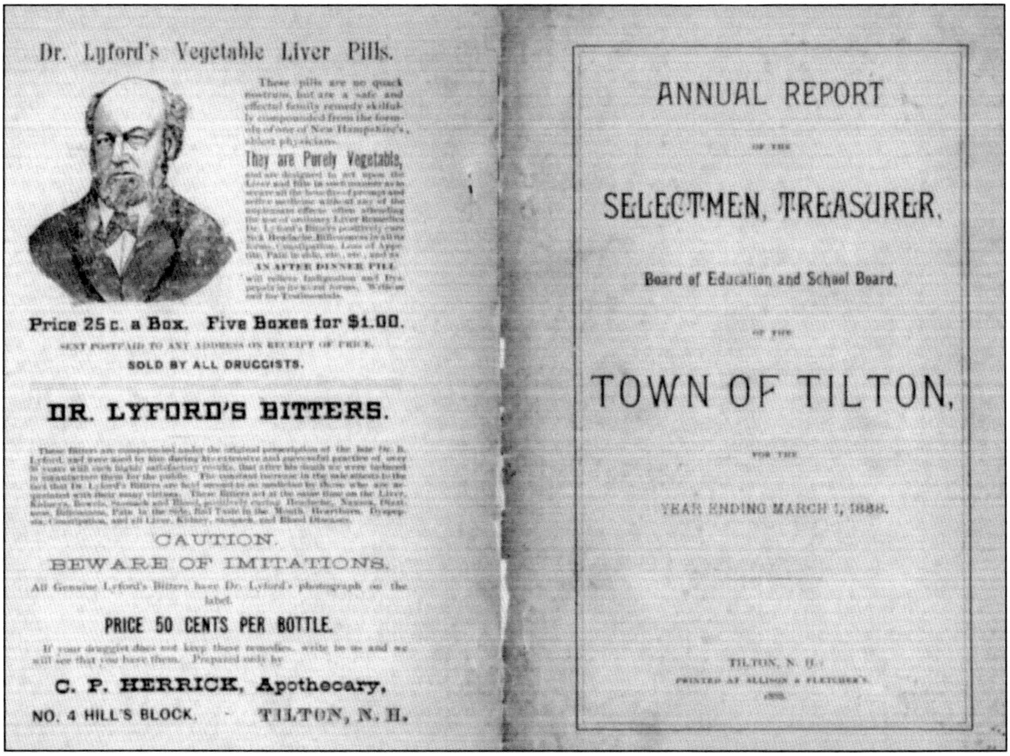

Dr. Lyford's Vegetable Liver Pills.

They are Purely Vegetable,

Price 25 c. a Box. Five Boxes for $1.00.

SOLD BY ALL DRUGGISTS.

DR. LYFORD'S BITTERS.

CAUTION.

BEWARE OF IMITATIONS.

PRICE 50 CENTS PER BOTTLE.

C. P. HERRICK, Apothecary,

NO. 4 HILL'S BLOCK. TILTON, N. H.

ANNUAL REPORT

SELECTMEN, TREASURER,

Board of Education and School Board,

TOWN OF TILTON,

For the year ending March 1, 1888, the *Tilton Town Report* of the selectmen, treasurer, board of education, and school board published an advertisement on the back cover of the annual report. A rare occurrence, prominent local businessman Charles Putnam Herrick exerted his influence in order to generate the advertisement. (Courtesy of the Randall family.)

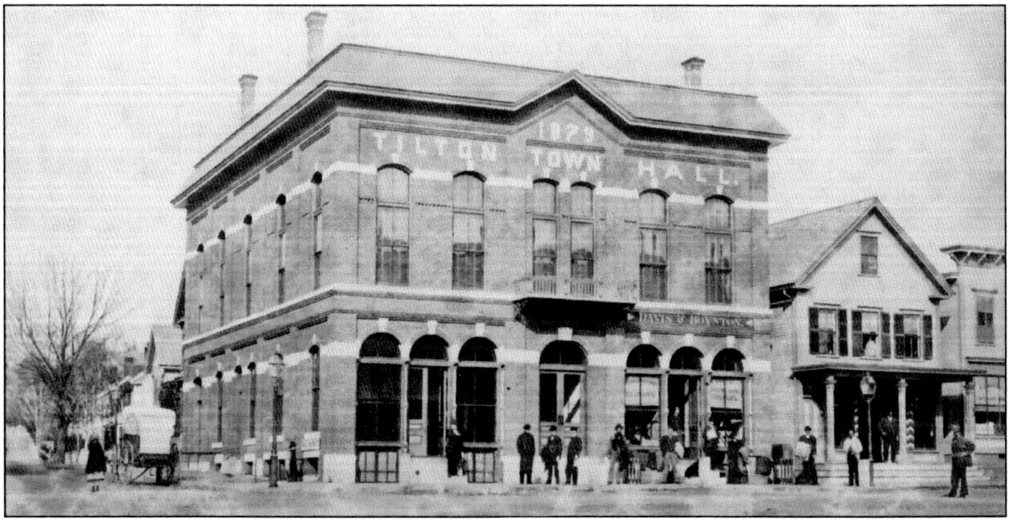

Tilton Town Hall, shown in this 1900 photograph, was a popular gathering place. The town's business was conducted upstairs. On the ground floor, there was a clothing store on the right and a post office on the left. On the School Street side of the building, steps led to a below-street meat market run by Batchelder and Couch. The wagon near the market was a common means of transportation at this time. (Courtesy of Mariam Melendez.)

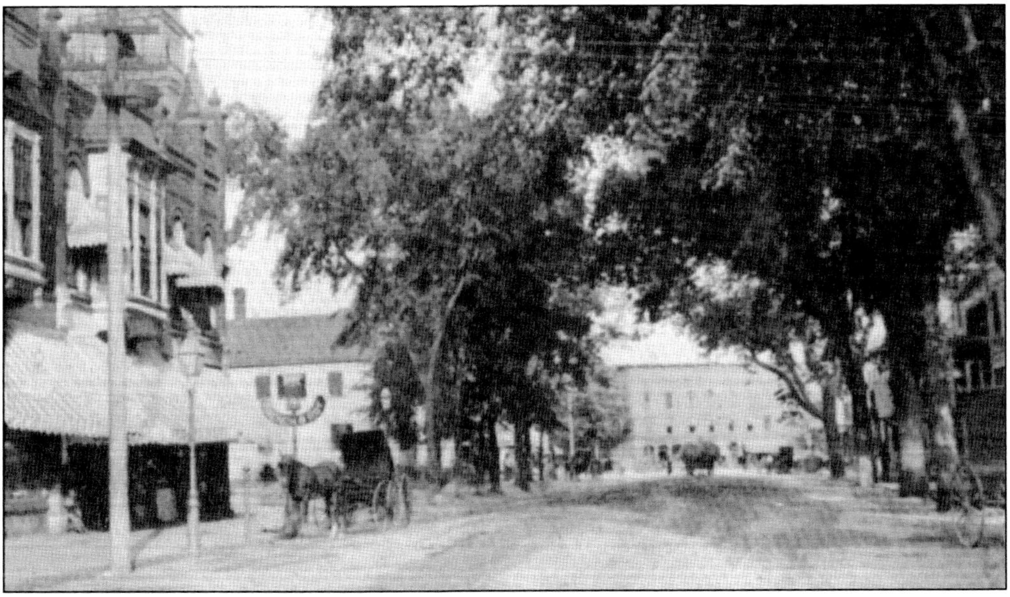

Looking east through the arch of grand elm trees that once lined the main street of Tilton around 1908, you can see the three-story Hill Block. The curved sign on the left over the horse reads French and Roy—the publishers of this postcard and several others throughout the book. (Courtesy of the Hall Memorial Library.)

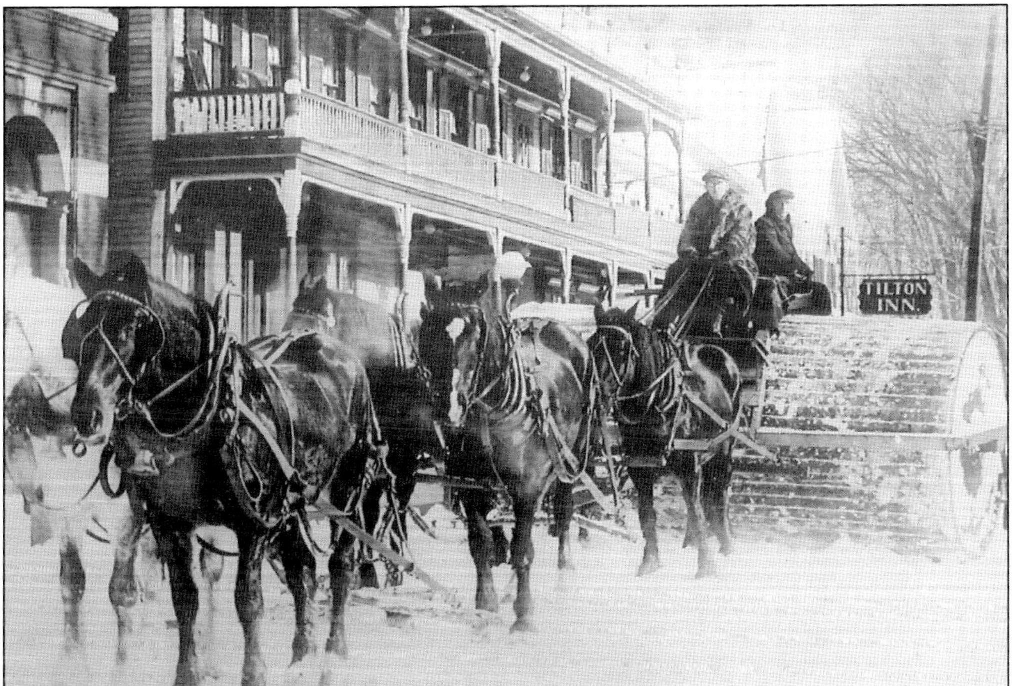

Ernest C. "Red" Elliott and an unidentified assistant are driving this horse-drawn snow roller, seen here in front of the Tilton Inn. This process of rolling and pressing the snow was, for many years, a successful and economic way to allow continued transportation during the winter season. (Courtesy of the Randall family.)

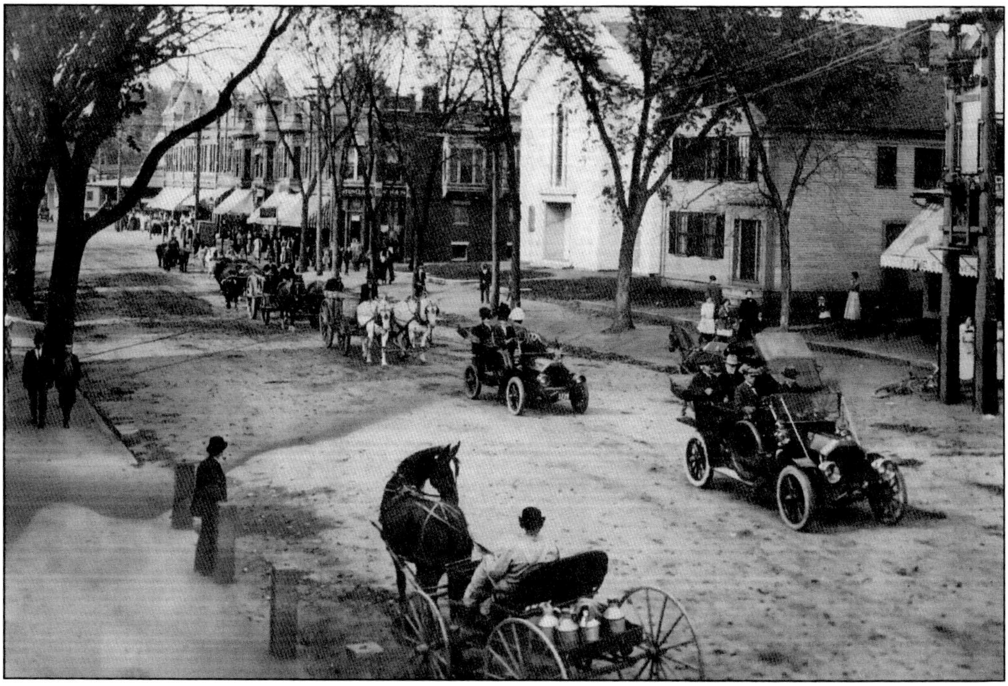

Going in an opposite direction than subsequent parades in Tilton, this early automobile and horse-drawn carriage procession was small in comparison to those of the future. The white house next to the Congregational Church was later replaced by a block of stores. A grand parade (below) even included a marching band with clowns. People are leaning out the windows in the Hill Block, and traffic is definitely at a standstill. The final vehicle in this parade is the pumper wagon that belonged to the Tilton–Northfield Fire Department. The soda fountain in Herrick's was probably very busy that day. (Above, courtesy of the Karl Barnard family; below, courtesy of the Randall family.)

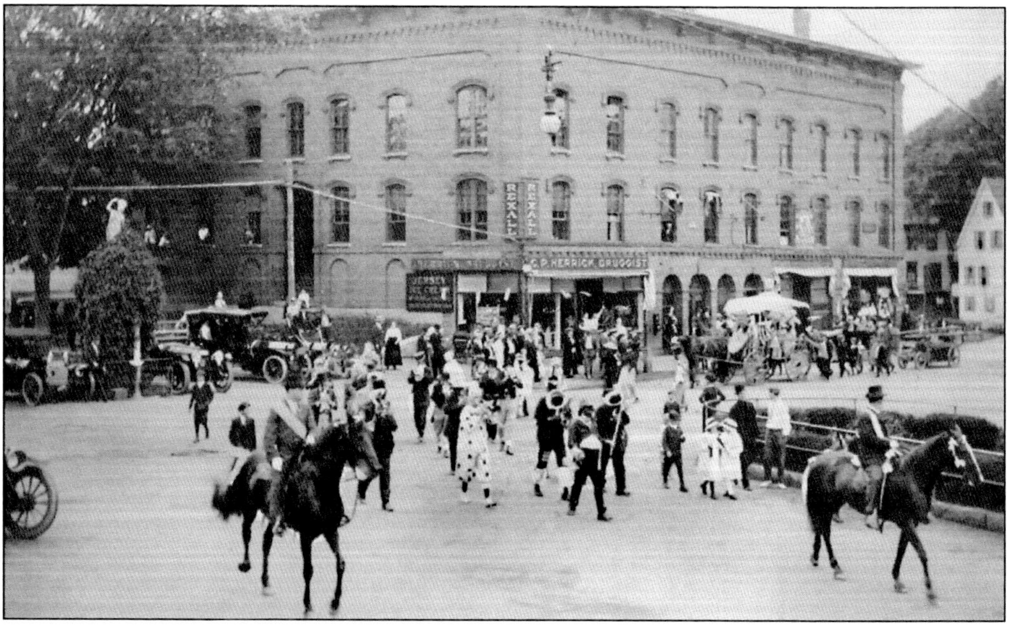

Parades were extremely popular events enjoyed by the residents of Tilton and Northfield. As a general rule, the parade route began near the fairground, went up Park Street, turned onto Elm Street, crossed the iron bridge (built in 1882) onto Main Street, and ended back at the fairground. This photograph shows a Labor Day parade turning onto Main Street. (Courtesy of the Hall Memorial Library.)

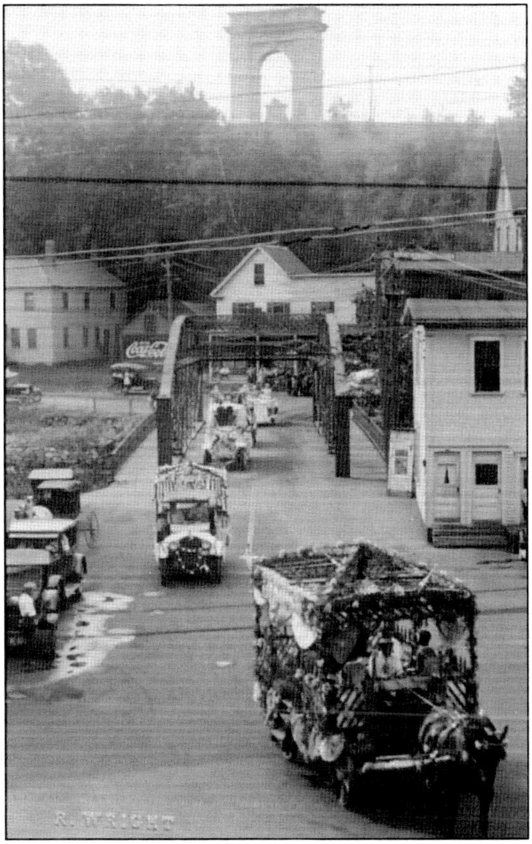

While waiting for an earlier parade to begin, these costumed ladies pose on their beribboned horse-drawn wagon. This float, sponsored by the Tilton Mills, shows examples of the woolen fabric they manufactured. The Tilton Mills were located at the foot of Mill Street. (Courtesy of Tilton Town Hall.)

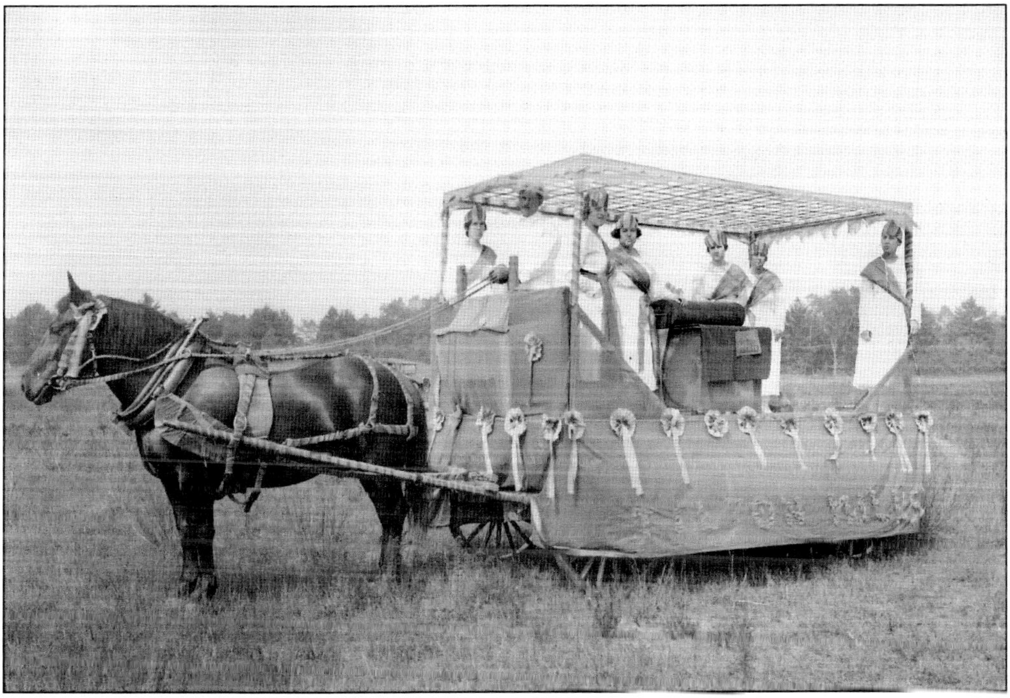

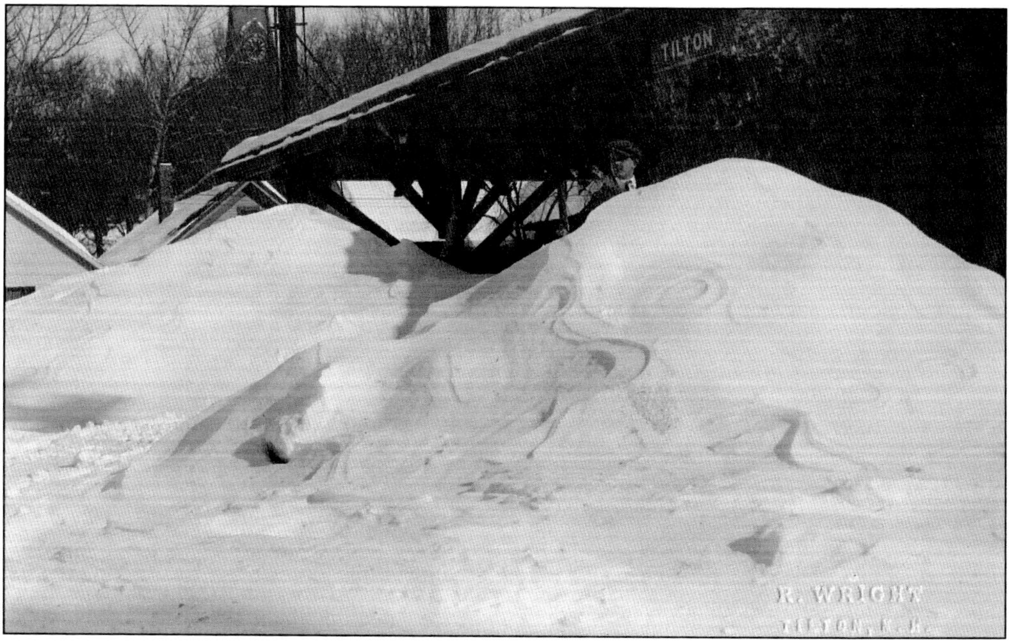

The banks of snow are piled high, and the wind has swirled it into beautiful patterns. This 1927 image by local photographer Roscoe Wright shows a winter scene at the Tilton railroad station. "When winter comes" is hand-printed on the postcard below. The snow is so deep that only the heads of two people are visible on the left side of the photograph near the soda sign. A chamber of commerce sign blows in the wind over the street. (Both photographs courtesy of the Moulton family.)

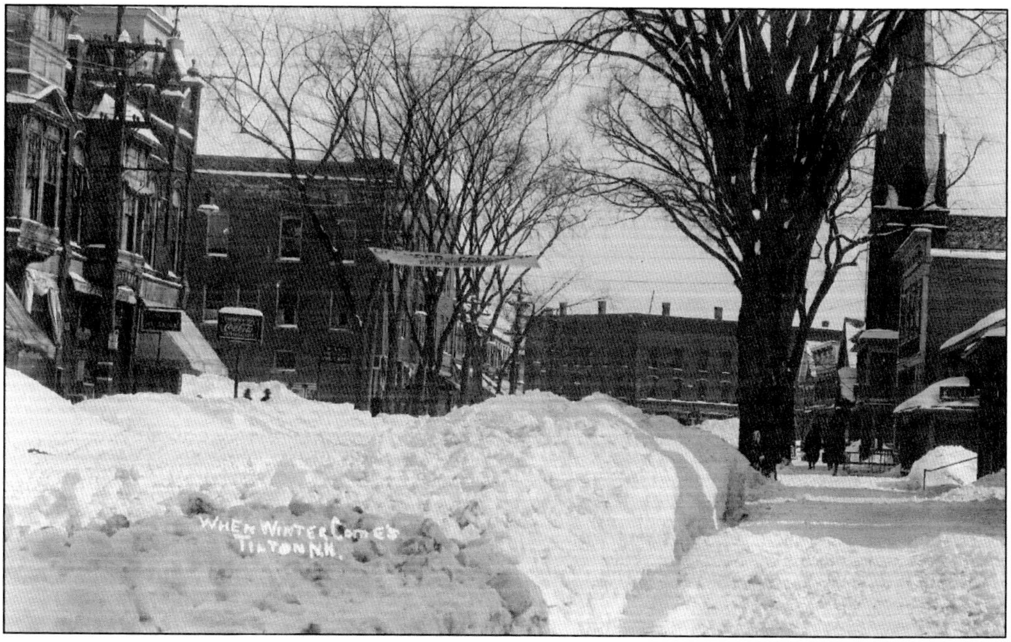

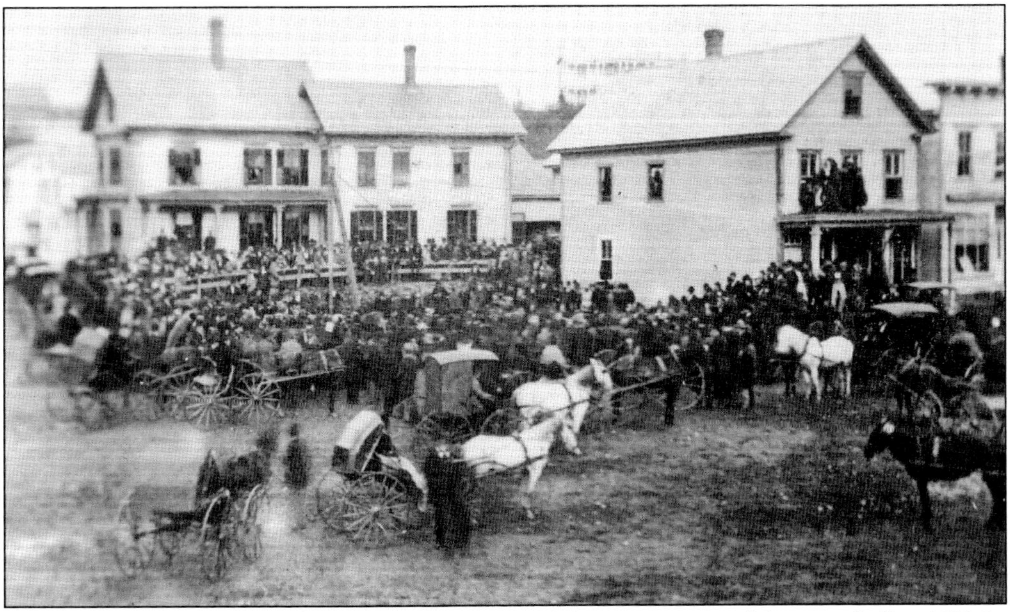

People came from all over town to watch the laying of the cornerstone of the town hall in 1879. In December 1880, the town voted to accept the building and abide by the donor's conditions—the most important being that the name of the town would never change. A gift to the people of Tilton from Charles E. Tilton, the fully furnished and appointed town hall has been the home to many other enterprises besides town business. In 1903, the post office occupied the left side of the first floor. The right side contained a barbershop, billiard and pool parlors, as well as a drop-off point for a Franklin laundry. Town business, including the annual town meeting, took place upstairs. (Above, courtesy of the Randall family; below, courtesy of the Hall Memorial Library.)

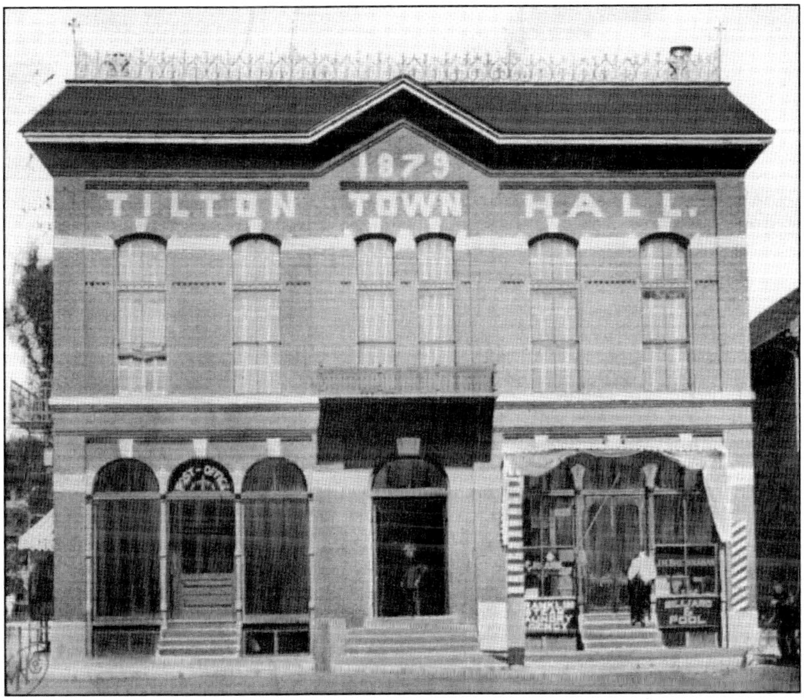

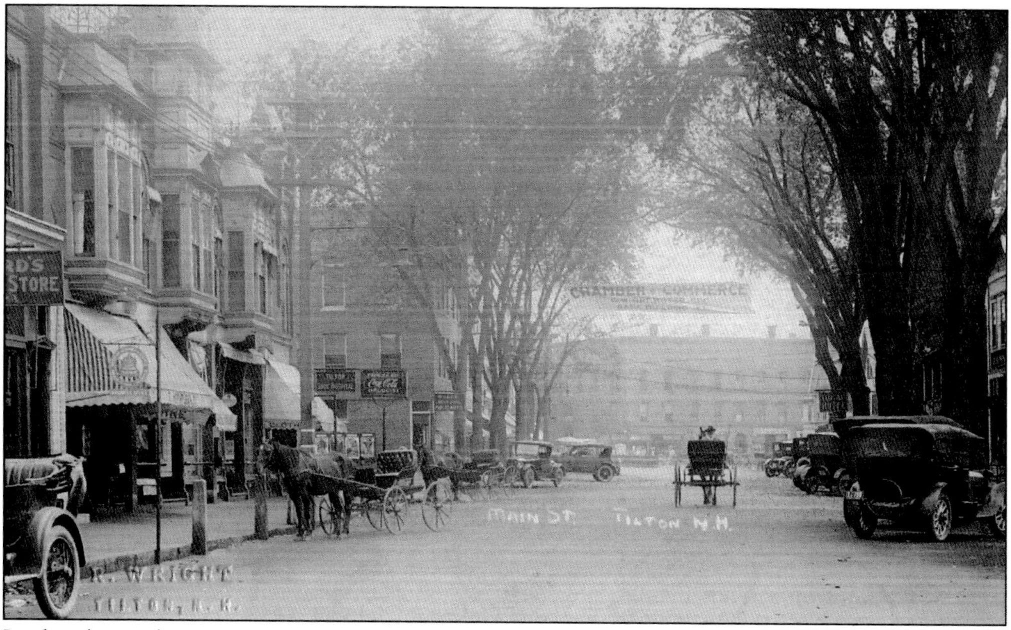

In the above photograph, the transportation transition is obvious on Main Street around 1918. The banner across the street reads, "Chamber of Commerce/C.W. Brewster, Sec/Bank Building." Starting on the left side of the street, signs indicate Simpson's Drug Store (only partially visible), a public telephone, the Tilton shoe hospital, and soft drinks available at French and Roy's drugstore. The sign beyond the drugstore indicates that the Livery Stable, located behind the stores, offers "Public Autos." The letters on the awning just before the church point out a clothing store, which was owned by brothers Arthur and Nazaire Twombly. Below is a notebook that served as an advertising opportunity for "The Corner Store with the Corner Door." (Both photographs courtesy of the Randall family.)

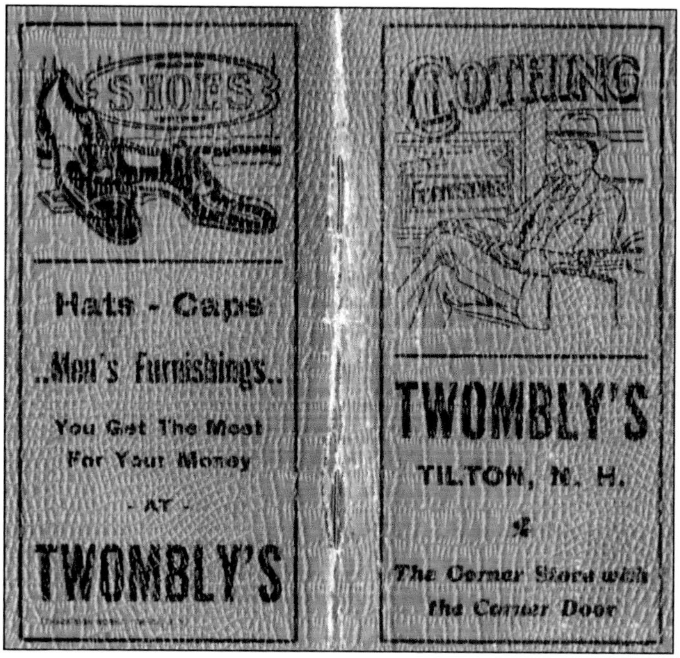

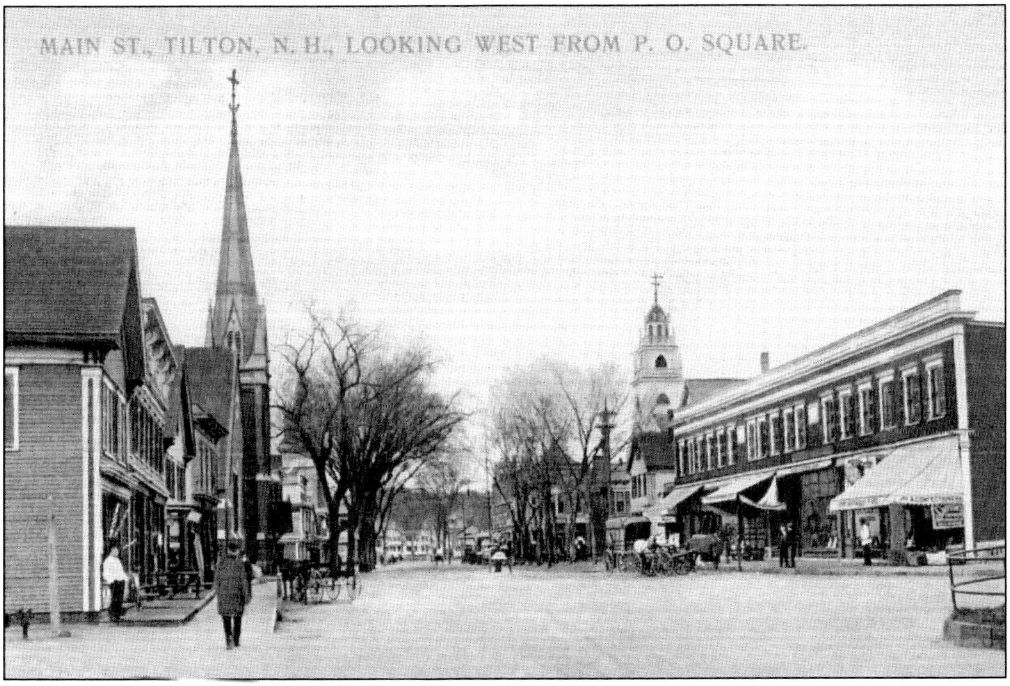

The above photograph looks west down Main Street in Tilton in the late 1800s. The store on the left is a barbershop. According to the awning, the store across the street is John Raffaelly's Confectionery. The steeples on the left belong to Trinity Episcopal Church and the Methodist Church, which can be seen through the trees. The steeple on the right is the Congregational Church. The photograph below looks east down Main Street in the mid-1940s, where elm trees form an archway over the street. Along the way, Ingalls Market was on the right and the Public Service Company of New Hampshire office that had a café next door was on the left. (Both photographs courtesy of the Hall Memorial Library.)

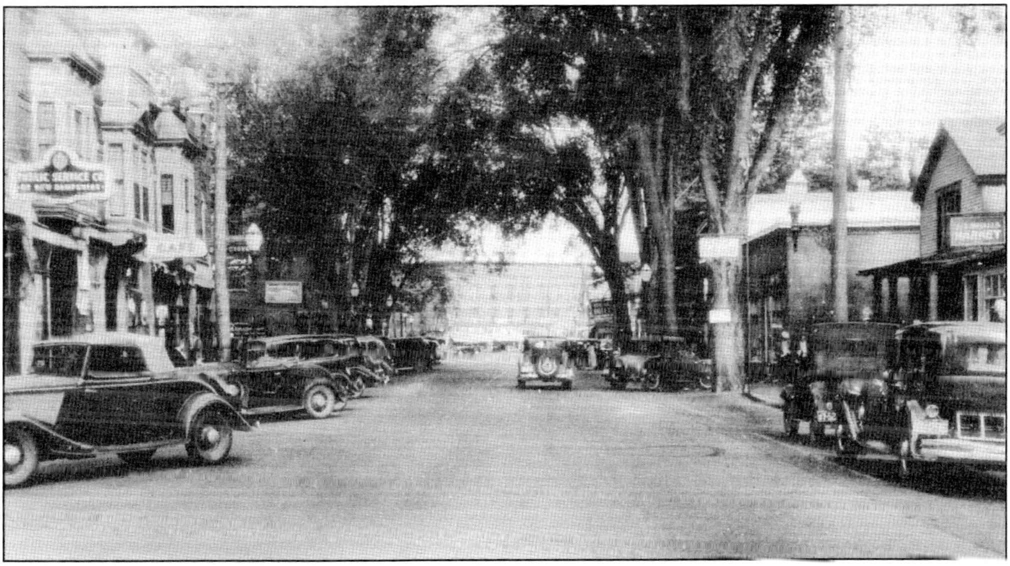

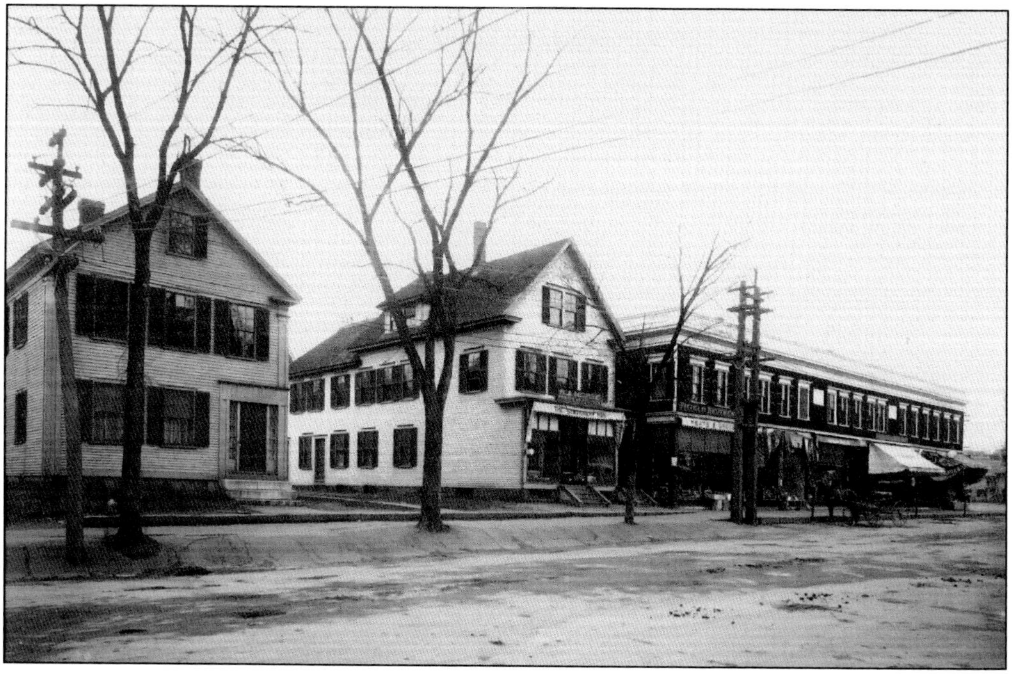

These two white buildings, on Main Street to the right of the Northfield-Tilton Congregational Church, were razed around 1915 when Maj. Charles E. Tilton purchased them to utilize the space for a block of commercial properties. In the photograph below, the Christmas tree in front of the monument indicates a busy shopping day on Main Street. One of the popular places for hot coffee or lunch was Pop's Diner, located on the corner of School Street and Main Street. The diner was run by "Pop" Maynard. The cars are from the late 1930s and early 1940s. (Above, courtesy of the Dodge family; below, courtesy of the Hall Memorial Library.)

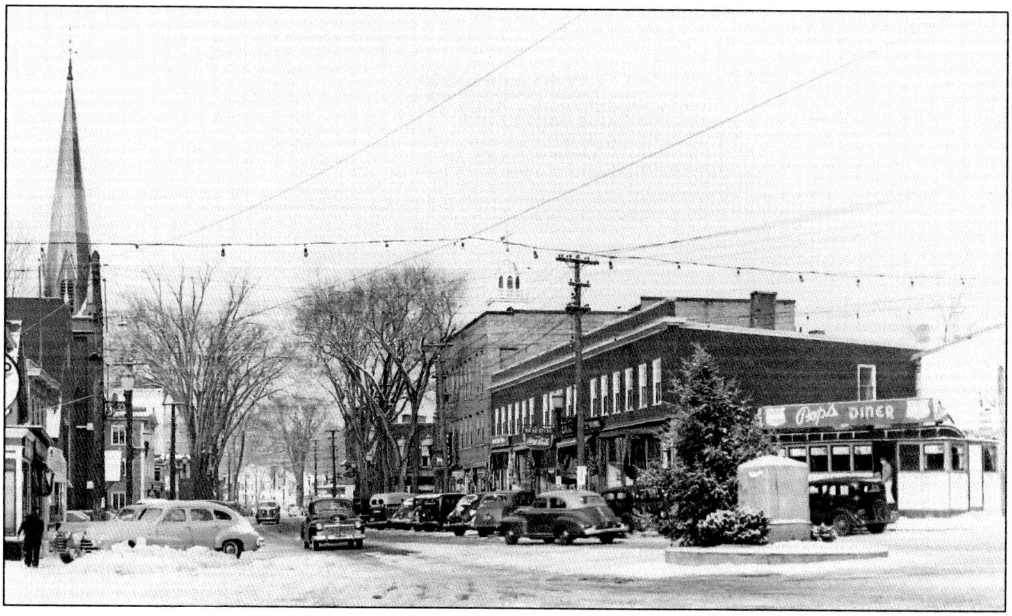

Three

Business and Industry

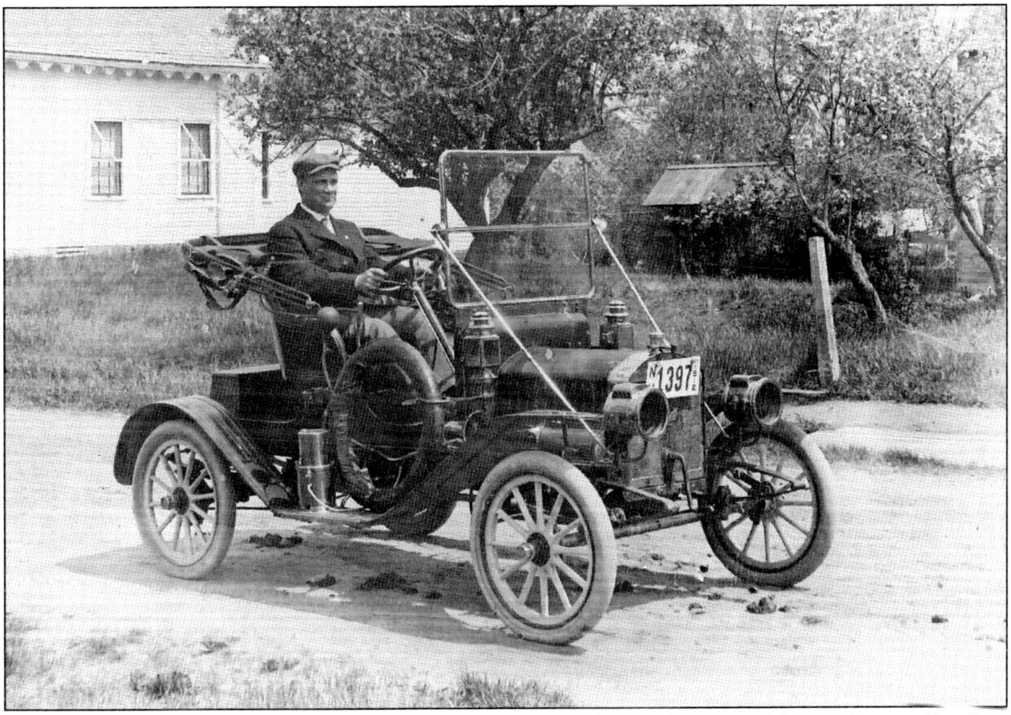

This visitor of the Barnard family farm on Lancaster Hill Road motored down Grange Road in his 1909 Model T Runabout with wooden spoke wheels. The date on the license plate is 1912. The contrast between the age of industrialization, symbolized by the motorcar, and the age of agriculture, symbolized by the manure on the road, is clearly demonstrated here. (Courtesy of the Karl Barnard family.)

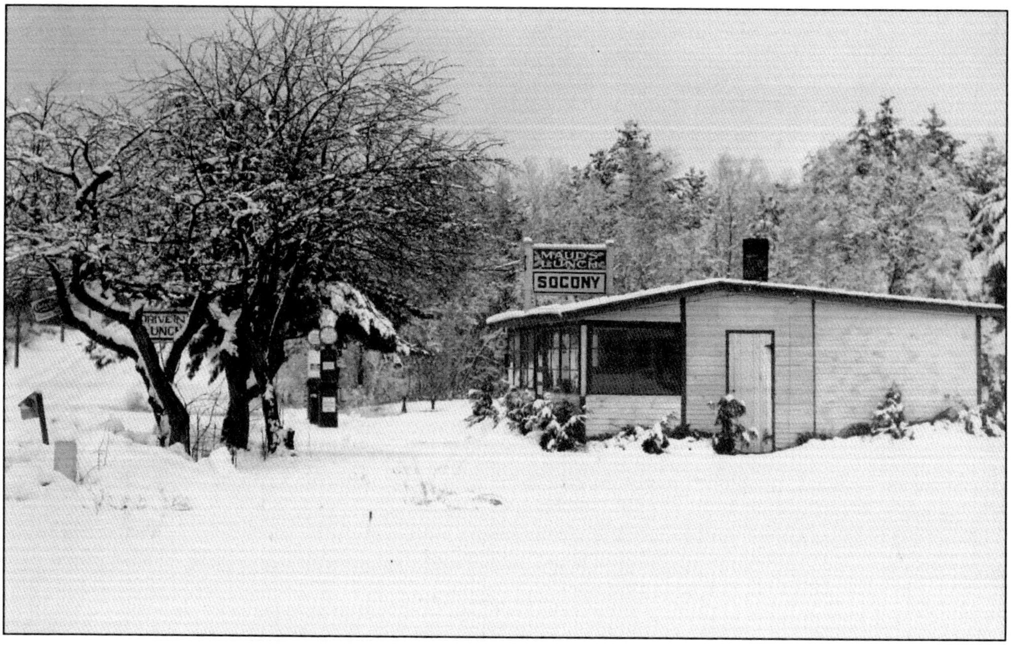

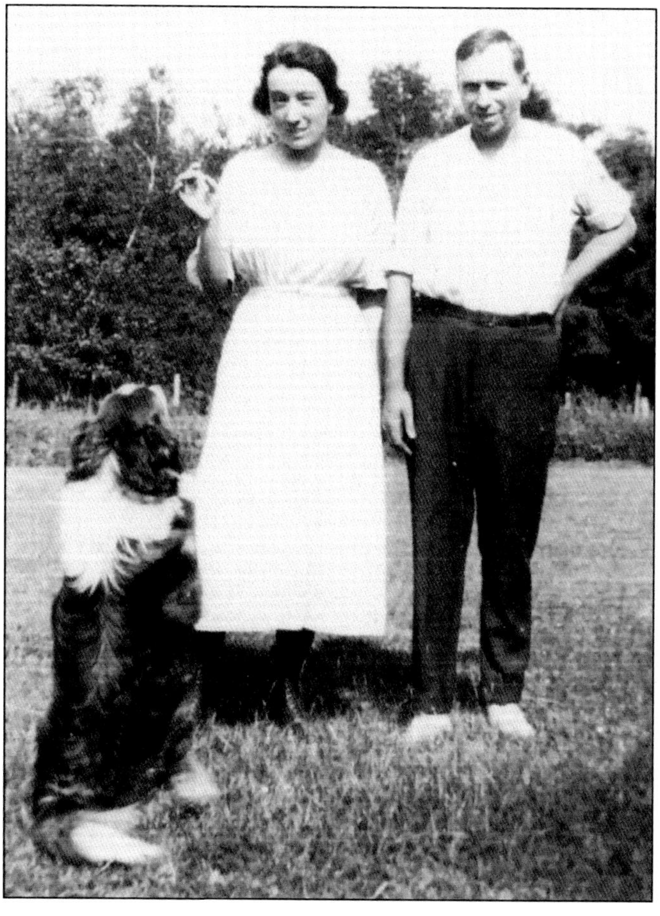

Located on Route 3, at the beginning of "the Plains" near the Sanborn Road, was this popular small restaurant and grocery store, shown above. Maude's Drive-in Lunch and Grocery was originally a hot dog stand. It became so popular that owners, Maude and Ralph Bickford, shown with their dog, added a dining room. Maude's home-cooked meals became well known throughout the area and tourists coming by the little establishment stopped for refreshments and/or supplies on their way to the Lakes Region. As the business continued to grow, gasoline became a frequently requested commodity that the Bickfords were soon able to provide. (Above, courtesy of the Hall Memorial Library; below, courtesy of Helen Hollister Holbrook.)

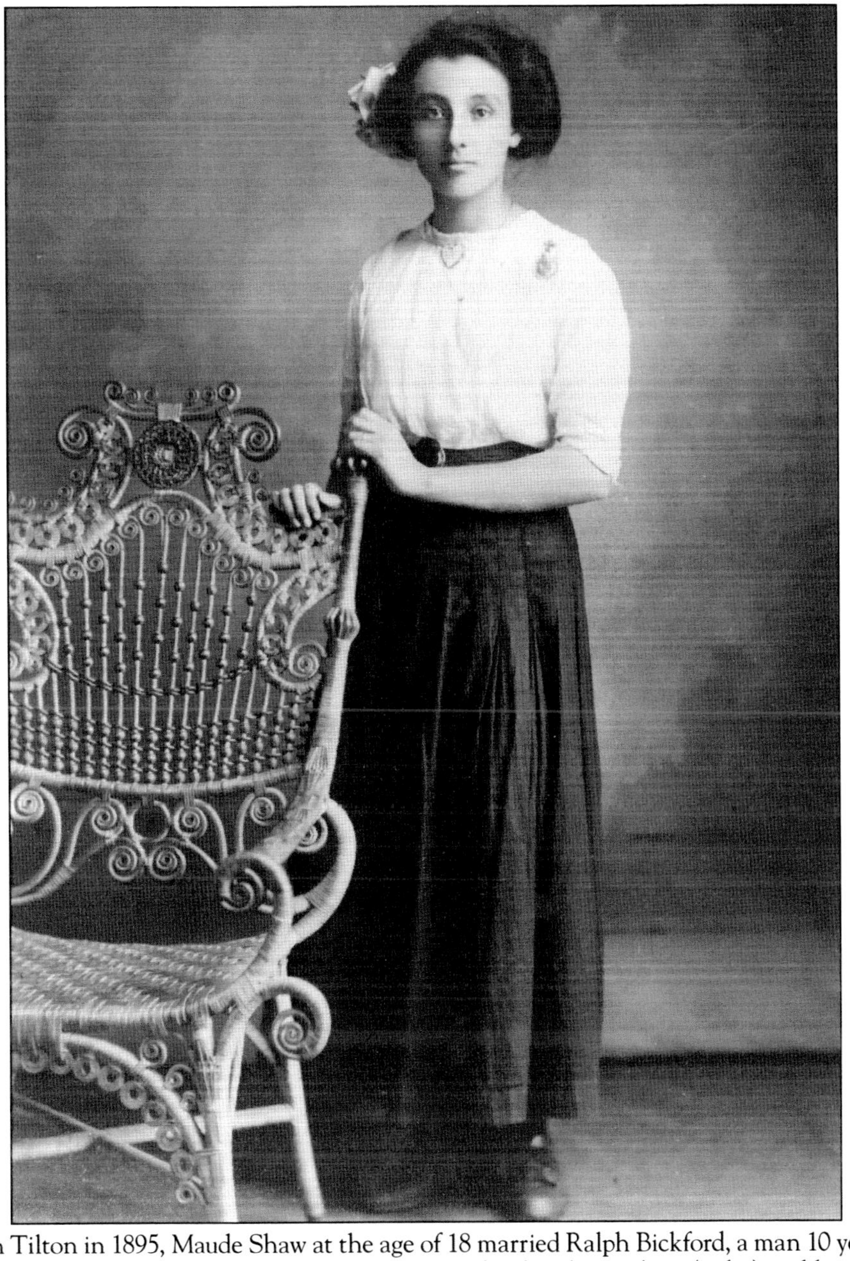

Born in Tilton in 1895, Maude Shaw at the age of 18 married Ralph Bickford, a man 10 years her senior. Shortly after their wedding, Ralph contracted infantile paralysis (polio) and became an invalid, as was Maude's father who lived with them. Due to a changed family situation, Maude and Ralph also became foster parents to her eight-year-old niece, Helen Hollister. According to Helen, her aunt worked successfully to return some use to her husband's limbs. Maude realized that their small home was a convenient place for campers from the Tilton Free Campground to borrow necessities, and from this Maude saw the opportunity to support her family. When World War II broke out, Maude could not get enough supplies to stock the store, so she accepted a position with the White Mountain National Forest as a spotter in the fire tower on Black Mountain in Benton, New Hampshire. Maude lived on the mountain from April to October from 1942 to 1945 with only her dog Fritzie to keep her company. (Courtesy of Helen Hollister Holbrook.)

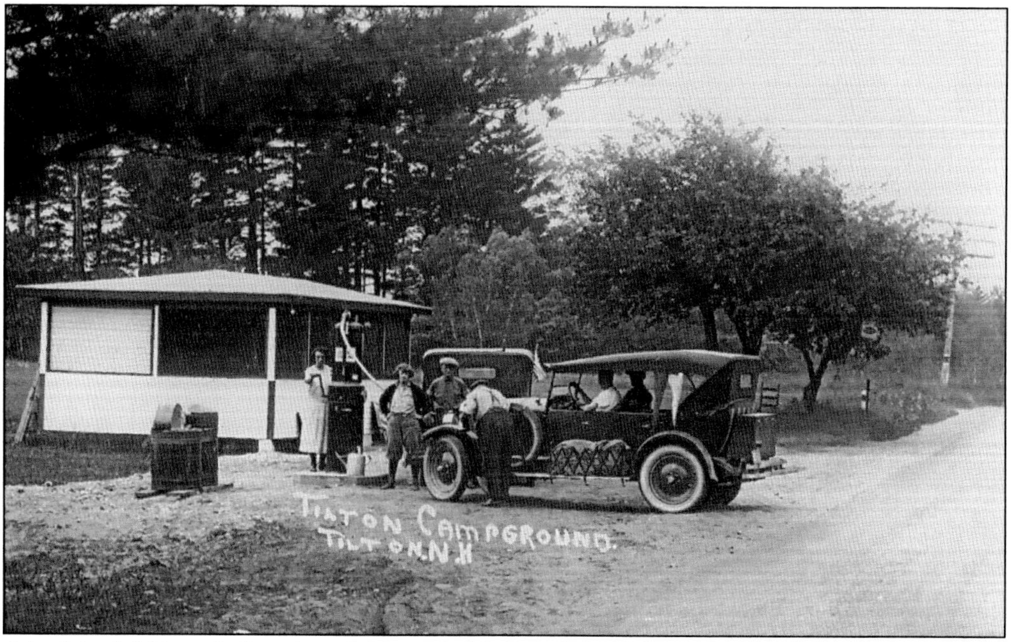

After Maude's Drive-In Lunch and Grocery added gasoline to their services, it was up to Maude, as the owner, to operate the crank on the gas pump. The car being serviced is a 1925 five-passenger Auburn touring car, with solid disc wheels. This vehicle was made in Auburn, Indiana, and sold for $1,350. On the rear of the vehicle is a trunk, which was an optional feature available at an additional cost. The Tilton Free Camp Grounds was located across the dirt road (Route 3). The upper sign reads, "Chamber of Commerce," and the lower sign reads, "Gypsies not allowed." According to Maude's niece, Helen Hollister, none were ever refused admittance. The smaller car, flying the American flag, is also an Auburn, with two doors rather than four. (Above, courtesy of Helen Hollister Holbrook; below, courtesy of the Hall Memorial Library.)

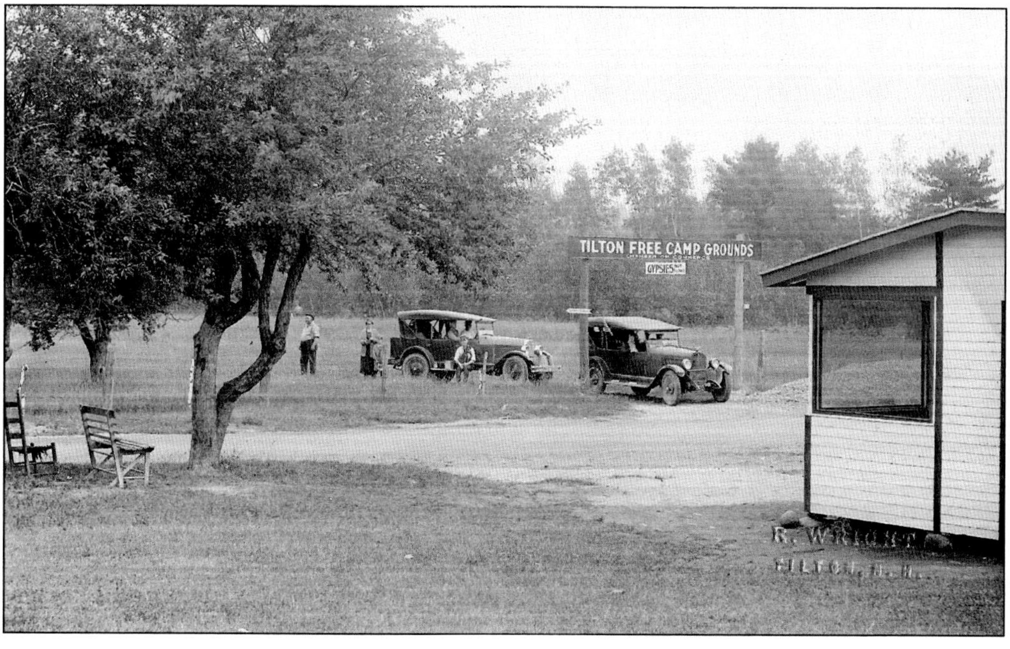

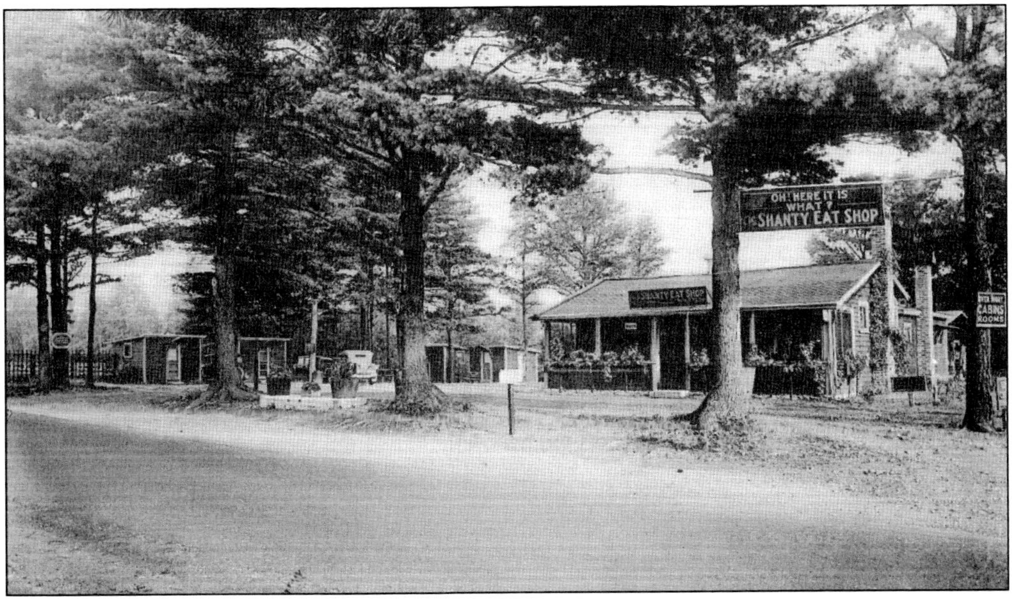

Around 1930, the Shanty Eat Shop on the Tilton Plains was located just east of the intersection of Sanborn Road and Route 3. The cabins were open only in the summer, but the restaurant was open year-round. "Bea" and "Bud" Blocker purchased this business in 1950, and the name was changed to the Midway Cabins and Restaurant. This was one of the earliest cabin colonies for tourists coming into the Lakes Region. The menu shown here is very basic, excluding the cost of each item. (Courtesy of the Hall Memorial Library.)

The Shanty Eat Shop

Tilton Plains

SPECIALTIES

Steak and Chicken Dinners — Fried Clams — Spaghetti-Italian

Waffles

Sandwiches: Club, Chicken, Ham, Egg

Salads: Shanty Special, Chicken, Egg, Fruit

Ice Cream — Cold Drinks

Home Cooked Food

Pies — Doughnuts — Cakes

Tea — Coffee — Milk

(Iced or Hot)

PRIVATE PARTIES ACCOMMODATED

Tilton Telephone No. 235-13

LUNCHES PUT UP TO TAKE OUT

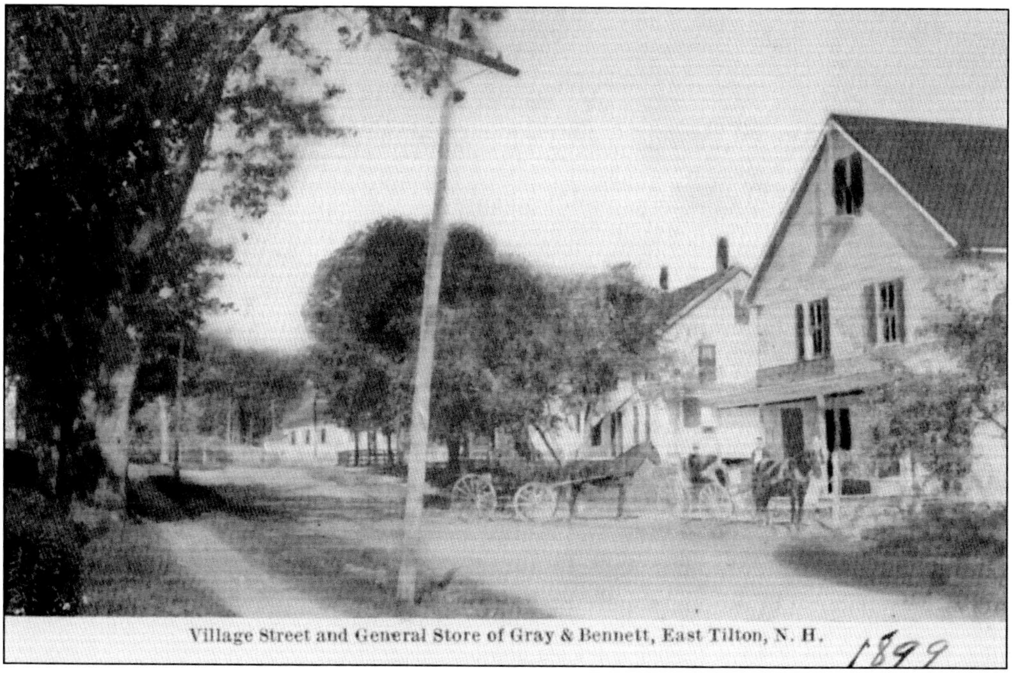

Church Street, the center of the community of Lochmere, is shown above in an 1899 photograph. The first building on the right was the General Store of Gray and Bennett. The white building next to the store was Harmony Hall, the second floor of which was used for entertainment, social events, and community gatherings. The photograph below shows the south end of Church Street going into Belmont. The white house on the left was on the Belmont side of the Winnepesaukee River. (Above, courtesy of the Randall family; below, courtesy of the Moulton family.)

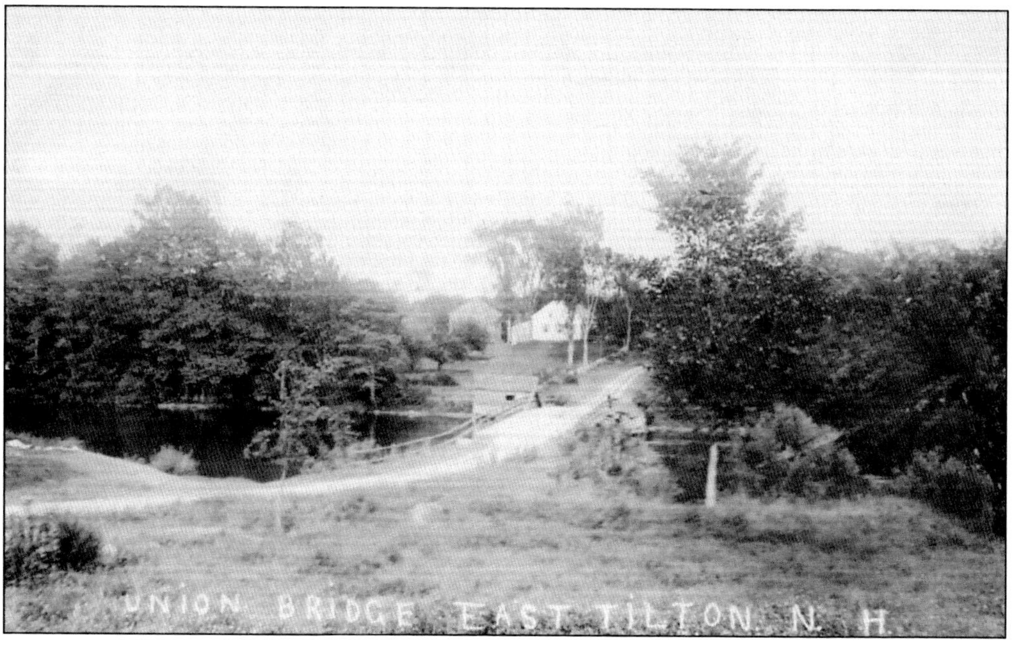

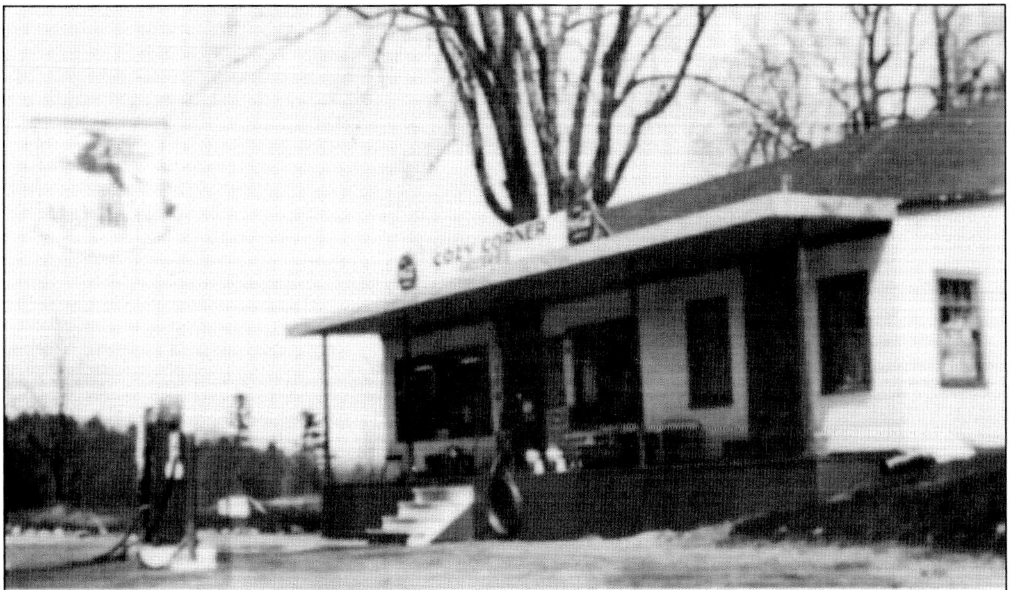

COZY CORNER STORE – LOCHMERE, NEW HAMPSHIRE

Cozy Corner Store presents the Pegasus trademark of Standard Oil Company/Mobilgas, indicating that they were a gas station as well as a small country store. Cozy Corner was located on the corner of Route 3 and Church Street in Lochmere, convenient to both area residents and tourists entering the Lakes Region. The photograph below shows the same corner when Church Street was the main street of Lochmere. Stories were told of gypsies camping with their horses on that triangle, where a town water pump was located. (Above, courtesy of the Moulton family; below, courtesy of the Randall family.)

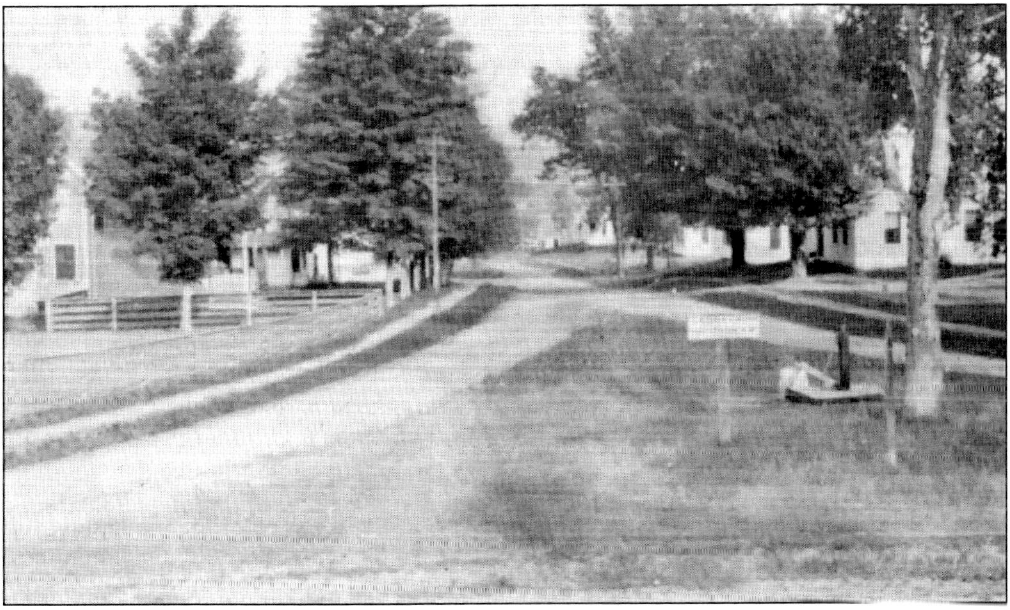

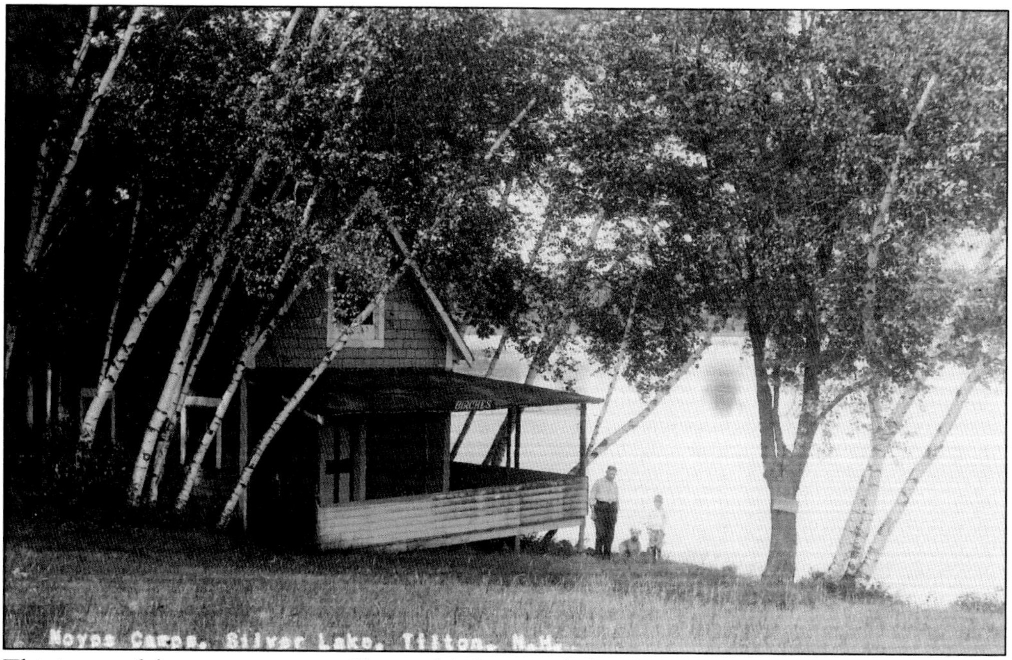

This is one of the many camps and beautiful clusters of white birch trees surrounding Silver Lake, formerly known as Little Bay. At a little more than a half-mile long, Silver Lake is a section of the Winnipesaukee River, which was a rich fishing source for Native Americans. It was the site of Fort Atkinson, a six-walled Colonial militia fort on the north shore of Little Bay. The fort's stone blocks were later removed to build a dam on the lake. The photograph below shows the Lochmere Dam, which is situated on the Winnipesaukee River. This dam allowed the mills in Lochmere to become self-sufficient through the use of the water as a power source. (Above, courtesy of the Hall Memorial Library; below, courtesy of the Karl Barnard family.)

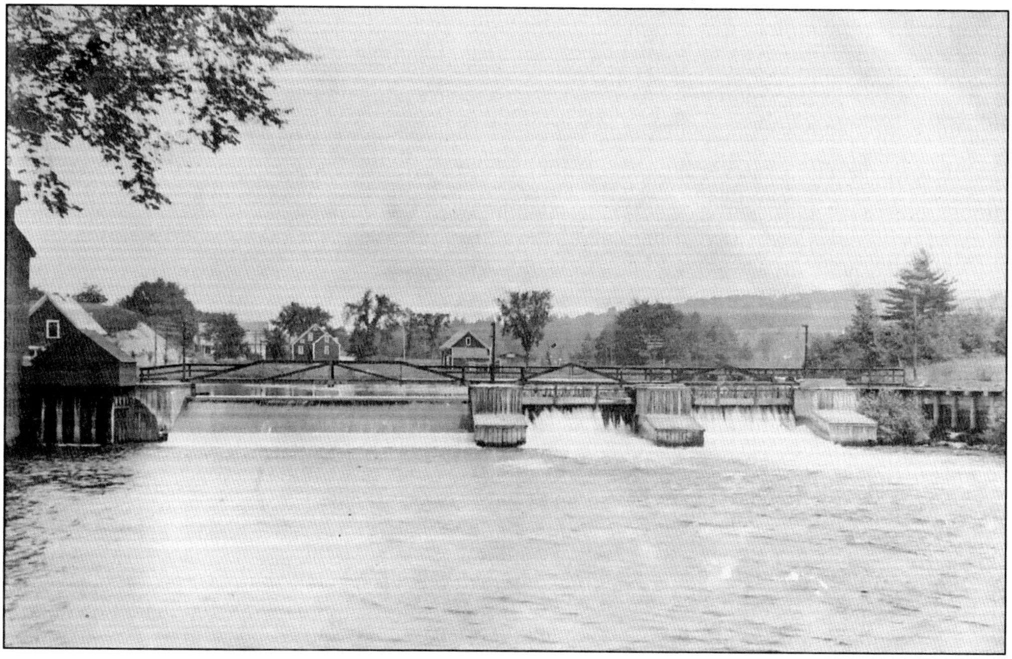

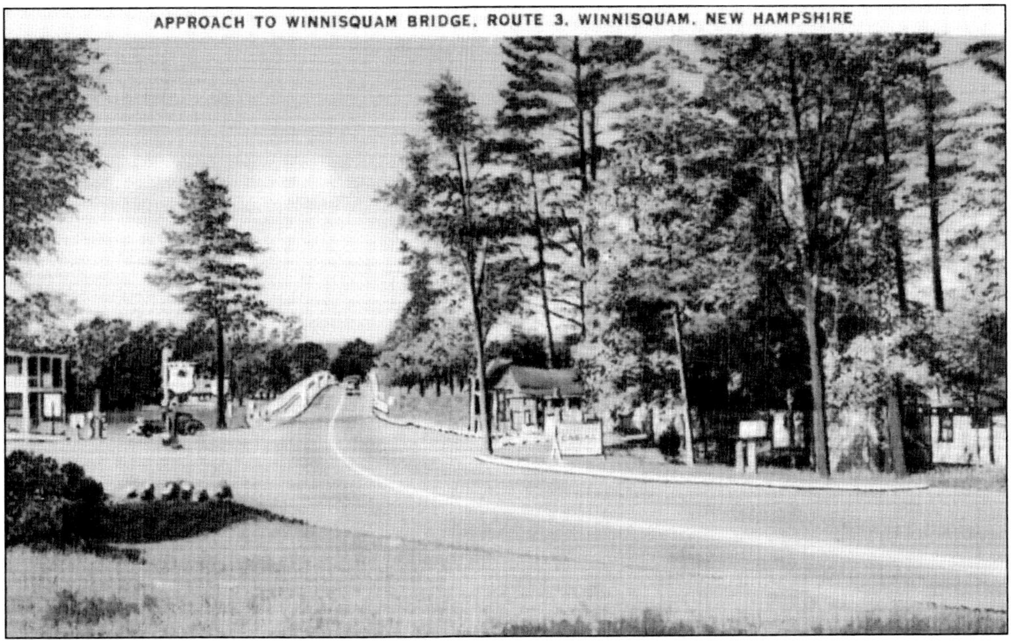

At the eastern end of Tilton, on the right hand side of the road approaching the Winnisquam Bridge, was a cabin colony—one of many in the Lochmere and Winnisquam area. On the left was a gas station and country store conveniently located for the tourist and local traffic. Just behind the country store, on the western shore of Lake Winnisquam, heading into Sanbornton, was a restaurant called The Sign of the Wings. It was the home base of the small seaplanes, which were available for rental flights over the Lakes Region. (Above, courtesy of Mike and Elaine Murphy; below, courtesy of the Moulton family.)

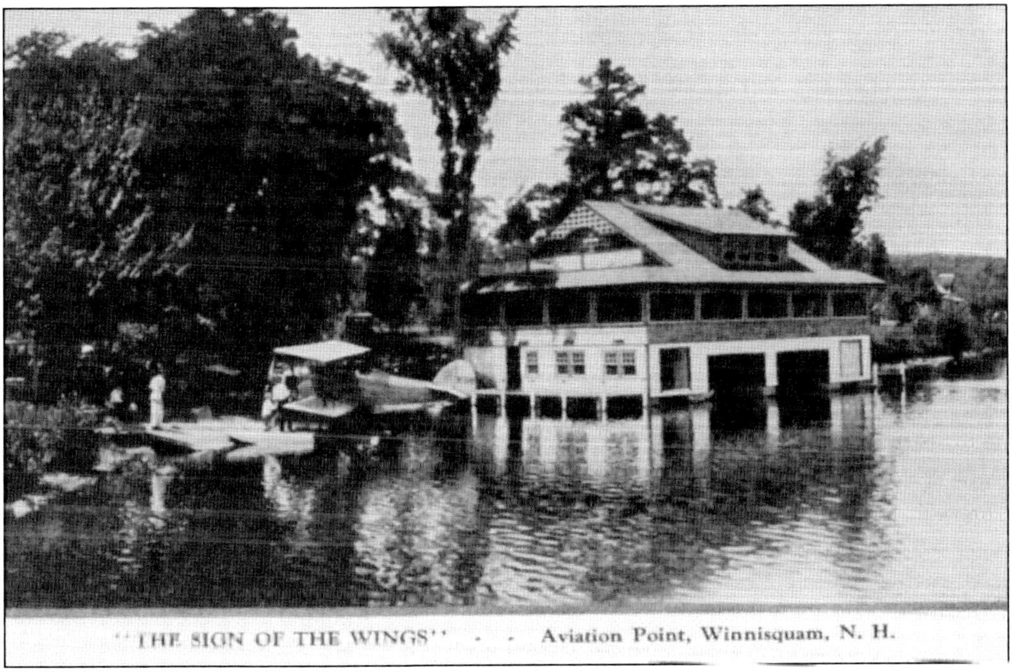

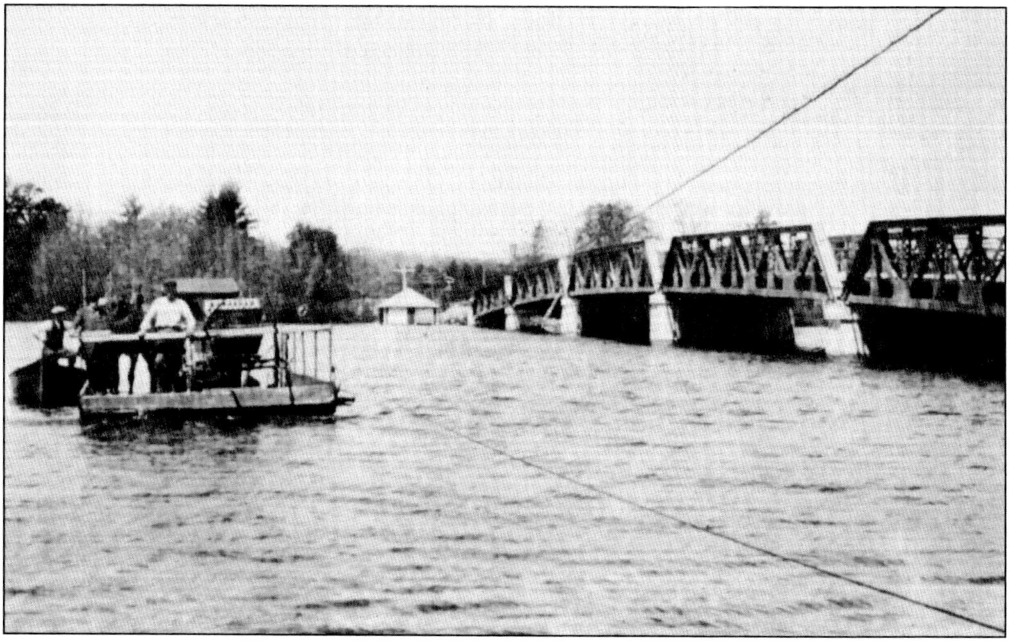

Winnisquam Bridge forms the boundary between Tilton, Sanbornton, and Belmont. This ferry drawn by cables was the only way for man or beast to cross Lake Winnisquam before the bridge was built. Built in 1915, the bridge (above) did not allow boats to pass beneath it. In the photograph below, the replacement bridge has a higher center. The new bridge reminded people of a mosquito; hence, its nickname "Mosquito Bridge." (Above, courtesy of the Karl Barnard family; below, courtesy of the Moulton family.)

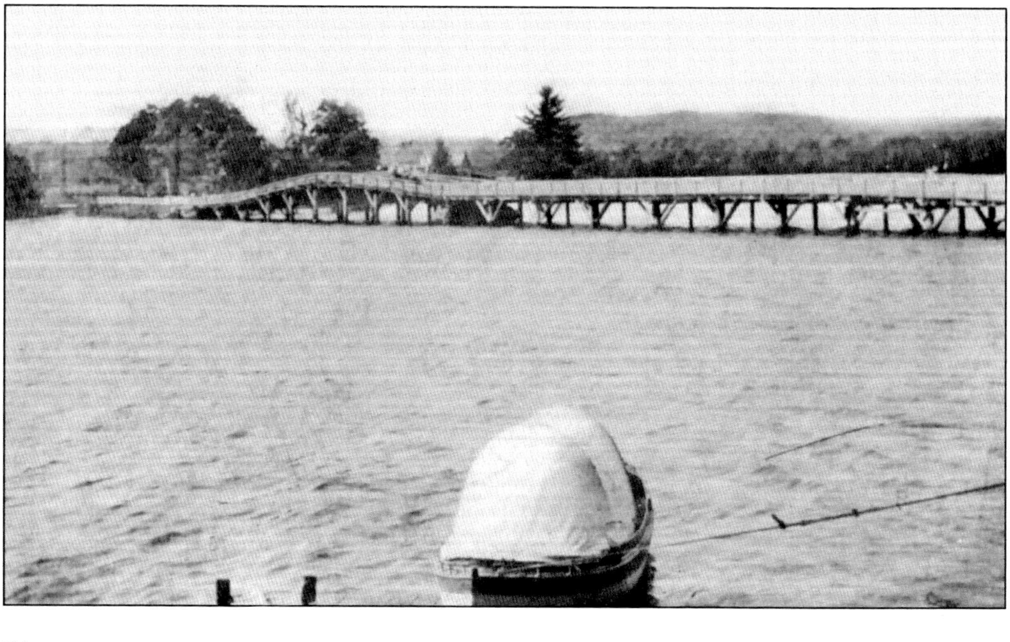

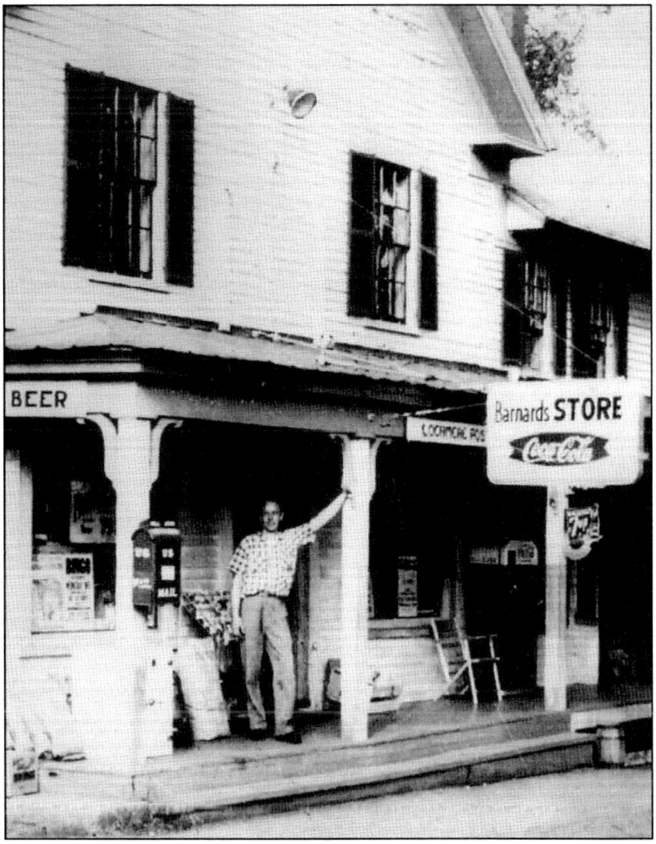

This 1950 photograph shows Lloyd Barnard, who was the owner of Barnard's Store in Lochmere for over 20 years. He was also postmaster for part of that time. The store was built around 1845, when Lochmere was attracting more residents. Some say that the hall upstairs was used for dances, and it may have been a Masonic Hall at one time. (Courtesy of Arthur Sanborn.)

Cadue's Garage was located across Main Street from the Tilton Inn and close to the river. This garage was one of the first Ford sales and service dealers in New Hampshire. The Texaco sign indicates that this was also a gasoline filling station. (Courtesy of Tilton Town Hall.)

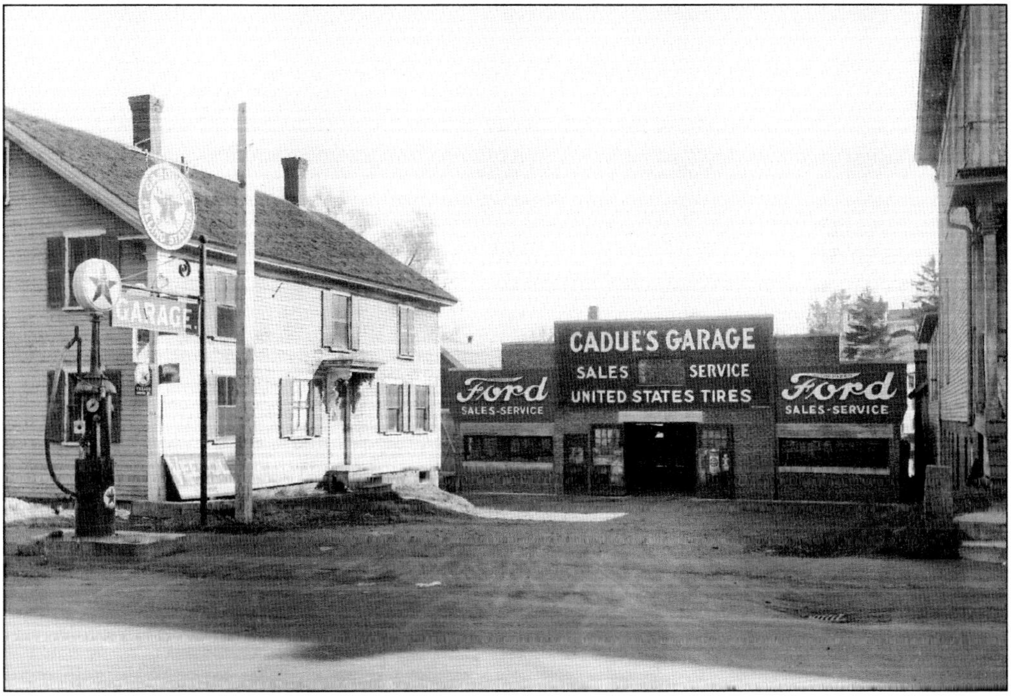

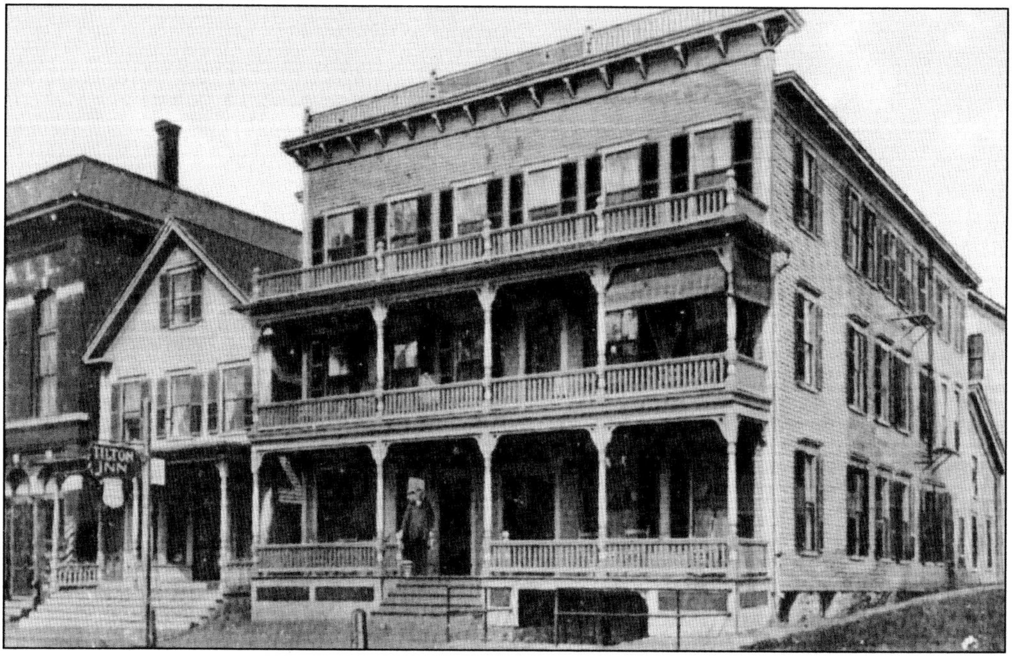

Built between 1875 and 1879, the Tilton Inn (above) was remodeled for a hotel in 1903. Between 1904 and 1912, it was enlarged to three stories with a two-story front porch. The Colby house, located between the inn and the town hall, was integrated structurally with the inn when the porch and the third floor were extended along the entire front, as seen in this 1924 postcard (below). At one time, the Colby house served as the post office until Jeremiah C. Tilton moved it back to the store where the town hall was later built. (Both photographs courtesy of the Hall Memorial Library.)

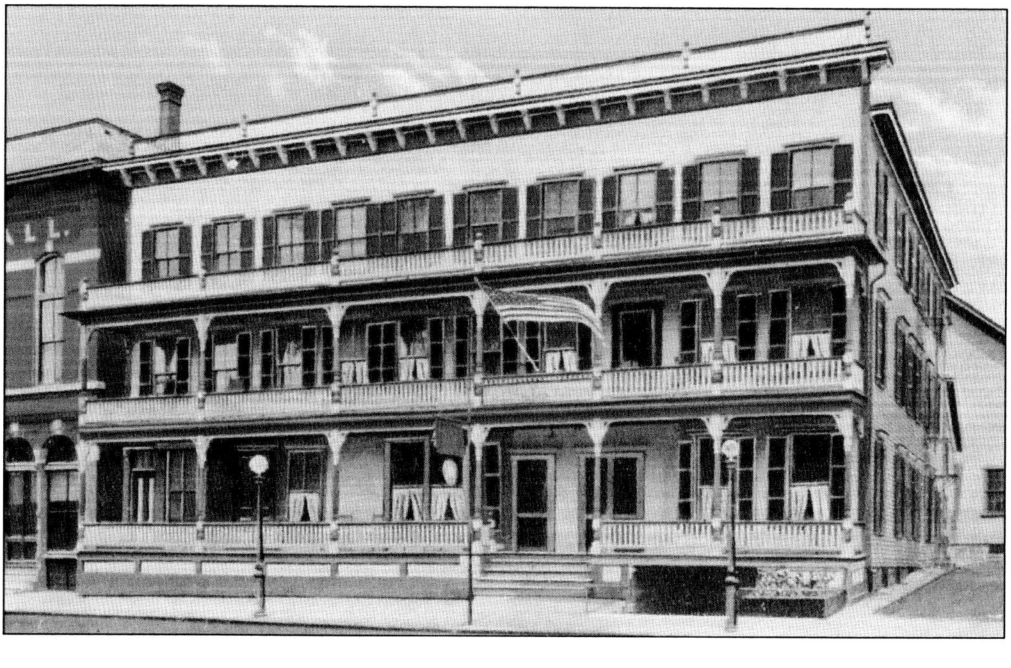

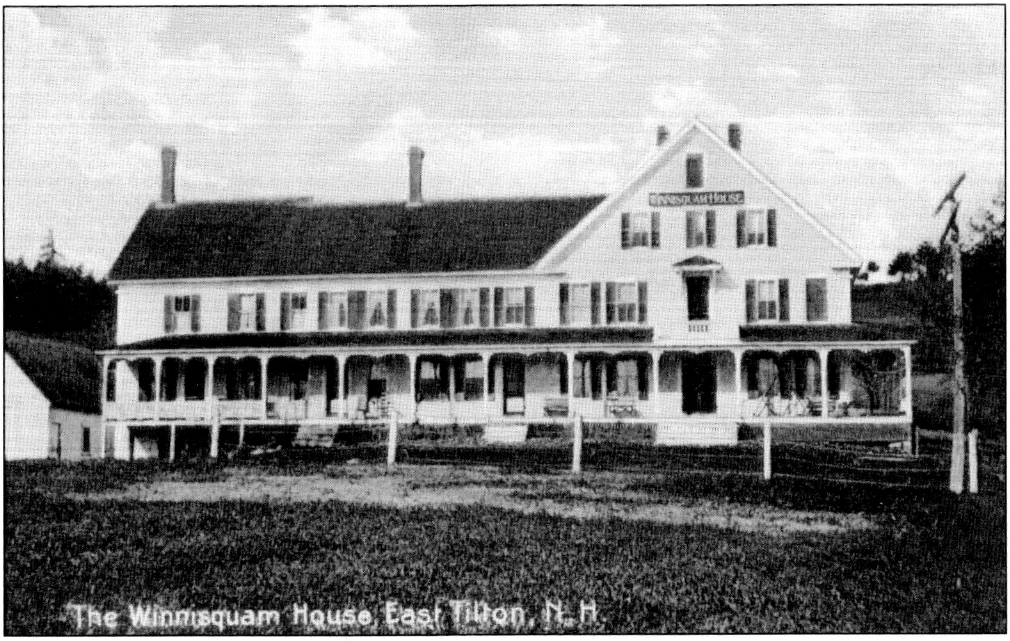

Shown above, the Winnisquam House may have been built by George Philbrook around 1875. At that time, it would accommodate 35 guests for $1 a day and $6 a week. It was open from July 1 to October 1. After the hotel was purchased by the Contigiani family in 1929, a restaurant was added, which made this a year-round facility. The photograph below shows another example of local accommodations with access to Lake Winnisquam. The Mai Cabins sat on a hillside on the north side of Route 3, heading east. It was owned and operated by Mai Brickett. (Above, courtesy of the Hall Memorial Library; below, courtesy of Mike and Elaine Murphy.)

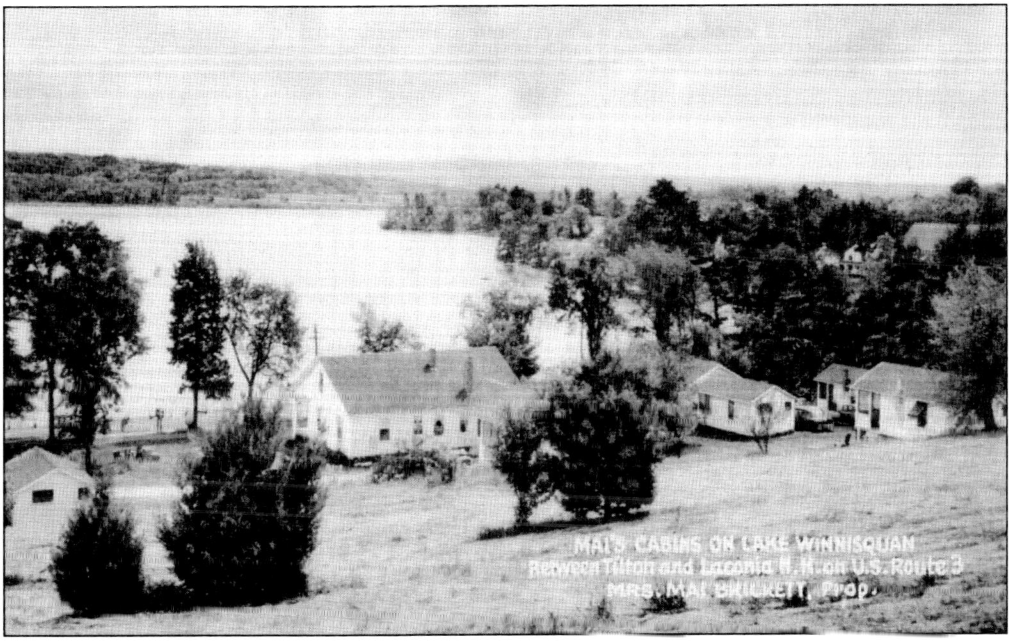

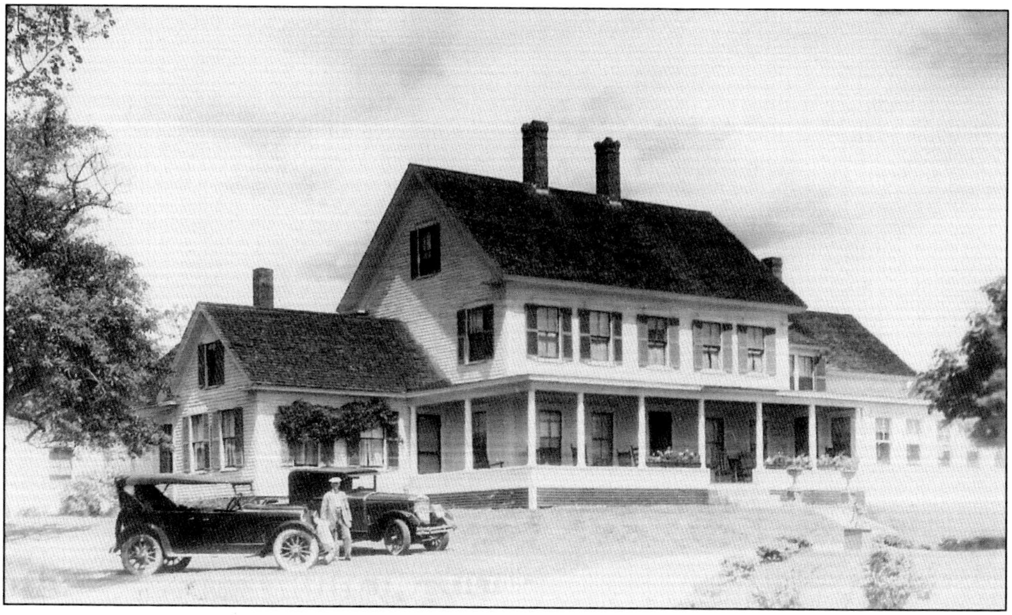

Lakeview Inn on Lake Winnisquam was a lovely two-story Colonial, well landscaped, and attractive to seasonal guests. In the photograph above, taken in the early 1930s, are two prime examples of the automobiles of the era. About the time of this image, the proprietor was C.J. Burns. Below is the Lakeside House with the small pond on the property located across the main road from Lake Winnisquam. In 1883, the proprietor of this establishment was Henry Q. Dalton. The majority of the tourist accommodations were located on or around the lake, such as Hillside House, Hilltop House, Meadowside Cabins, and the Ladd Hill Cabins. (Both photographs courtesy of the Moulton family.)

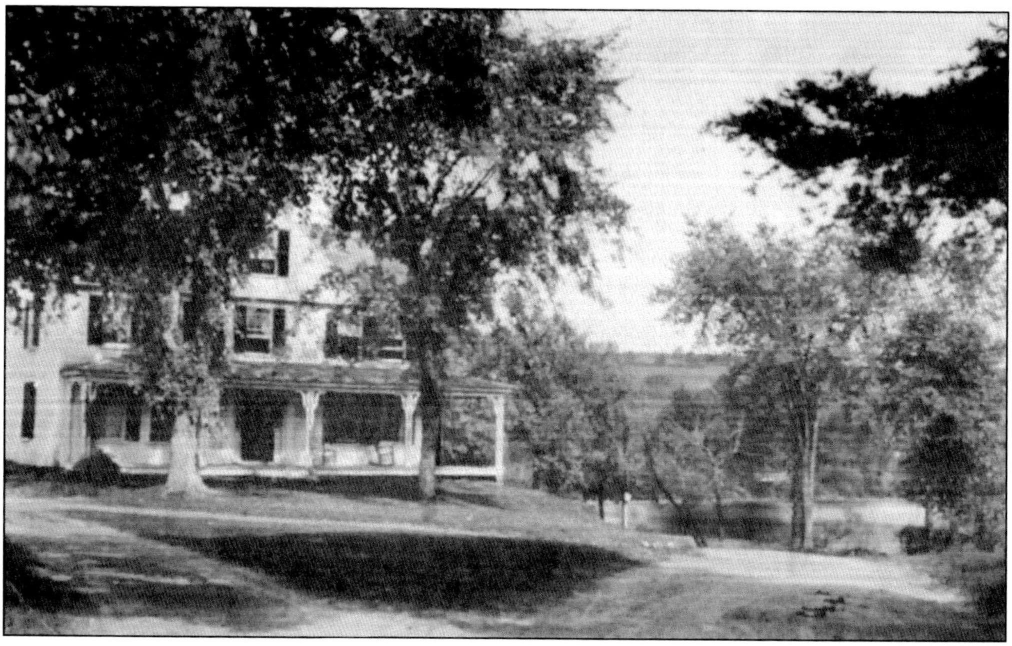

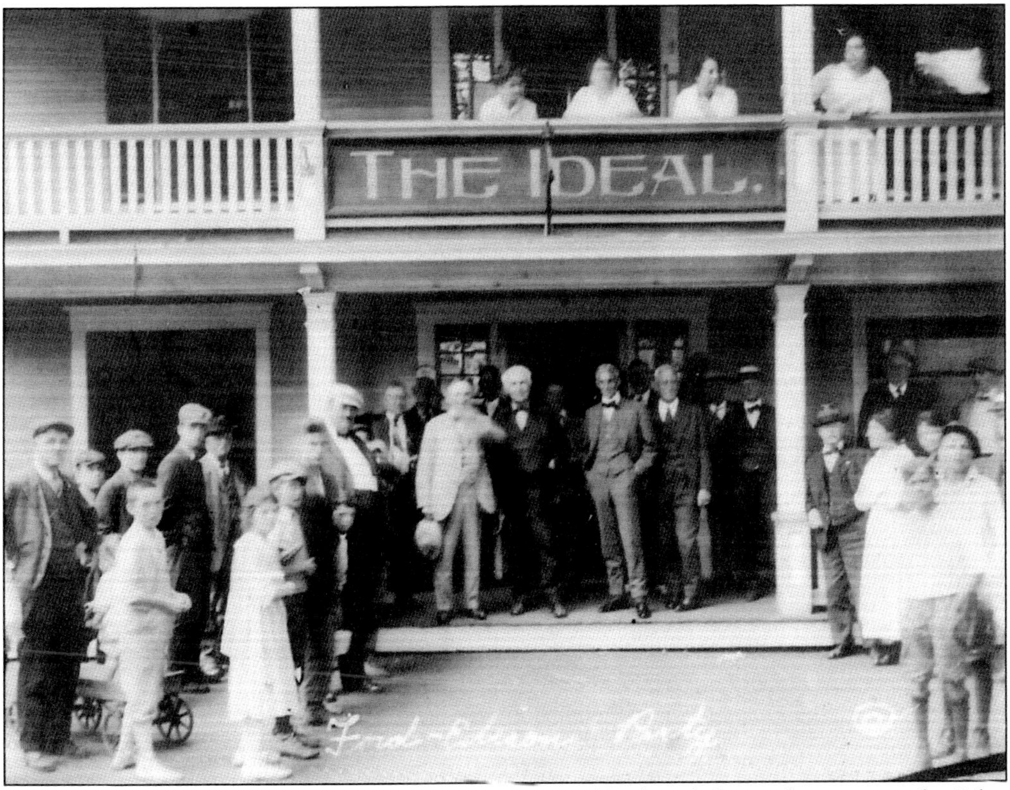

Standing on the porch of the Ideal Hotel on August 11, 1919, from left to right are naturalist John Burroughs, inventor Thomas Alva Edison, and industrialists Henry Ford and Harvey Firestone. These men stayed at this establishment after the truck transporting their camping equipment was separated from the other three cars in their caravan. While in Tilton, Edison, Firestone, and Ford toured the Arthur S. Brown Manufacturing Company or "Endless Belt factory," as well as Brown's extraordinary Victorian home and gardens. In the 1911 photograph below, the Ideal Manufacturing Company is visible next to the hotel. The Ideal Manufacturing Company produced women's clothing. (Above, courtesy of Donald Robert; below, courtesy of James and Elaine Lamanuzzi.)

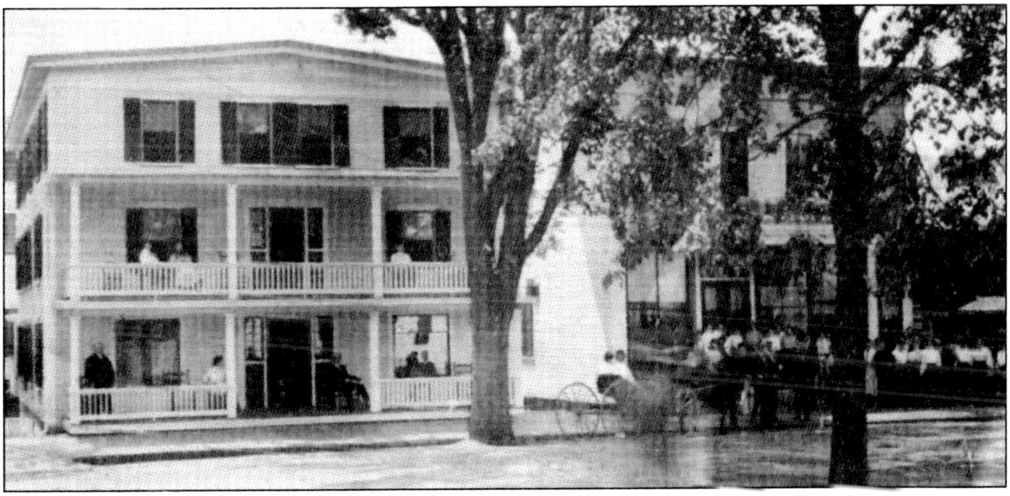

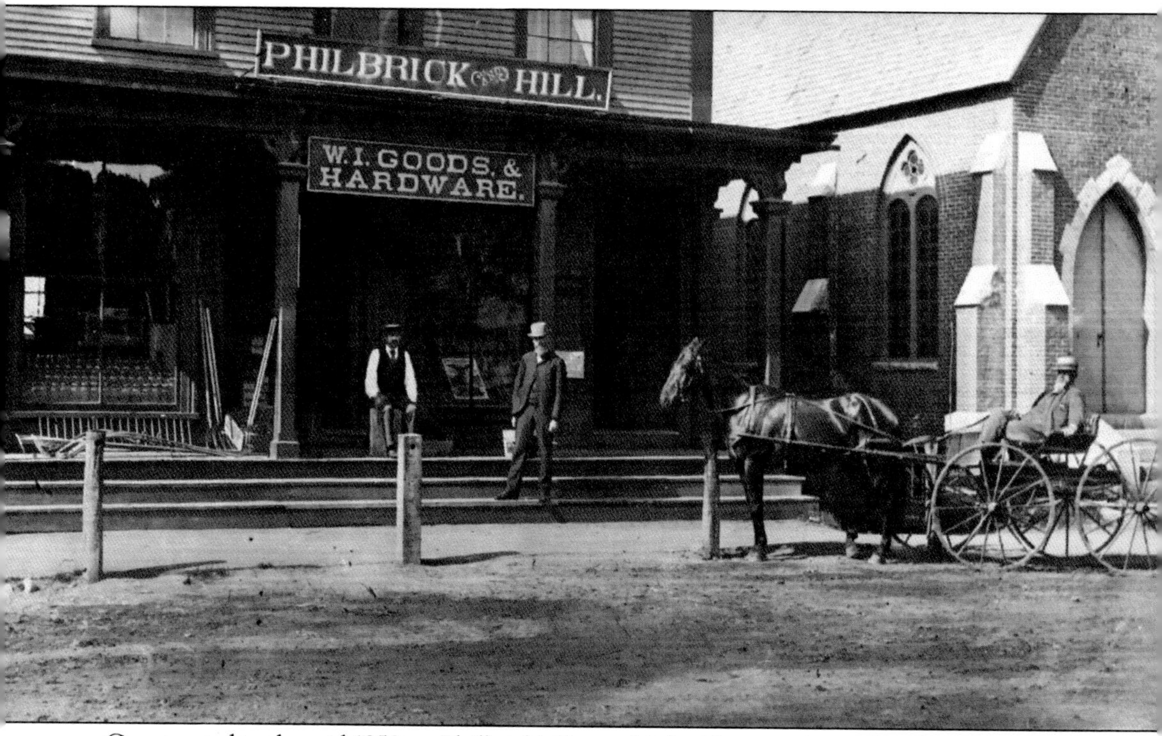

Constructed in the mid-1850s as Philbrick's Store, this building was located in the center of town. Later known as Philbrick and Hill, they sold groceries, hardware, and small farm implements. Note the pitchforks displayed on the porch. In the 1890s, Edwin H. Bryant purchased and operated it as a meat market while at the same time selling the items listed above. The sign above the doorway indicates W.I. (wrought iron) Goods & Hardware were their most popular items. Beginning in 1921, Bryant's son Maurice along with Oakes K. Lawrence operated the establishment primarily as a hardware store. When Bryant retired, Lawrence purchased the business, keeping the name Bryant and Lawrence. The gentleman in the horse-drawn buggy is believed to be Asa Cate, a prominent attorney. (Courtesy of the William Lawrence family.)

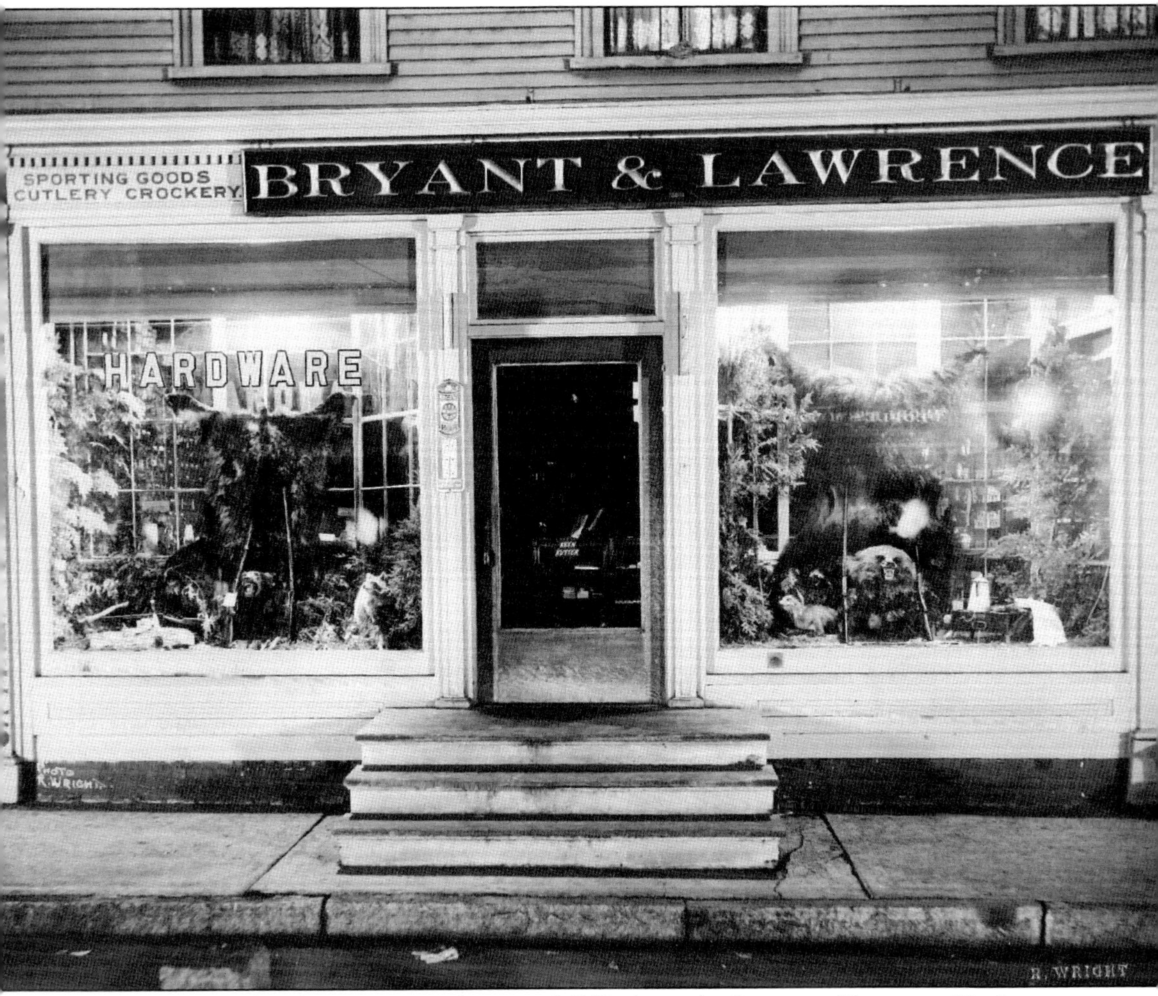

This photograph, taken by Roscoe Wright around 1930, shows the Bryant and Lawrence Hardware Store on Main Street with the porch removed. Note the sign running vertically on the left of the building that reads, "stoves and ranges." The horizontal sign nearby reads "cutlery, crockery, sporting goods." Oakes Lawrence's in-laws (the Moseses) were avid big game hunters and some of their preserved trophies made interesting window displays. Sporting goods available included guns, ammunition, knives, fishing rods and reels, tackle and tackle boxes, snowshoes, and traps of all kinds. Surprisingly, historical documents noted that pianos and organs were also available at this establishment. The Bryant and Lawrence Hardware Store is the oldest continuously operating establishment in Tilton. (Courtesy of the William Lawrence family.)

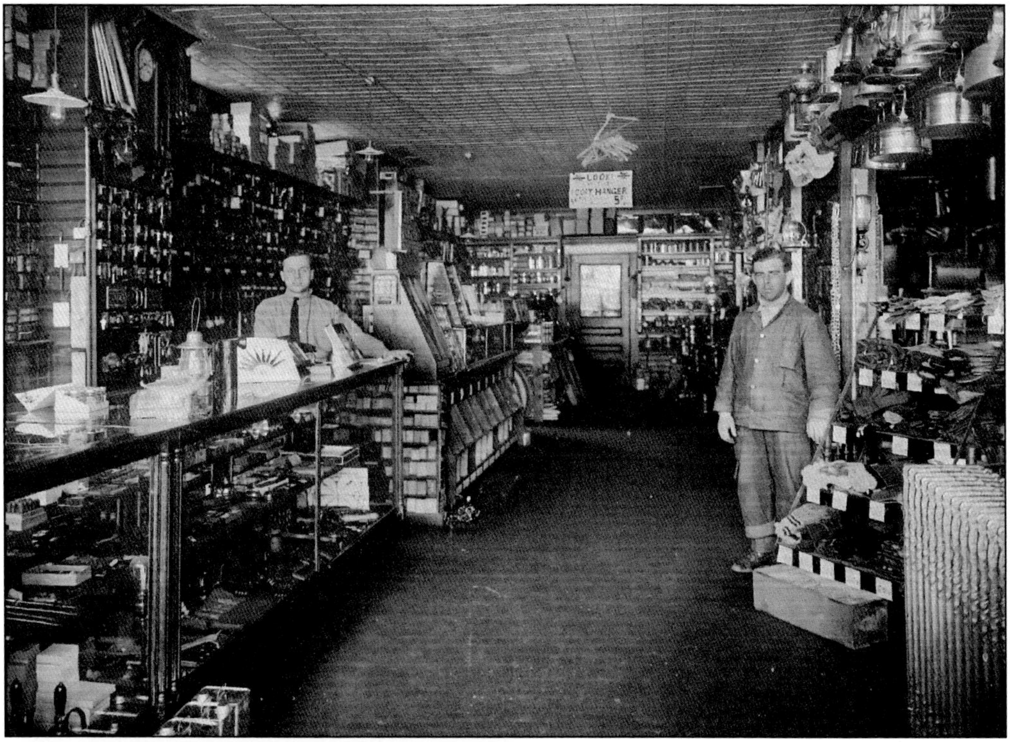

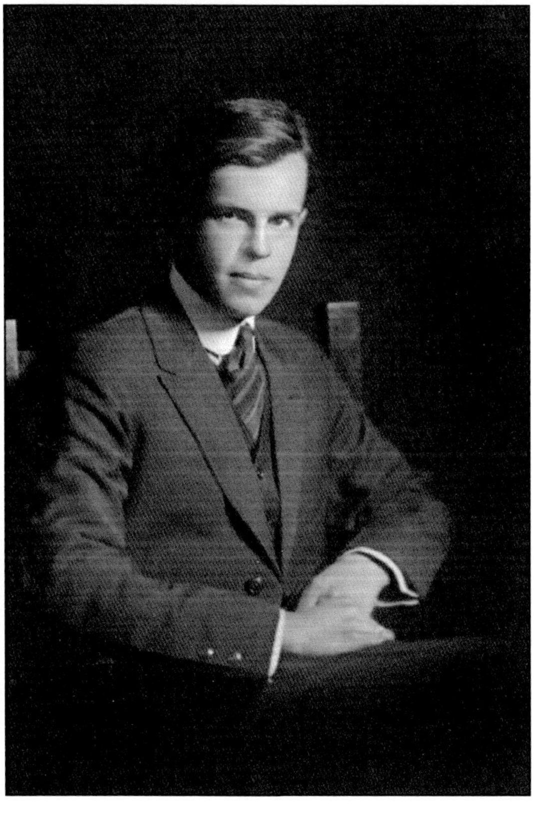

In 1918, upon graduating from Tilton Seminary, Charles A. French (below) went to work for Edwin Bryant. He retired from the same store 55 years later. In 1921, Maurice Bryant, Edwin's son, took over the store in partnership with Oakes K. Lawrence. In the photograph above are Maurice Bryant (left) and Charles French. Note that the wooden coat hangers hanging from the ceiling cost 5¢ each. (Both photographs courtesy of the William Lawrence family.)

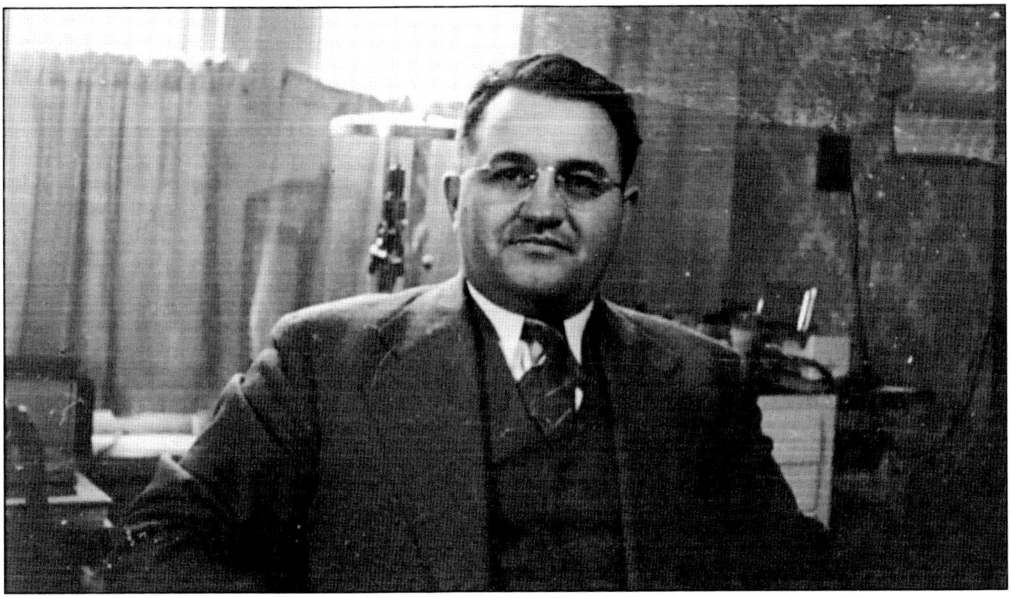

Dr. Archie Grevior was a very popular general practitioner and well-loved member of the community. He was also the physician for the students of Tilton School and the residents of the New Hampshire Soldiers' Home. He was on the Tilton–Northfield School Board when the new high school was built, donated a piano for the auditorium, and gave a Good Sportsmanship Award every year at graduation. (Courtesy of Martha Grevior Turnblom.)

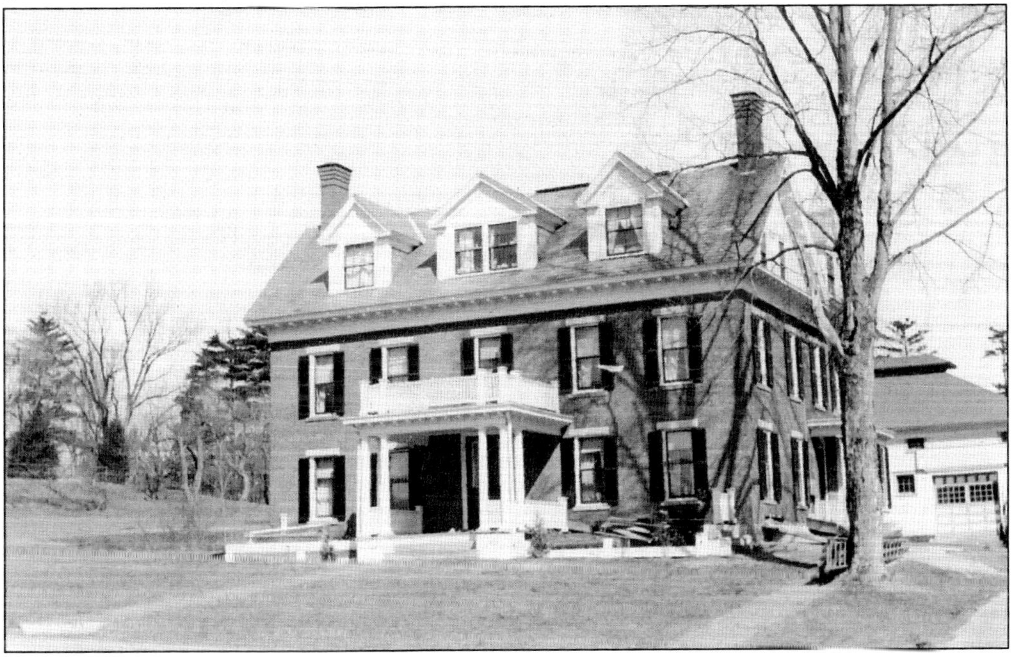

The charter of the State Bank of Sanbornton Bridge was granted in June 1853. This was the first bank in town. The initial meeting was held in August in the front room of this house, owned by cashier Charles Minot. In February 1865, the bank was renamed the Citizens' National Bank of Sanbornton Bridge (and eventually Tilton). The bank moved to the Charles E. Tilton Block after 1886. (Courtesy of Martha Grevior Turnblom.)

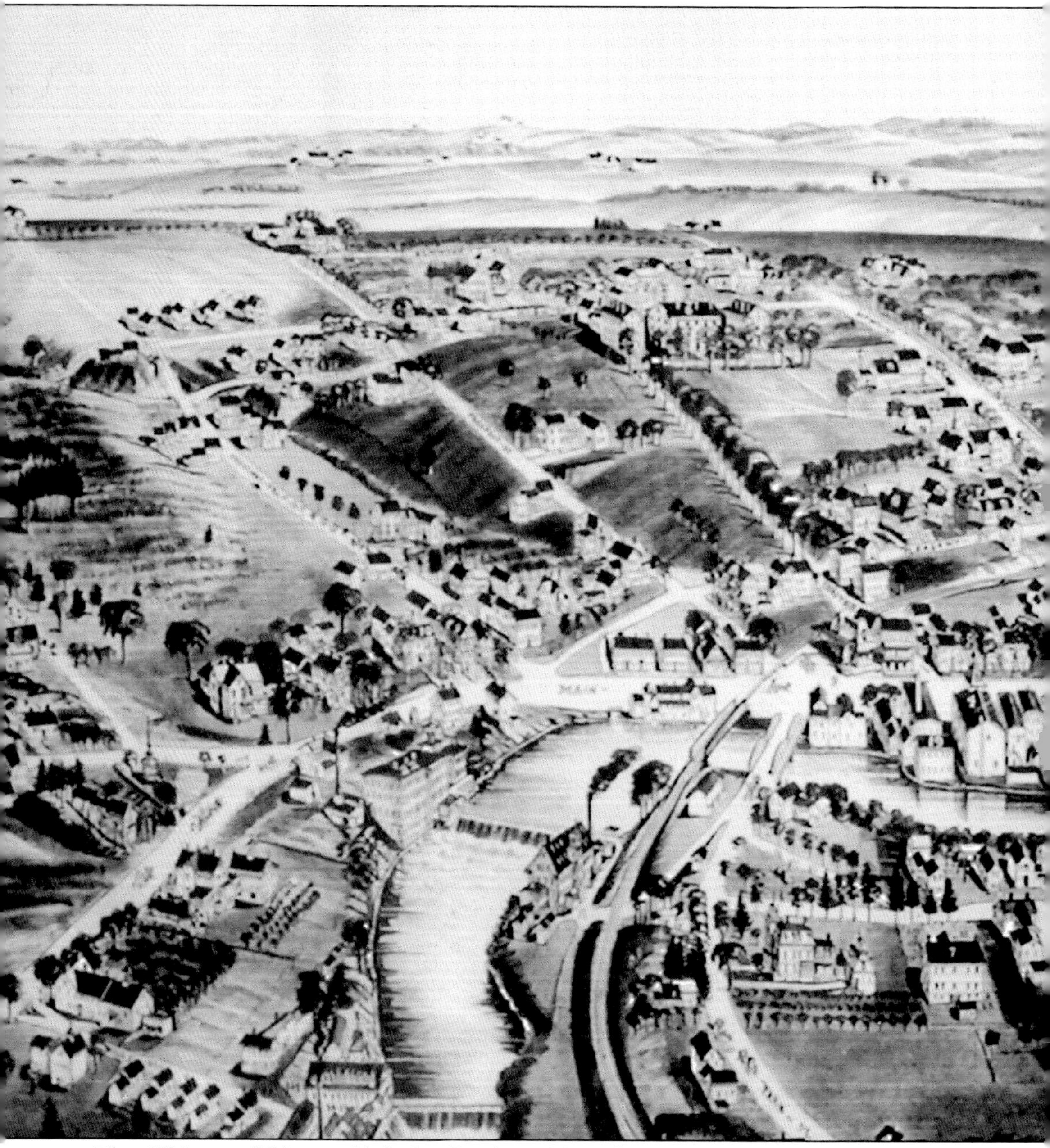

This 1884 map of Tilton, published in Brockton, Massachusetts, was drawn by one or more artists who traveled throughout New England producing maps for small towns. In this map (as in many others), only the most populous areas of the town are depicted. The battlements in front of the home of Charles E. Tilton are quite exaggerated, and Tilton Island Park appears larger than it was.

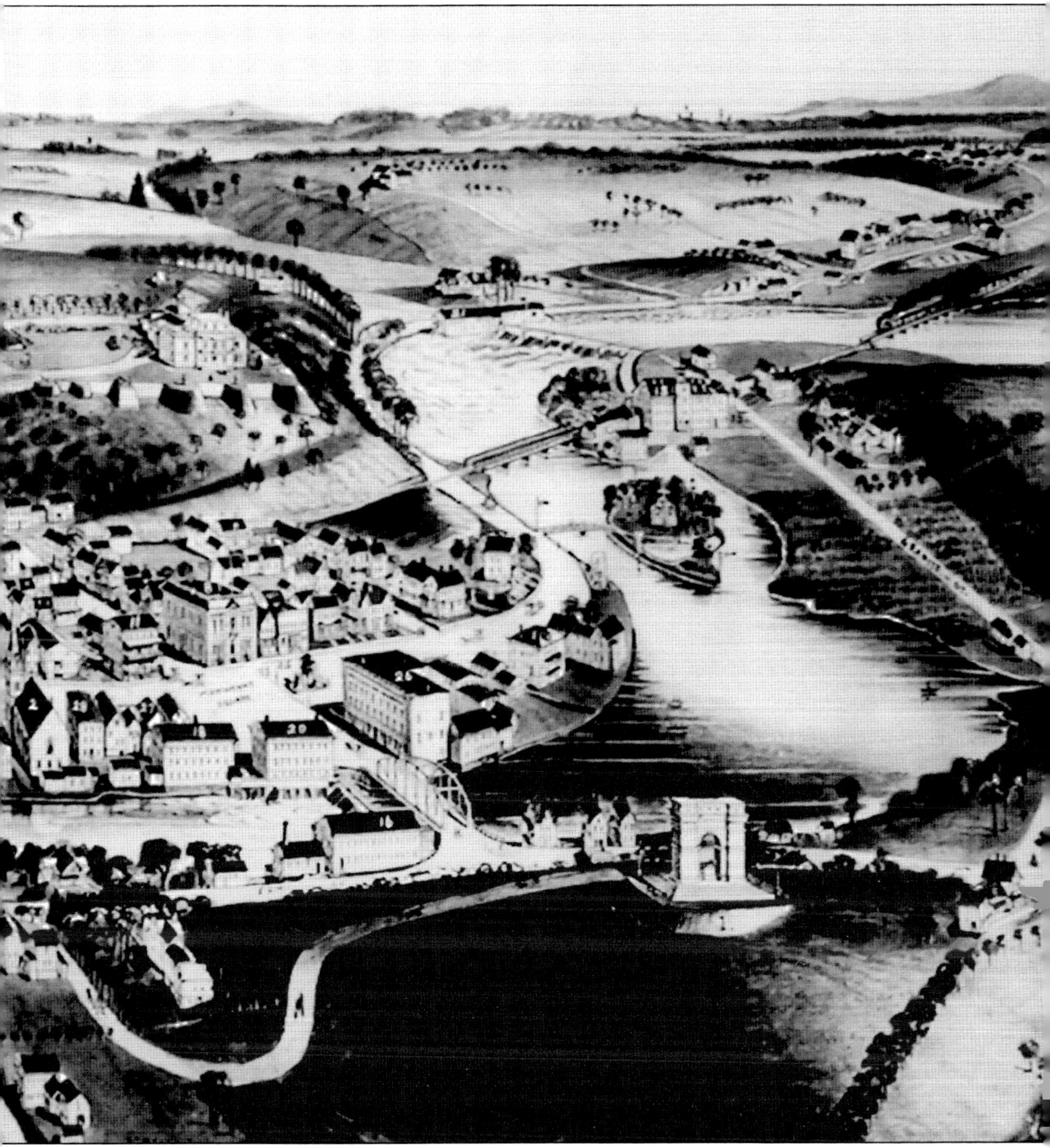

Pillsbury Lane, the street that connects School and Prospect Streets beyond Tilton School, was called Elmwood Street in the 1880s. The two mountain ranges at the top of the photograph are the Belknap Range and the Ossipee Range. From the mountains southward are the open fields associated with the large farming communities. (Courtesy of the Randall family.)

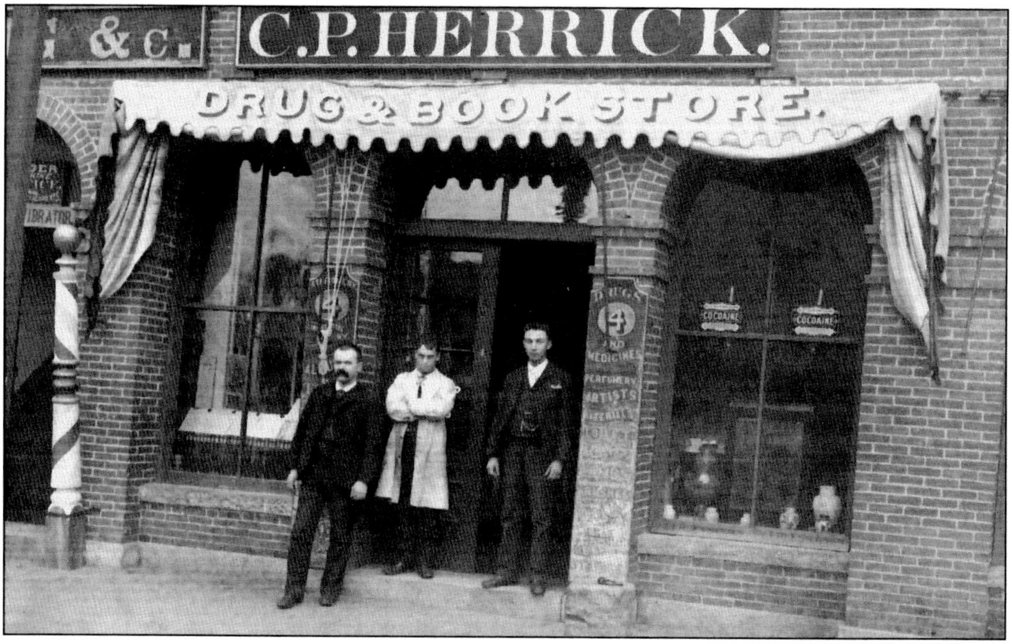

Born in 1854, Charles Putnam Herrick bought the store pictured above in 1883. Herrick was a licensed pharmacist, and his first store sold pharmaceuticals, books, and general merchandise. The men to Herrick's left are George Stewart and Waldo Bryant. In the photograph below, the Herrick pharmacy had moved to the corner of the Hill Block and became a distributor of Rexall products. Owned by Charles Alexander Riva, the Pastime Theatre (shown below) occupied Herrick's previous location. Riva was born in Canada and died in Tilton in 1923. (Both photographs courtesy of Mariam Melendez.)

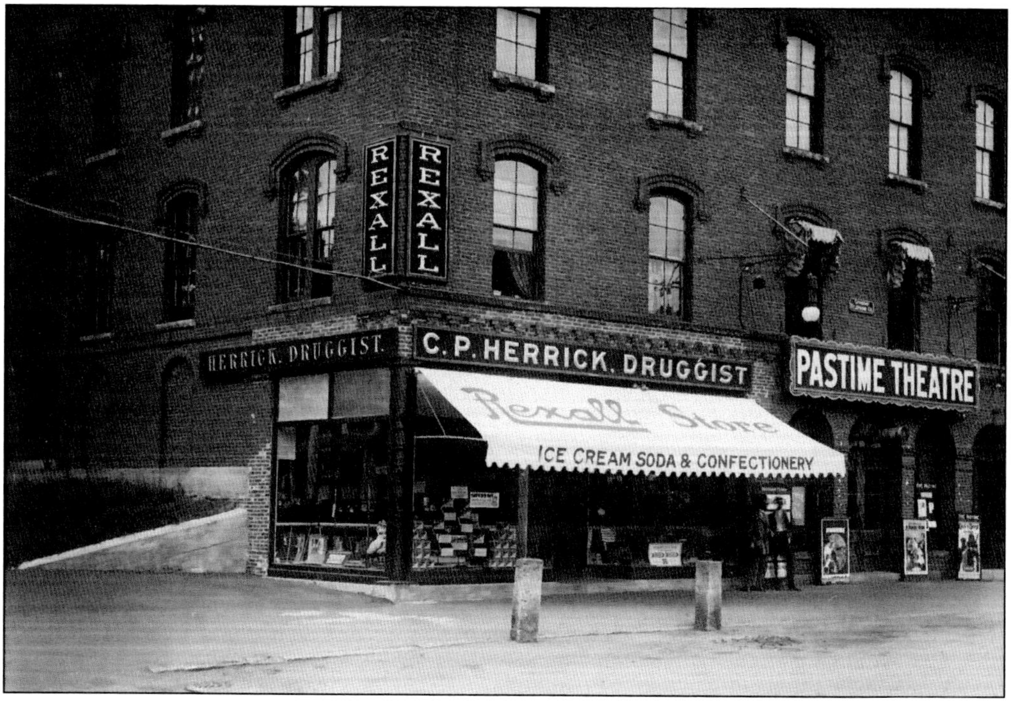

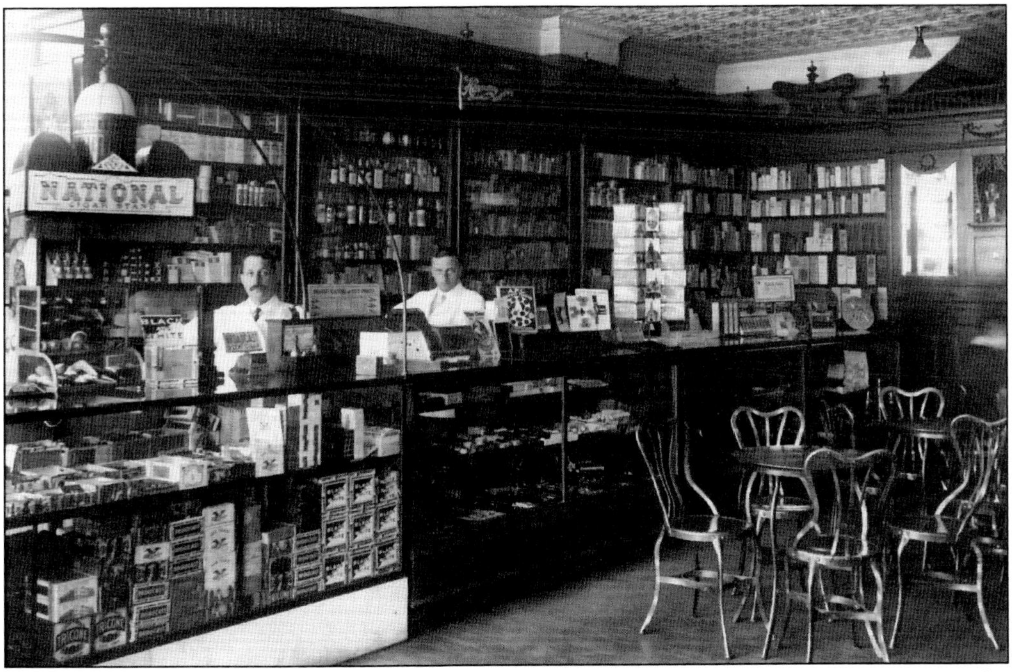

Inside Herrick's Drugstore, at its prime location on the corner of Bridge and Main Streets in the Hill Block, is a vast variety of products available for purchase. The tin ceilings and spindled, and decorative shelving added to the distinguished character of the store. On the opposite side of the interior are a marble-trimmed soda fountain and a display case of confectionaries. The gentlemen are, from left to right, Charles Putnam Herrick, Waldo Bryant, and George Stewart. (Both photographs courtesy of Mariam Melendez.)

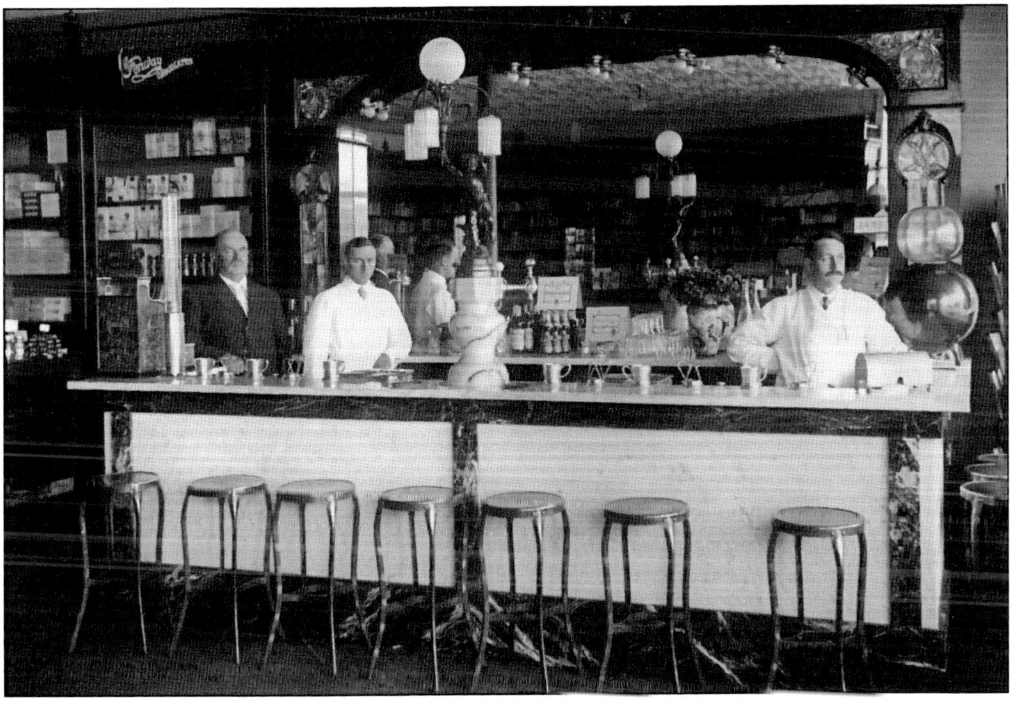

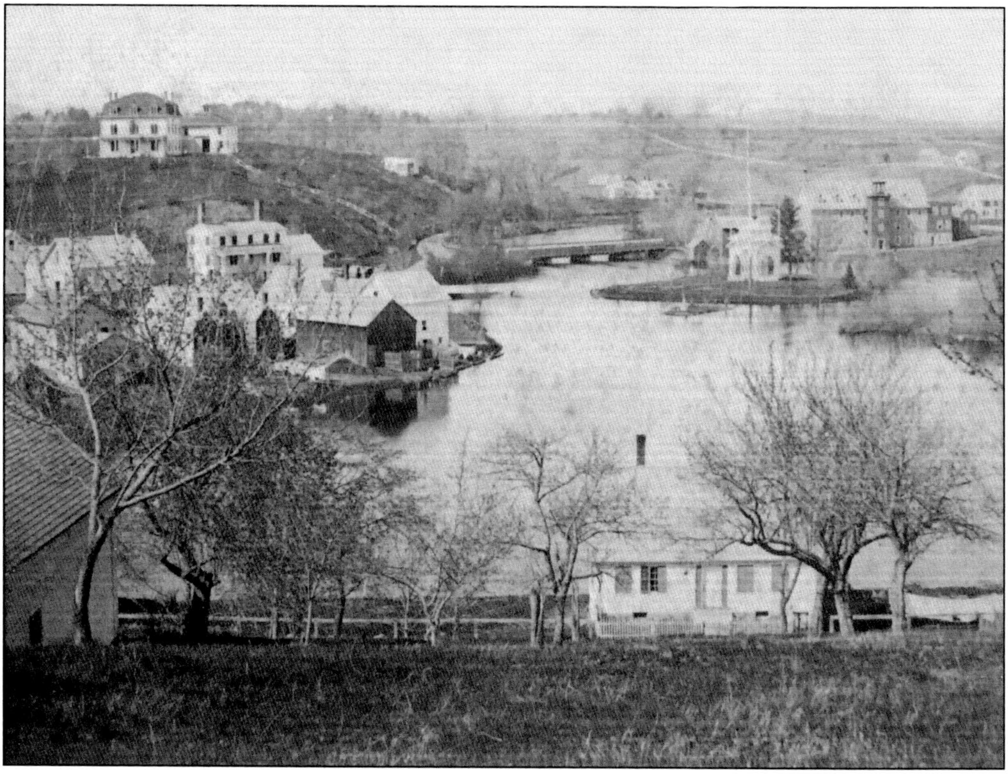

Taken from Arch Hill and facing the river, this photograph shows many aspects of life in Tilton. On the right is one of Northfield's mills, and in the center is the railroad bridge crossing the river. At the top of the hill on the left is the home of Charles E. Tilton before the porches were added to the house. (Courtesy of Mariam Melendez.)

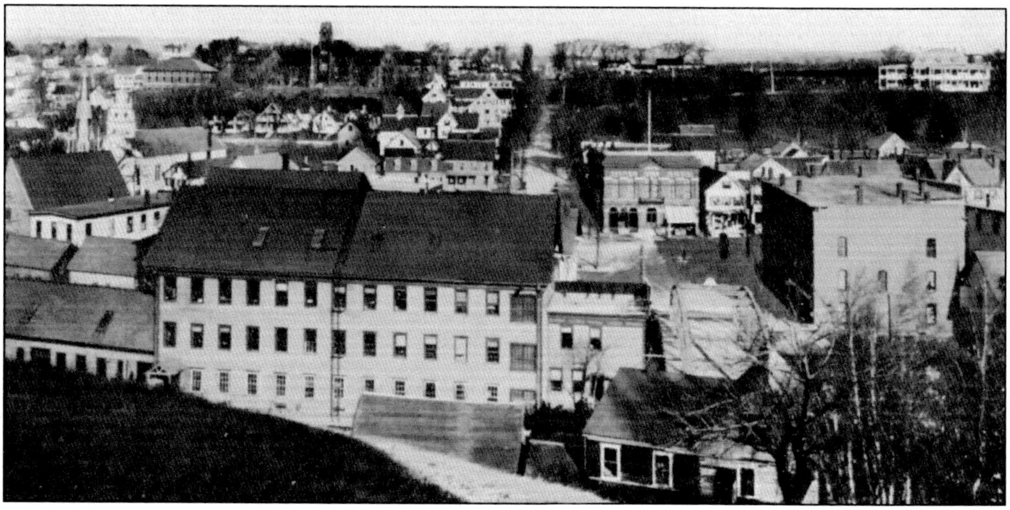

This bird's-eye-view of Tilton from *Memorial Arch* in Northfield shows School Street to the north, Episcopal Church to the west, and Hill Block to the east. Hill Block obscures the view of the Tilton Inn before it was expanded. In the foreground, the arched metal bridge crosses the Winnipesaukee River—the boundary between Tilton and Northfield, as well as Belknap and Merrimack Counties. (Courtesy of the Hall Memorial Library.)

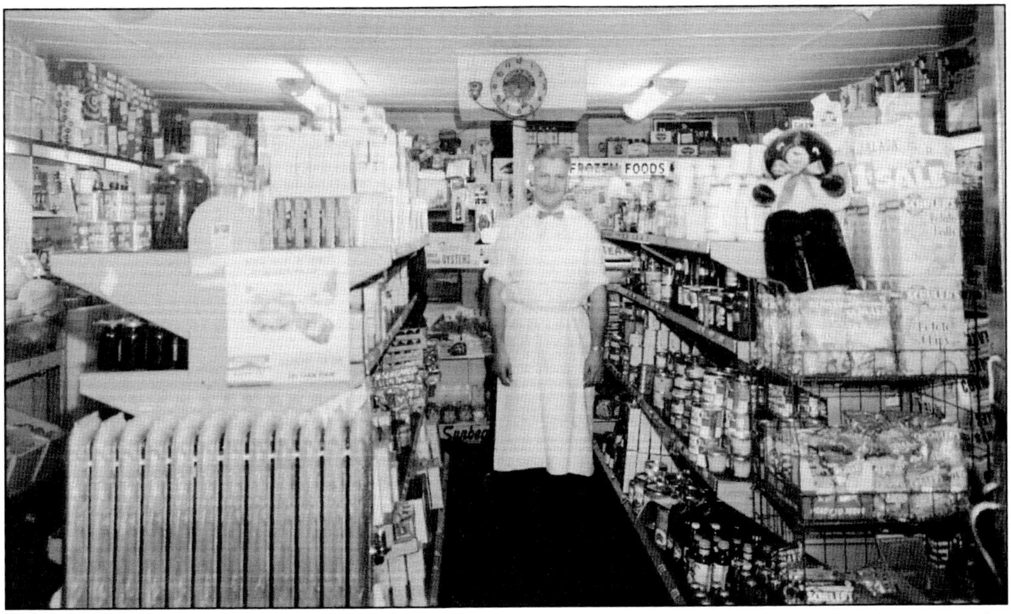

Myron Meserve (shown above) walked into Gile's Cash Market on opening day to buy sugar for his mother. Everett Gile asked him if he wanted to work there. Myron said "yes," ran home with the sugar, and came back to the store that became his second home for the next 64 years. He bought the store in 1943 and changed its name to Meserve's Market. Meserve, who was born in 1907, became a pillar of the community—serving as a selectman, a trustee of the Congregational Church, a past master of Doric Lodge, F&AM, and a member of the Tilton–Northfield Rotary Club, among other organizations. Shown below is Gile's Cash Market. Gile stands to the right with two unidentified employees. Advertising is visible on the windows, including eggs for 45¢ a dozen. (Courtesy of the Meserve family.)

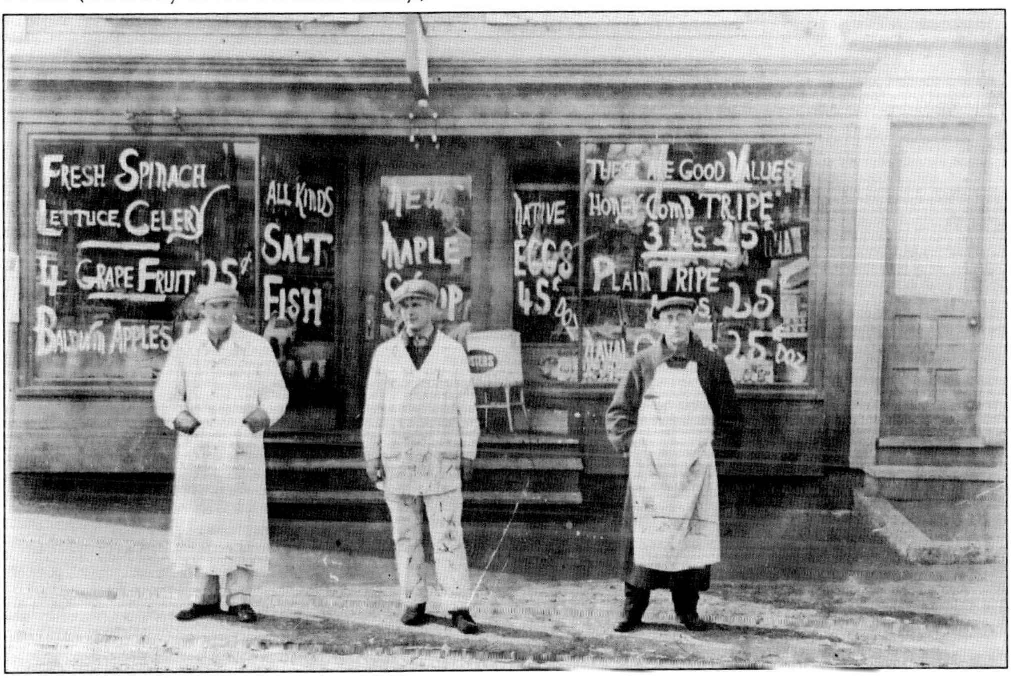

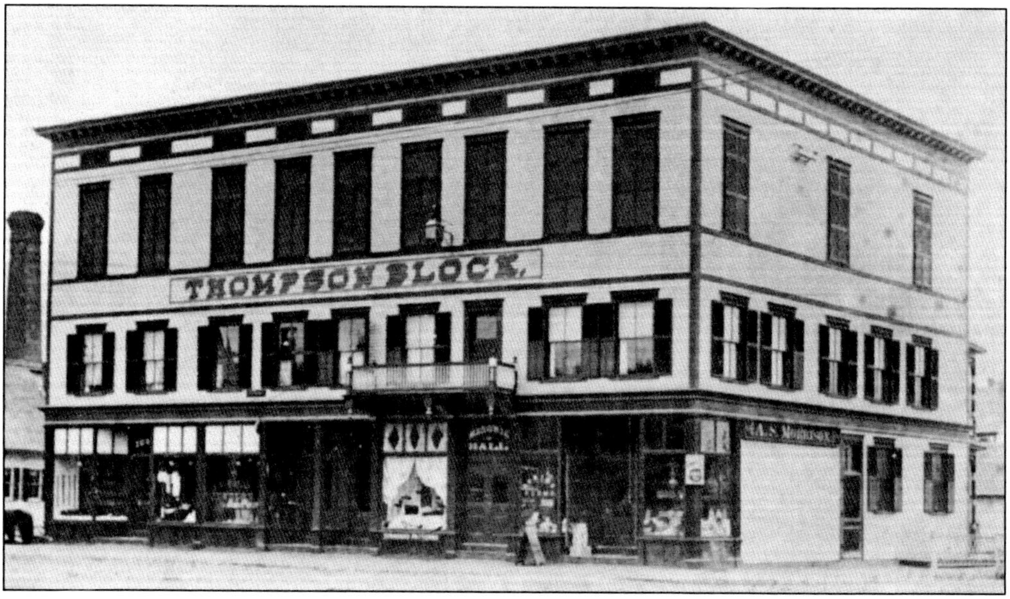

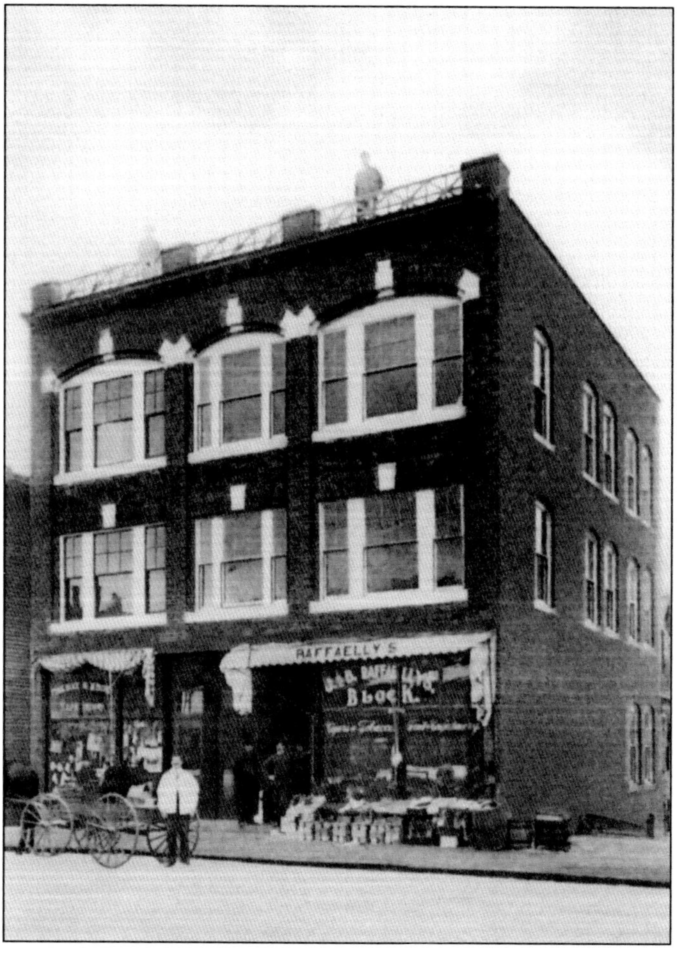

The three-story Thompson Block was constructed on the corner of Main and Park Streets. The third floor was used for storage, and the second floor was used for apartments. The residents of the apartments had access through a single door onto the small balcony. On the ground floor, there was a public dining room and jewelry store. The decorated window was probably the millinery shop of E.R. Jackson (see page 107). The Masonic Hall was also in this building. A.S. Morrison was the owner of the small grocery store on the corner. This block was consumed by fire in 1919, and the Raffaelly Block was later built on this site. Businesses in this block were shoe and boot repair and the Raffaelly's, which sold tobacco, fruit, and other staples. (Above, courtesy of Louise and Bill Joscelyn; below, courtesy of Gayle and Phil Twombly.)

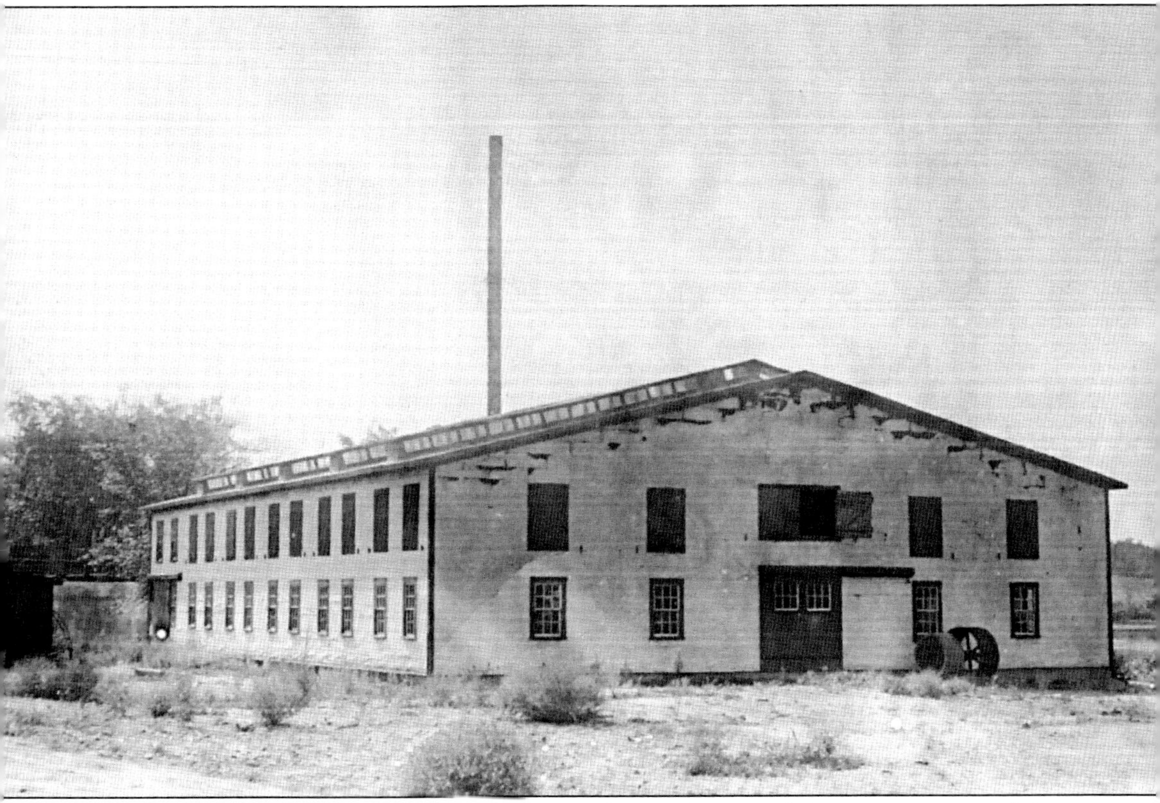

The leather board and pulp mill in Lochmere was the predecessor of the power station of the Public Service Company. The mill contained vats in which old newspapers, rags, and pulpwood were made into mash. The mash was then screened, pressed, and dried into a hard, four-foot-square board. It was reported that there was a most unpleasant odor emanating from the mill, and it was also noted that the water around the mill had a reddish color. The bundles of rags and papers came by train, and the wood burned by the mill was brought across the ice from Belmont in the winter. The resulting leather boards were used as innersoles for shoes, among other things. Two corporate businesses were involved in this process: the first was P.C. Cheney Pulp Company, and the second was George E. Collins Leatherboard Company. Much of this information came from *A History of Lochmere, New Hampshire*, by the Lochmere Woman's Club, 1974–1975. (Courtesy of the Moulton family.)

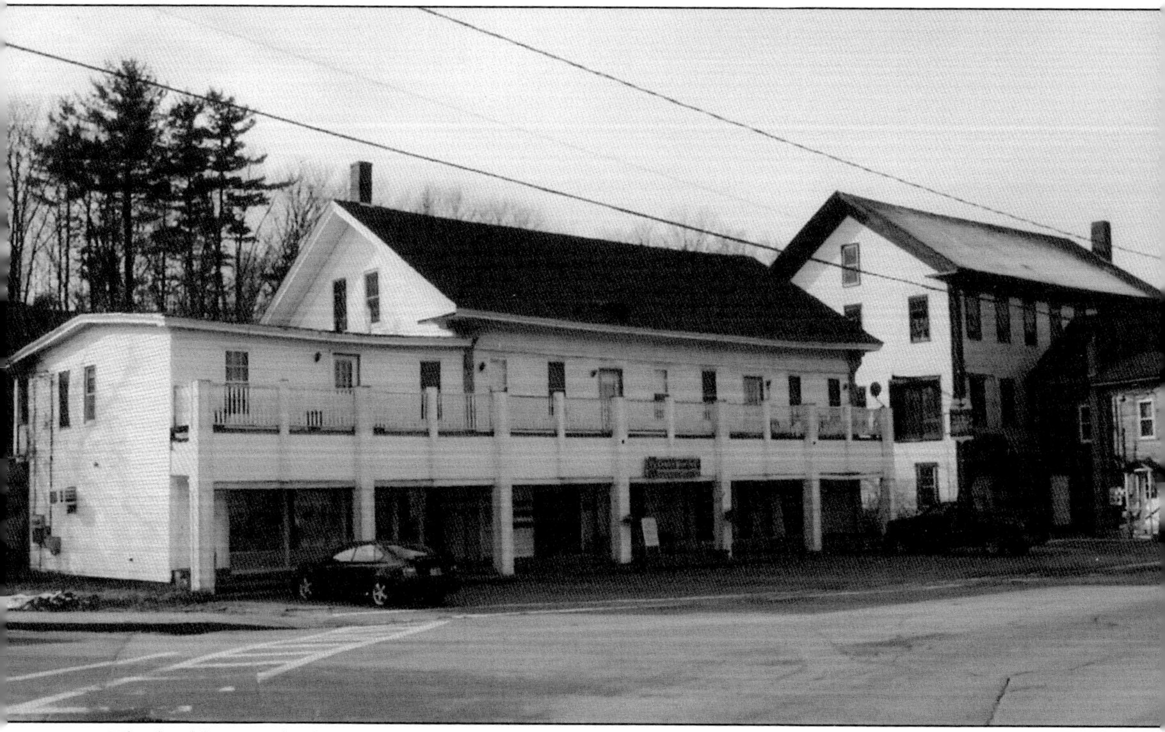

The building to the left occupies the site of the first manufacturing industry at Sanbornton Bridge, i.e. Tilton. Built as early as 1788, it was a trip-hammer, scythe-shop, and gristmill conducted by Tilton & Smith. In 1872, Hazen Copp expanded the two-story gristmill and fitted it with modern improvements. In 1880, Charles W. Blood ran the mill. Copp built the three-story factory to the right, occupied by Arthur M. Dodge's hosiery manufacturing facility. In 1899, the upper story was added when the building was converted to a shoe factory. The machinery in both mills was run by the same falls. In the smaller part of the building to the left was Raymond N. Colvin Hosiery, where they made ribbed shirts and drawers. (Photograph by Dennis Evans.)

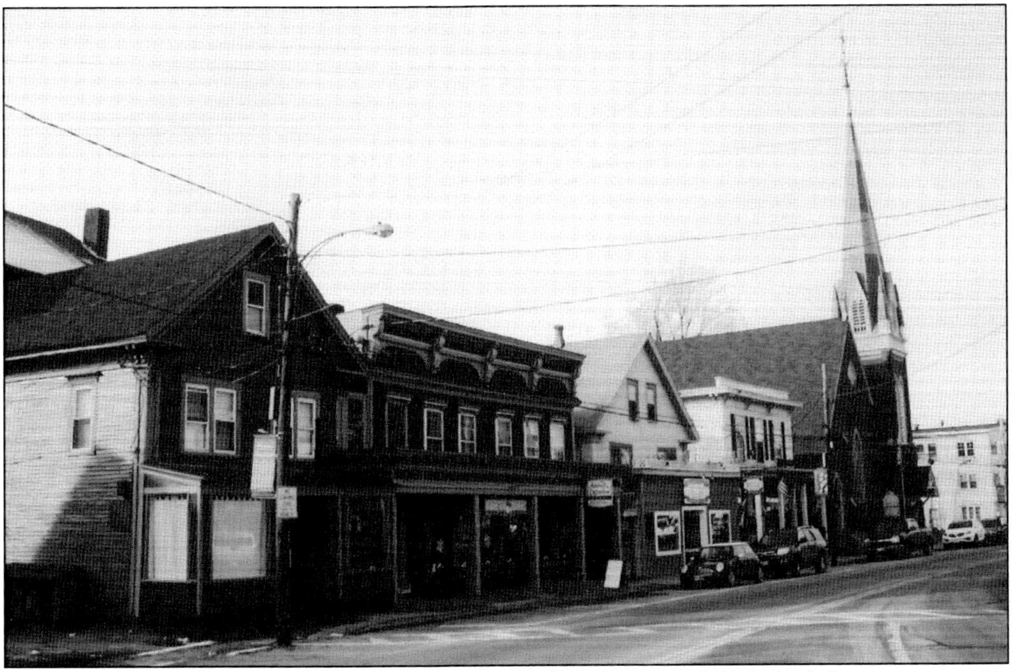

The second building from the left in this photograph is the Copp Block, built by contractor T.J. Davis for Hazen Copp around 1893. The building was a two-story, shed-roofed, Victorian commercial block. In the 1920s, the block received an addition with a flat roof—forming a traditional storefront. Across Main Street from the Copp Block and the Gristmill was the entrance to School Street, shown in the photograph below. The two-story house on the left belonged to Hazen Copp and his family. It had escaped the extensive fire of 1903, which destroyed the Loverin Hotel. The hotel was located on the corner of School and Main Streets, just south of the Copp home. (Above, photograph by Dennis Evans; below, courtesy of the Hall Memorial Library.)

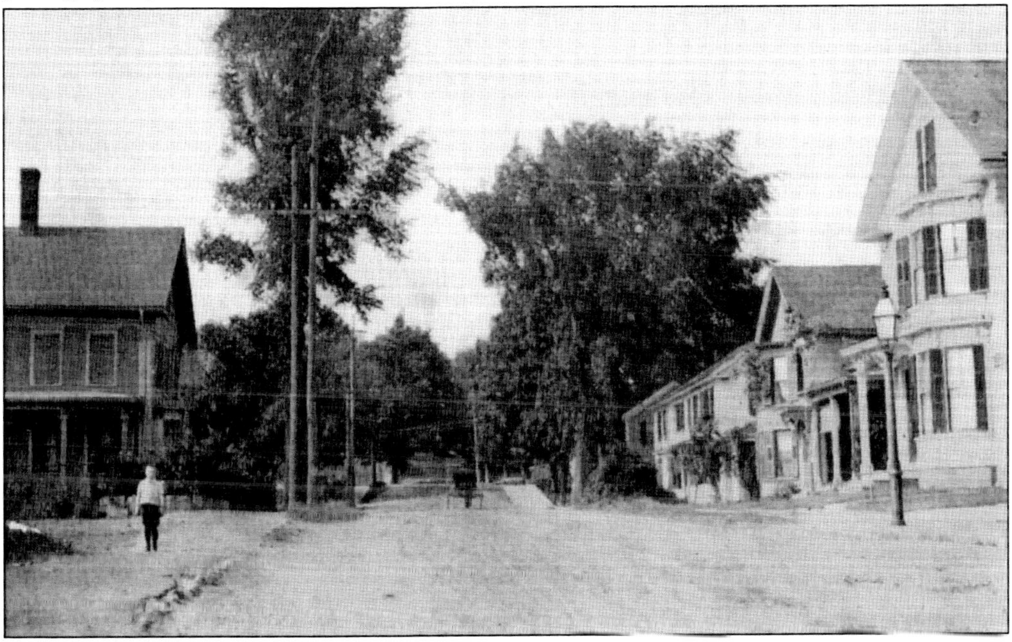

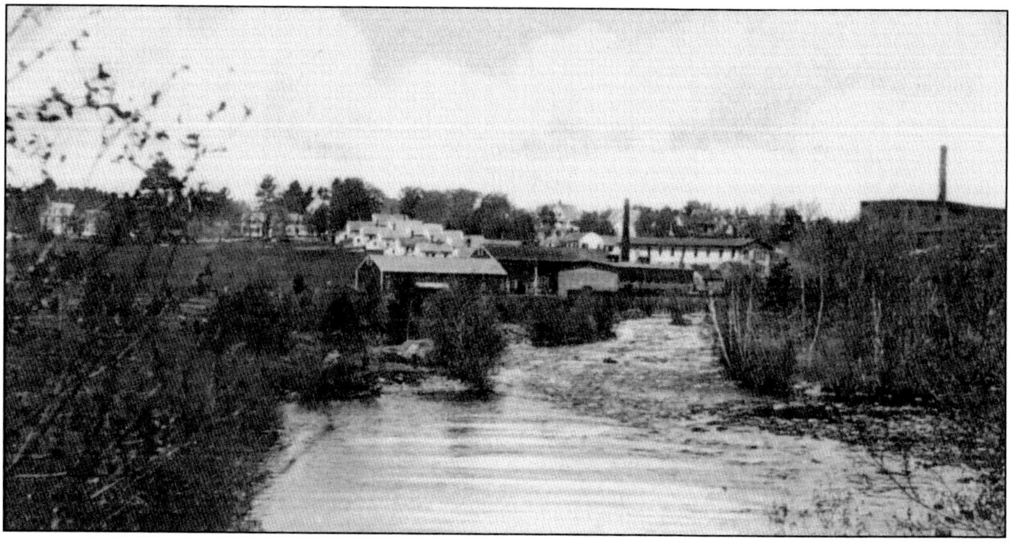

Mill Street, shown above with a double line of white houses, was called Tilton Lane in the mid-1800s. Both names were appropriate, as Tilton Mills was located at the foot of the street. Mill employees occupied these homes, and some of those on Peabody Street. The woolen mill and wire shop are shown in the photograph below. These belonged to Abigail Tilton until her husband's death. She was later joined in partnership with Selwin Bancroft Peabody. He subsequently became the sole proprietor, and it was at his mill that the celebrated Tilton Tweeds were made. In addition to tweeds, he also introduced certain styles of cashmere material, which became very popular. (Above, courtesy of the Hall Memorial Library; below, courtesy of the Dodge family.)

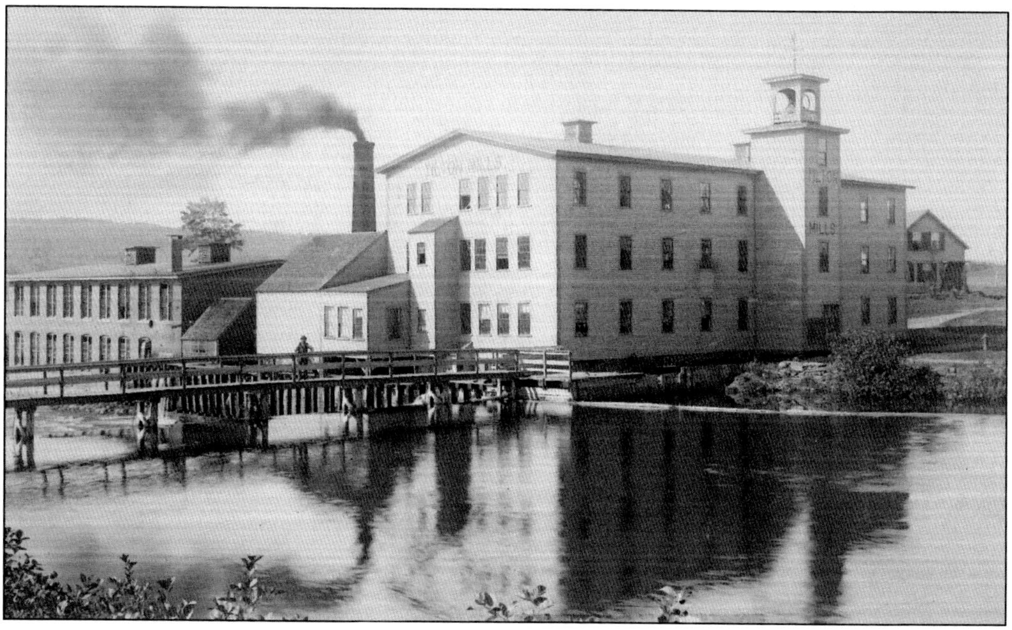

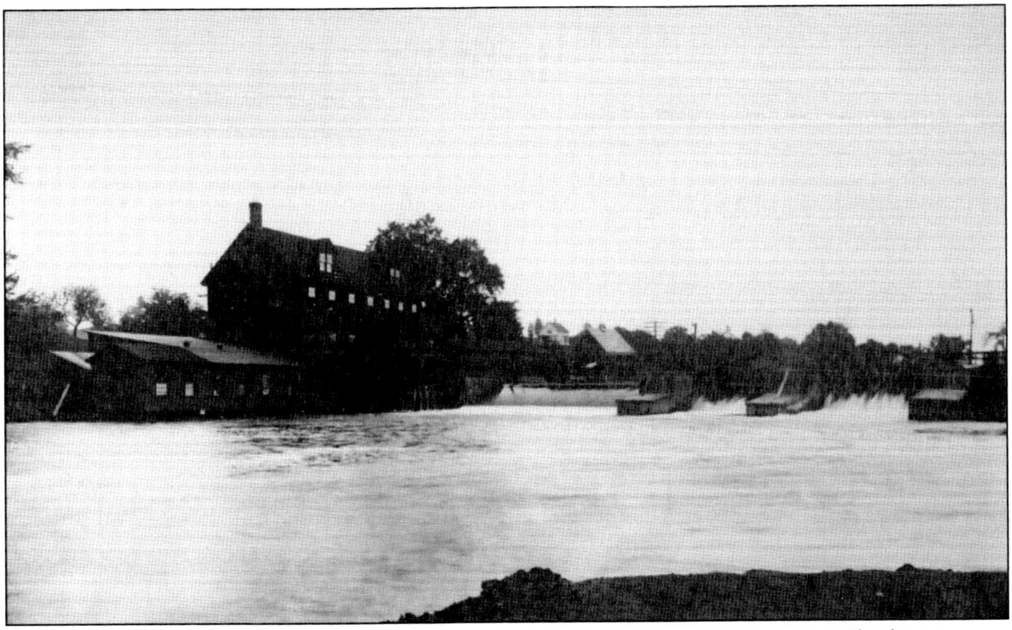

Pictured above is the Box Factory of the George H. Tilton Hosiery Company. The hosiery was moved from the Northfield side of the river to the Box Factory on Main Street for packing and shipping. Transport was expedited by the walkway, which was built on the top of the dam between the two mills. Endless Belts appears in the photograph below. Although the company struggled when it began in 1912, with the collaboration of Supt. Ludovic Shiatte and bookkeeper Gertrude Knapp, Brown received a patent for an endless power transmission belt in 1925. Building its success on this patent, the company went on to employ residents from Tilton, Northfield, and surrounding communities for generations to come. (Above, courtesy of the Randall family; below, courtesy of the Meserve family.)

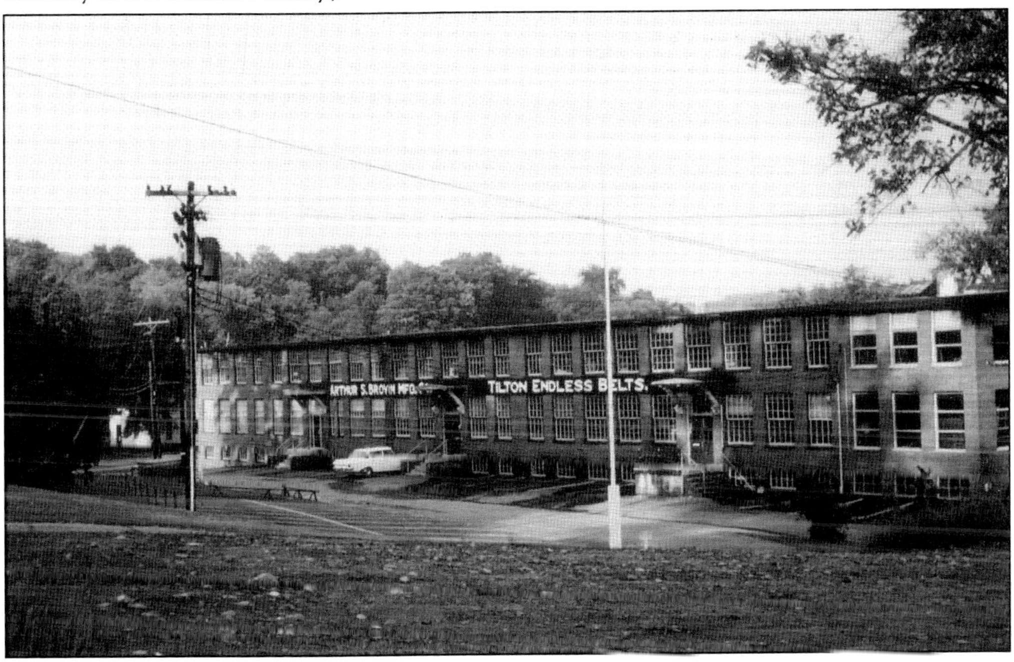

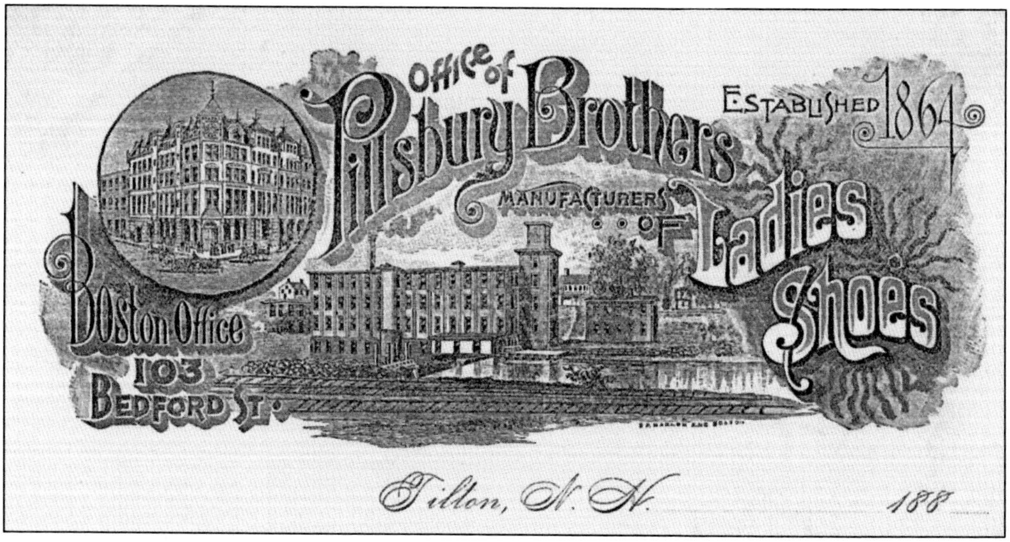

The Pillsbury Brothers' letterhead is shown above. This ladies' shoes manufacturing company had an office in Boston where it was established in 1864. Built in 1868, the mill shown below produced shoes, woolens, cotton cloth, and leathers under different ownerships. In 1885, Alpha J. Pillsbury opened a second shoe manufacturing facility on this site. In 1890, Pillsbury sold the shoe business and formed a company with Selwin Peabody, who had long been engaged in the manufacture of woolen cloth. In 1901, this company was incorporated and became Tilton Woolen Mills. (Both photographs courtesy of the Dodge family.)

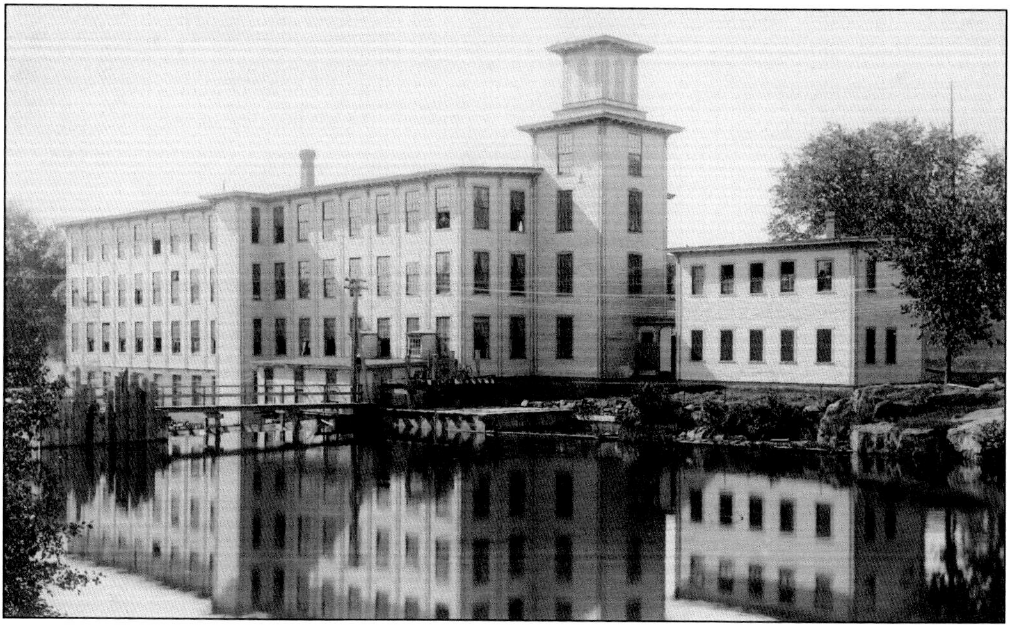

Four

Community Life

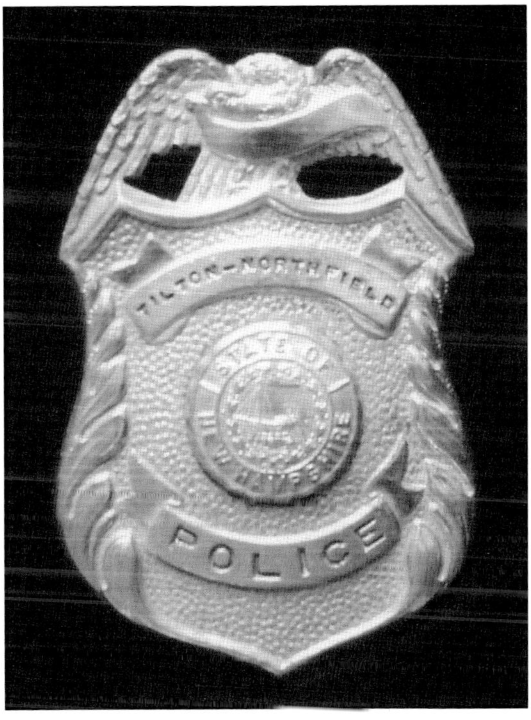

This Tilton–Northfield police badge exemplifies one of the cooperative civic responsibilities. For many years, the police department (sometimes with very limited resources) covered all of both towns. As the towns grew, the police department became strained with various obligations, and more officers and official vehicles were required. (Courtesy of the Meserve family.)

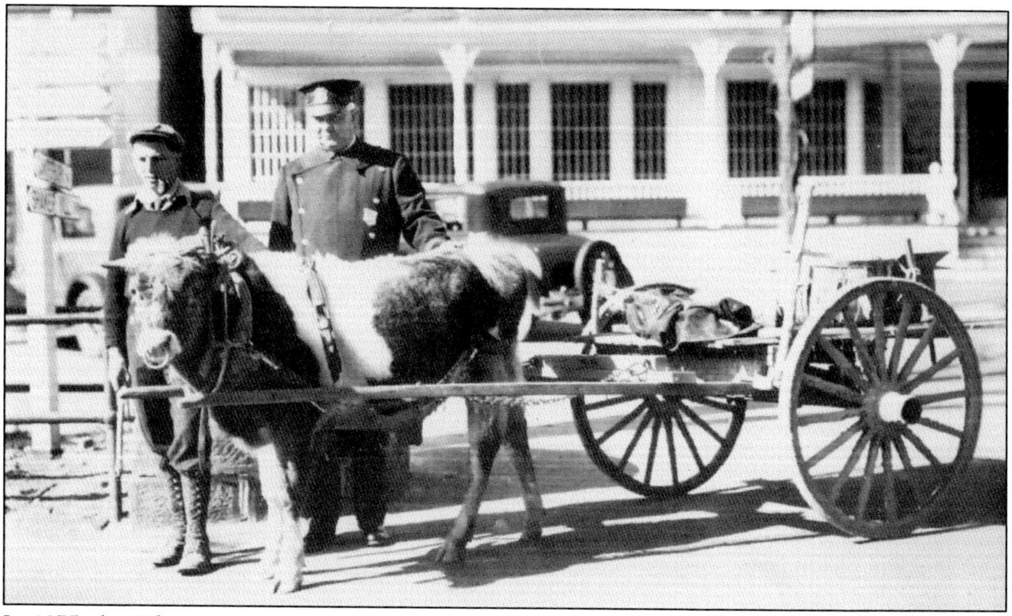

In 1875, the *Tilton Town Report* made mention of a constable and a policeman for the first time. Police protection in Tilton was a long established collaboration with Northfield. The police station for the two communities was in Tilton Town Hall, and the jail was downstairs in the same building. Officer John Driscoll and an unidentified man pose with the man's wagon. (Courtesy of the Hall Memorial Library.)

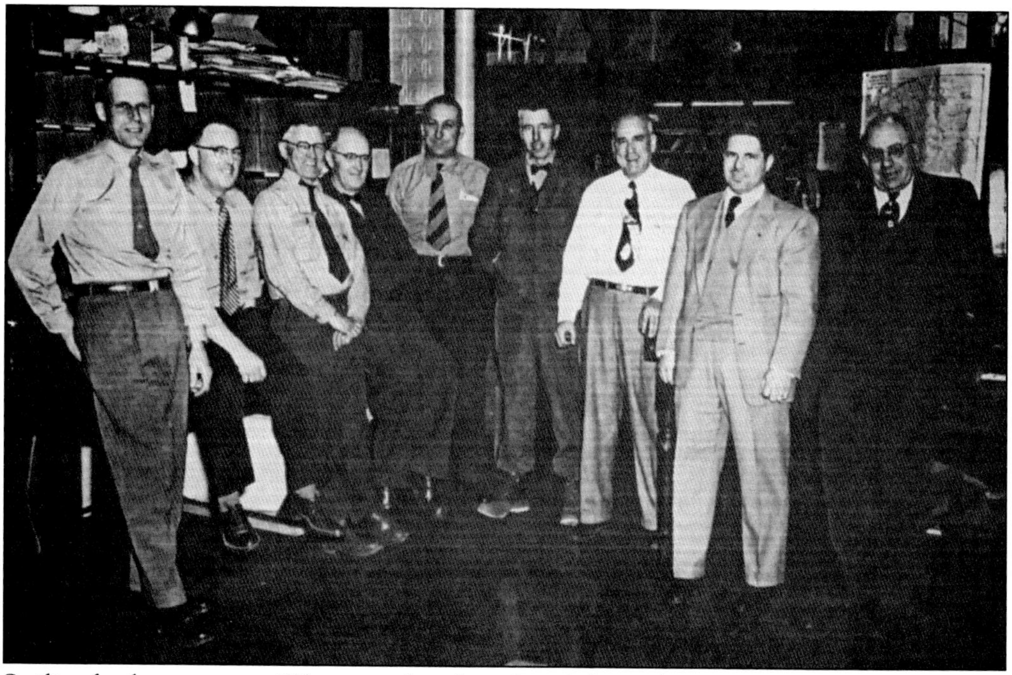

Smiling for the camera are Tilton postal workers, from left to right, George Currier, Paul Pelletier, Ted Whittier, Leo French, Sebastian Pucci, Jim Simpson, Herb Howe, Charles Fitzgerald, and Fred Terrien. This photograph was taken in the late 1940s when the post office was located at the ground level of the town hall. (Courtesy of the Randall family.)

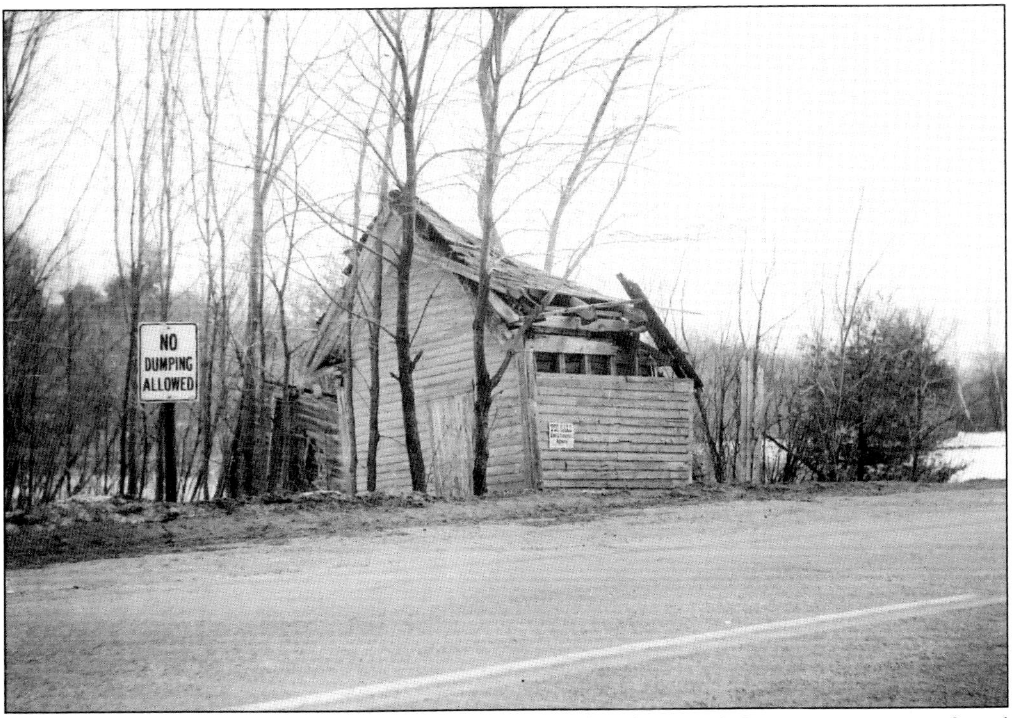

This former jailhouse was on the corner of Brook Road and Route 3. It was sometimes referred to as the "Hobo Hotel," as many of the hobos removed from the trains stayed there overnight. It may have been built when Tilton was Sanbornton Bridge. In later years, the police station for Tilton and Northfield was located in Tilton Town Hall, which housed a more substantial jail. The automobile accident below, which required the attention of police officer Roy "Sliver" Sanborn, took place in 1927 when a train collided with this 1927 Hudson Super Six sedan. The car was pushed to the sidewalk on the north side of Main Street. (Above, courtesy of Marjorie Rudolph; below, courtesy of the William Lawrence family.)

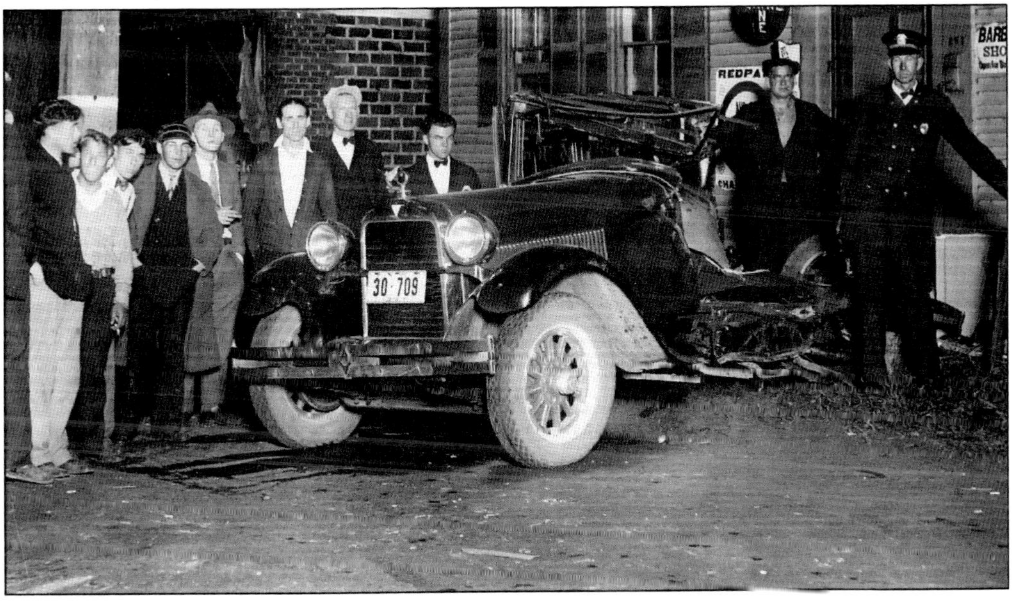

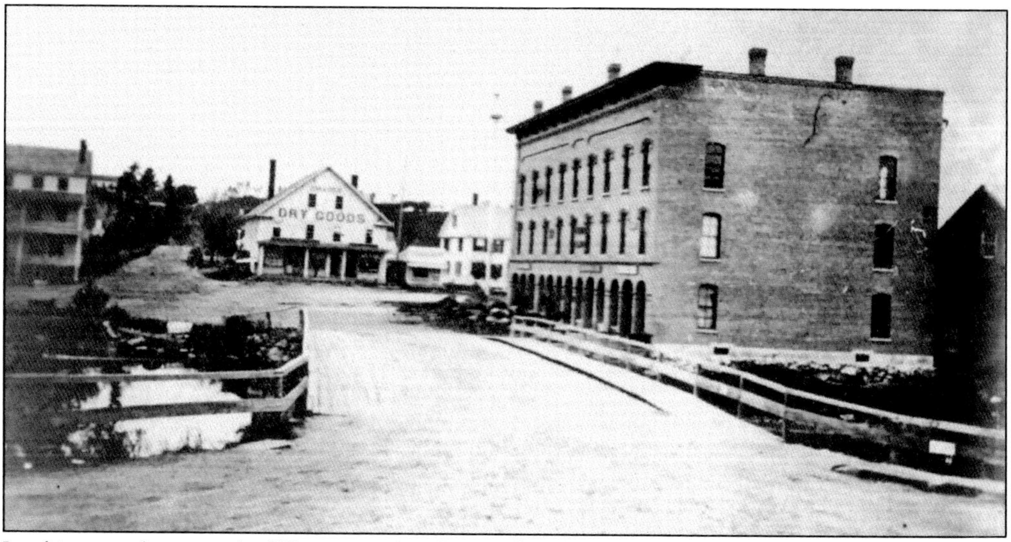

Looking north across the Winnipesaukee River, this photograph above shows (from left to right) the Dexter House, a dry goods store, a private home, and the Hill Block. The most significant building here is the dry goods store on the corner of Main and School Streets. A Mr. Duncan of Concord is said to have owned and occupied a small store on this location as early as 1789. This property became the site of Tilton Town Hall in 1878. The Dexter House, shown below, was built by Jeremiah Tilton in 1825 and was the first hotel in town. It was later owned by his son, Col. Samuel Tilton. (Both photographs courtesy of the Randall family.)

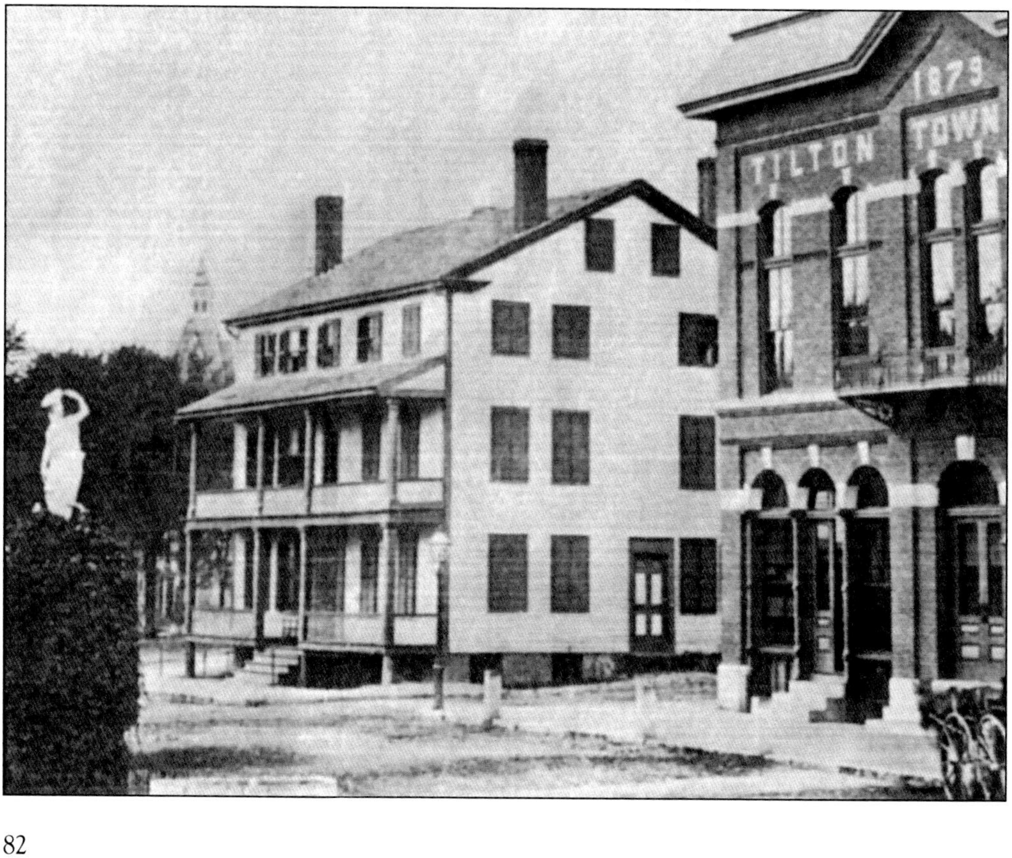

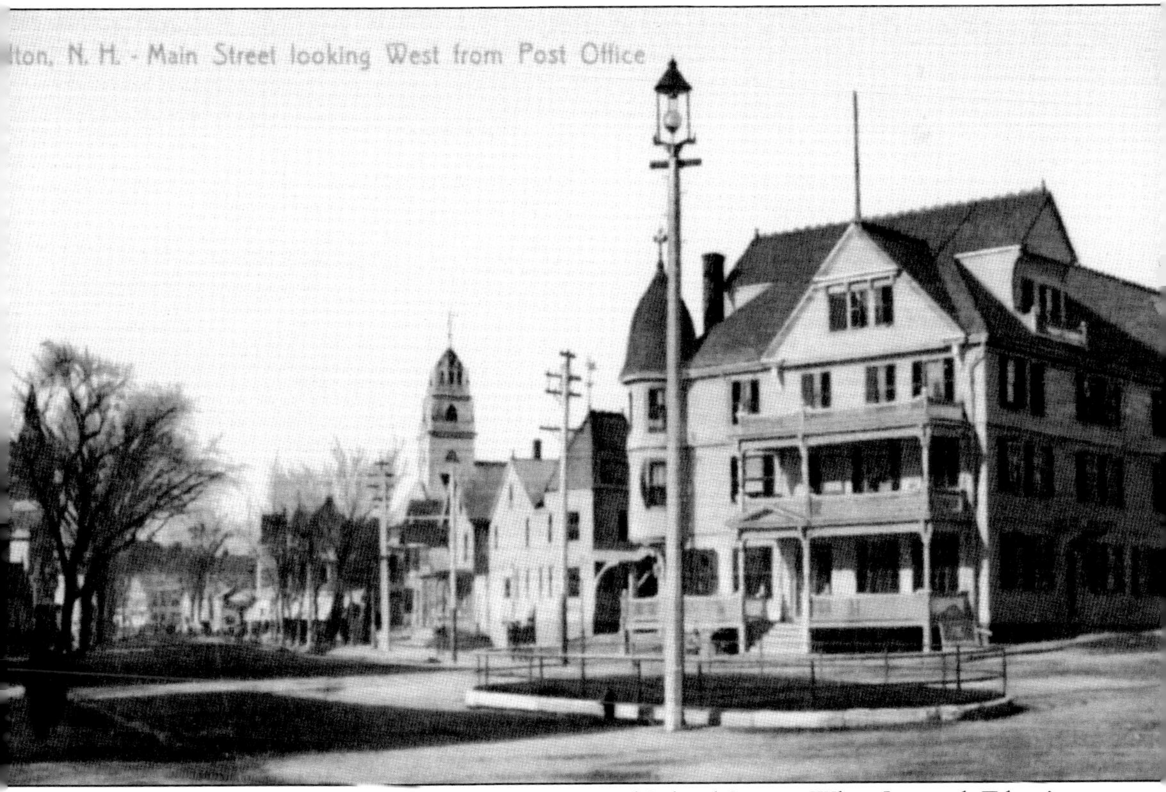

The Loverin Hotel is located on the corner of Main and School Streets. When Jeremiah Tilton's son Samuel became the owner of the hotel, another story was added, making this a very imposing building. It had three porches, four stories, and a turret on the western corner. According to the *1888–1889 Franklin and Tilton Directory,* the Loverin Hotel was the only hotel in town at that time, and the proprietor was John F. Bryant. At 3 a.m. on July 23, 1903, a fire destroyed this hotel, the Livery Stable, and Morse's Printing Office. With reports of inadequate water pressure, the need for a better-equipped fire service and alarm system was brought to the attention of the town. The fenced-in area by the light post was eventually the site of the *World War I Memorial Monument.* (Courtesy of Cecile Robert.)

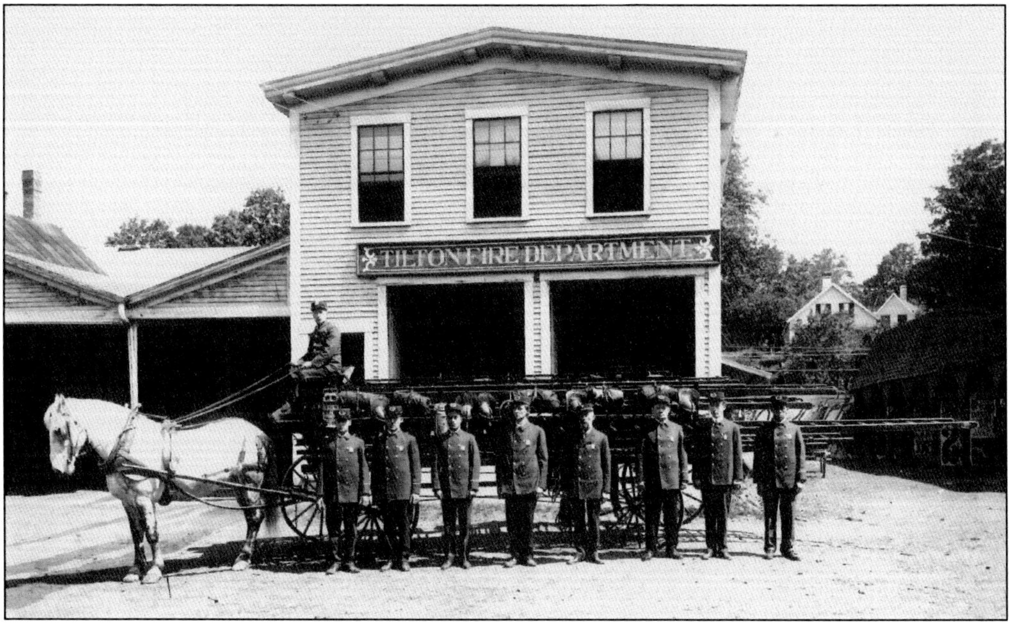

In 1867, the Tilton and Northfield Fire Precincts used two-hand engines. The larger one required 50 men to operate it. The smaller, operated by fewer men, one was more efficient. In the photograph above, firemen are shown in the late 1800s with a horse-drawn ladder truck. In 1944, the *Tilton Town Report* noted, "Now each fireman has his own rubber boots, rubber coat, and helmet." Prior to 1950, the Fire Precinct also provided night watchmen. Pictured below is a view of the Loverin Hotel fire of 1903. One of the firemen can be seen at the top of the pole. (Above, courtesy of Tilton Town Hall; below, courtesy of the Moulton family.)

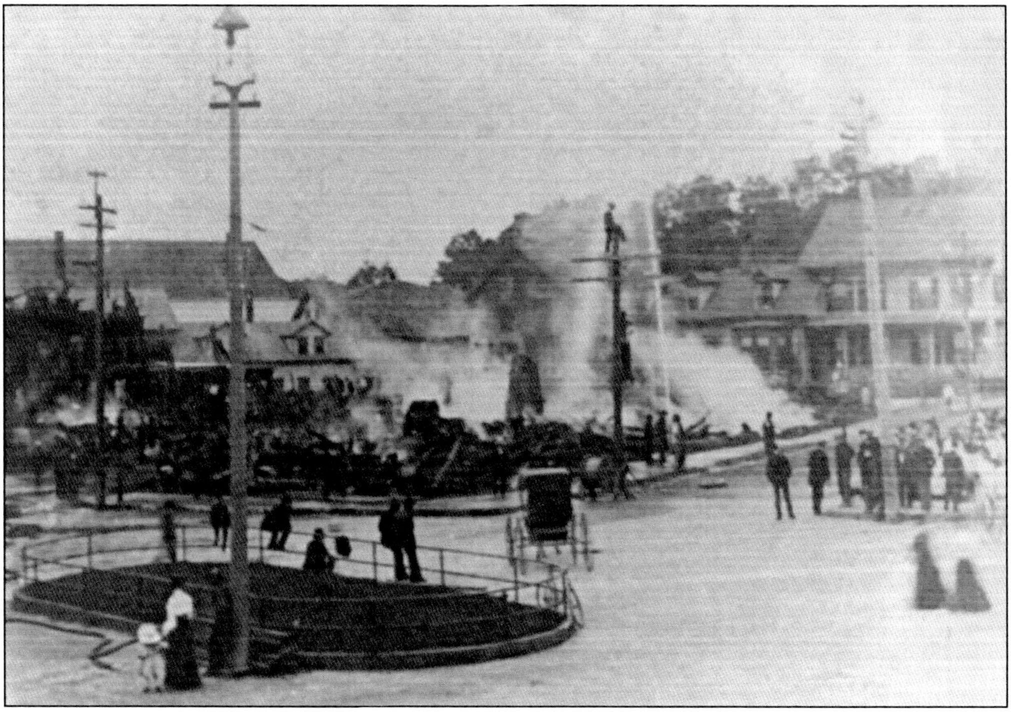

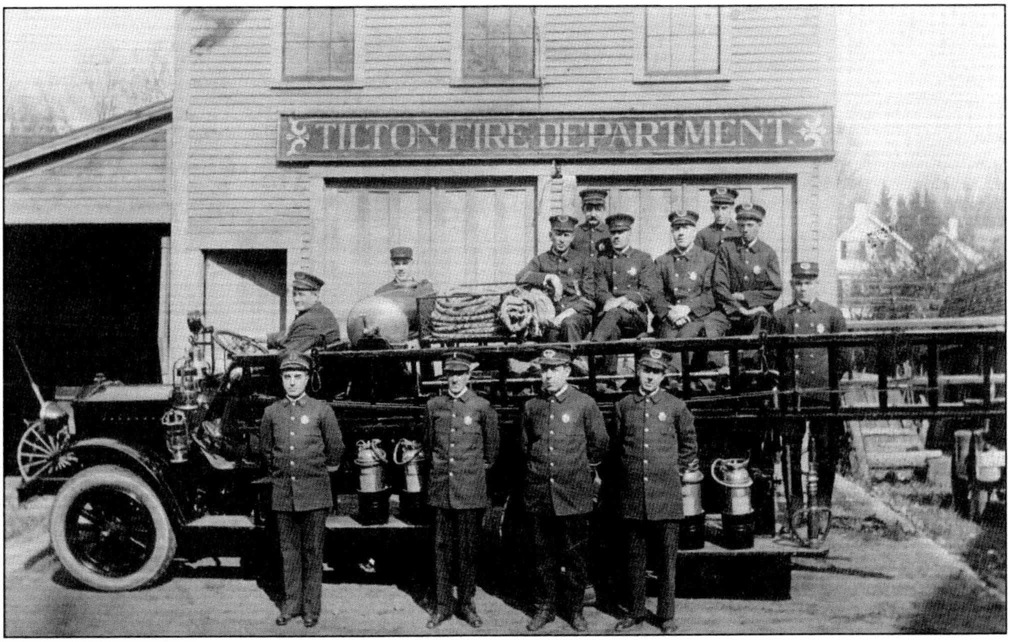

The Tilton Fire Department, composed of men from both Tilton and Northfield, pose with their ladder truck in front of the Center Street station. The following are, from left to right (first row) George Plummer, unidentified, Ludovic Shiatte, and Asa Manning; (second row) driver Walt Bosworth, Bill Flyn, Polie Daigneau, unidentified, Fred Pickering, unidentified, Gus Goodale, Bill Simpson, and John Simpson. The hand-hose cart from earlier days is seen in the shed on the left. In the photograph below are, from left to right, Walt Daniels, Lawrence Dubia, Joseph Roberts, and Chief Roy Jordan Sr.—on the scene after a fire at the Ideal Hotel on March 25, 1944. (Above, courtesy of James and Elaine Lamanuzzi; below, courtesy of the Roy Jordan family.)

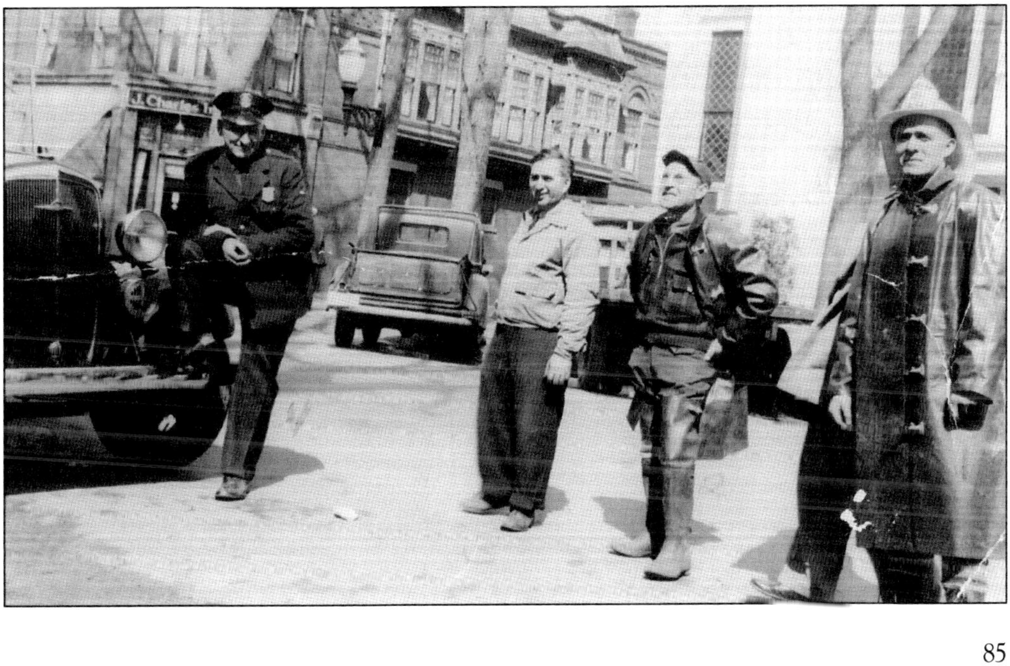

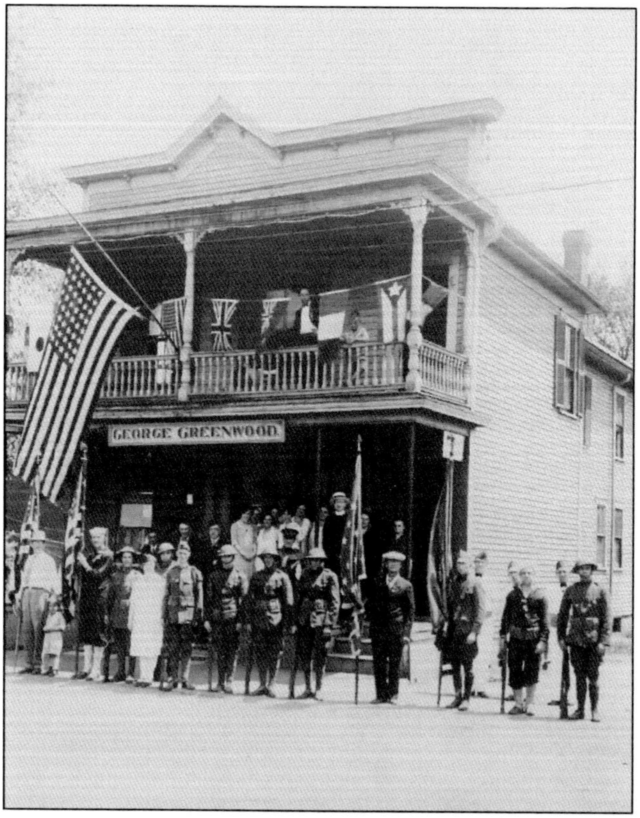

World War I veterans stand at attention in front of the American Legion Hall, which was upstairs over George Greenwood's plumbing supply store. This whole building eventually became the Legion's home. Whiteman–Davidson Post 49 received their covenant in September 1945, as did their auxiliary. World War II veterans (below) who formed the Legion's first Drill Team in 1946 are, from left to right (first row) Ernie Stebbins, Bud Deragon, George Limoge, Joe Dakin, Bill O'Connor, and Paul Barton; (second row) Wilbur Crossett, Vern Simpson, Robert Beaulieu, Larry Dubia, and Davy Davies; (third row) Roy Jordan Jr., Roy Harbour, Erttel Stanley, and Robert Harbour. (Both photographs courtesy of the Whiteman–Davidson Post 49, American Legion.)

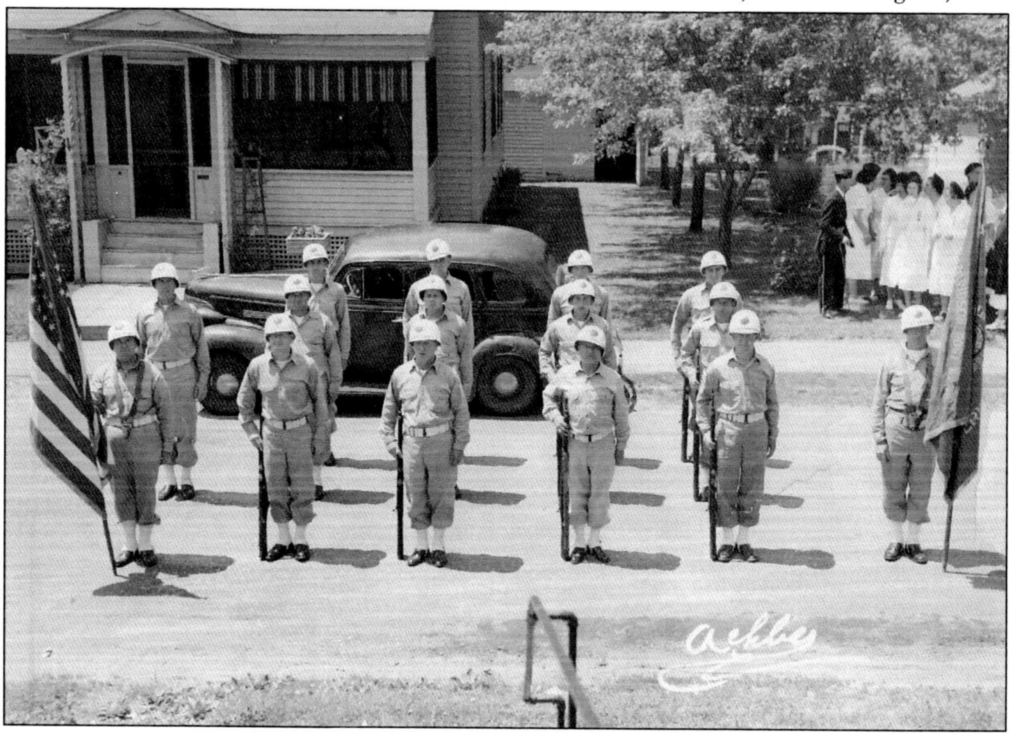

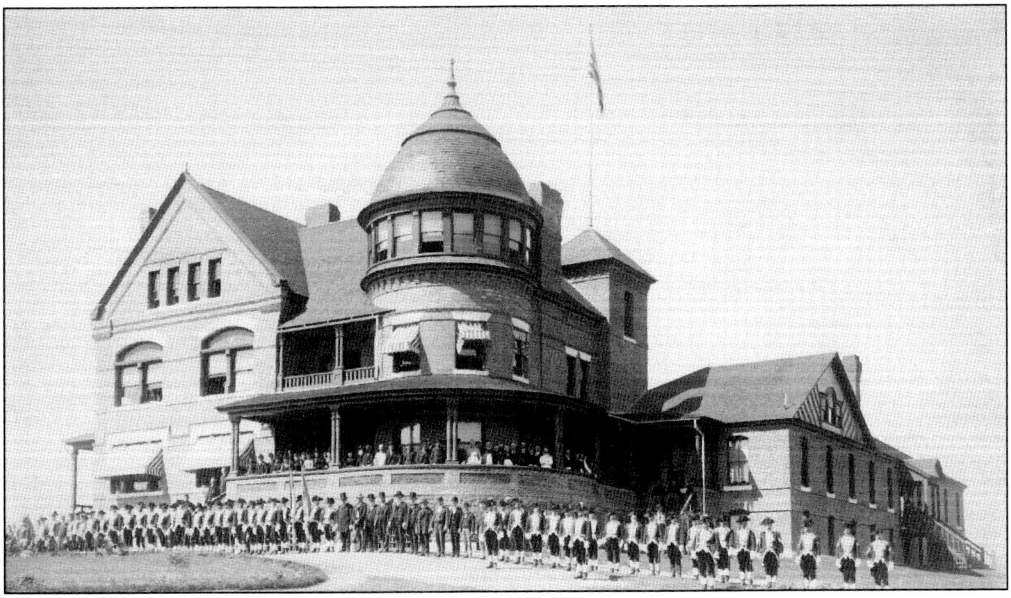

A veterans' board of managers, composed of prominent New Hampshire citizens, met to select a site for a Soldiers' Home. Member of the board, Charles E. Tilton, offered to give the State of New Hampshire a 30-acre site known as the Savage Farm, which was located near an early settlement called Tin Corner in Tilton. The dedication ceremony for the New Hampshire Soldiers' Home took place on December 3, 1890, which may have been the date of the above photograph by T.C. Moon. Three days later, the first veterans were admitted to the home for the care of Civil War veterans. Constructed in 1913, an addition to the farmhouse, shown below, was used as a hospital. (Above, courtesy of Tilton Town Hall; below, courtesy of the Hall Memorial Library.)

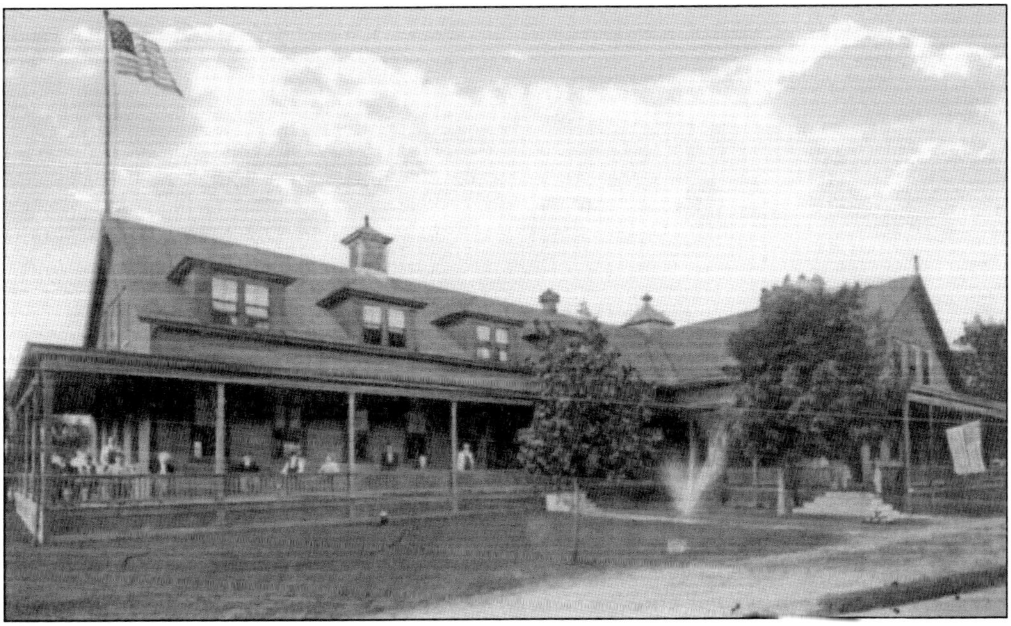

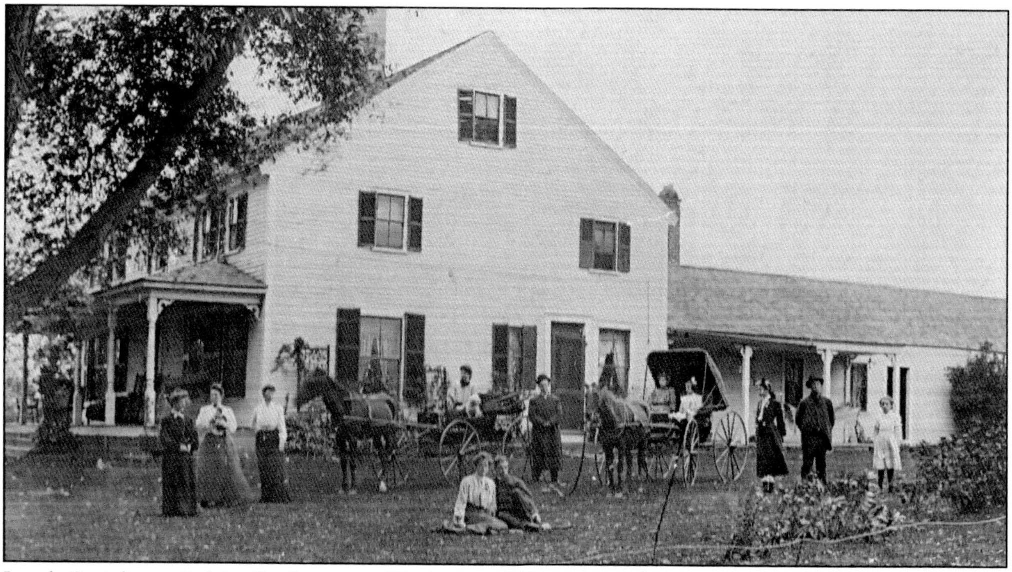

Jacob Smith settled in Sanbornton Bridge in 1768, married Betsey Cass, and established the Smith Farm. This 1778 home, the second to be built on Clark Road, was occupied by generations of the Smith family until the late 1930s. In the late 1800s, Margaret and Charles Smith (below) renovated the house and added the porch. In the early 1900s, the owners began taking in tourists, and the house became known as the "Fairview Inn." In the late 1930s, the home was empty for several years until the Shaw family purchased it in 1946. (Both photographs courtesy of the Plessner family.)

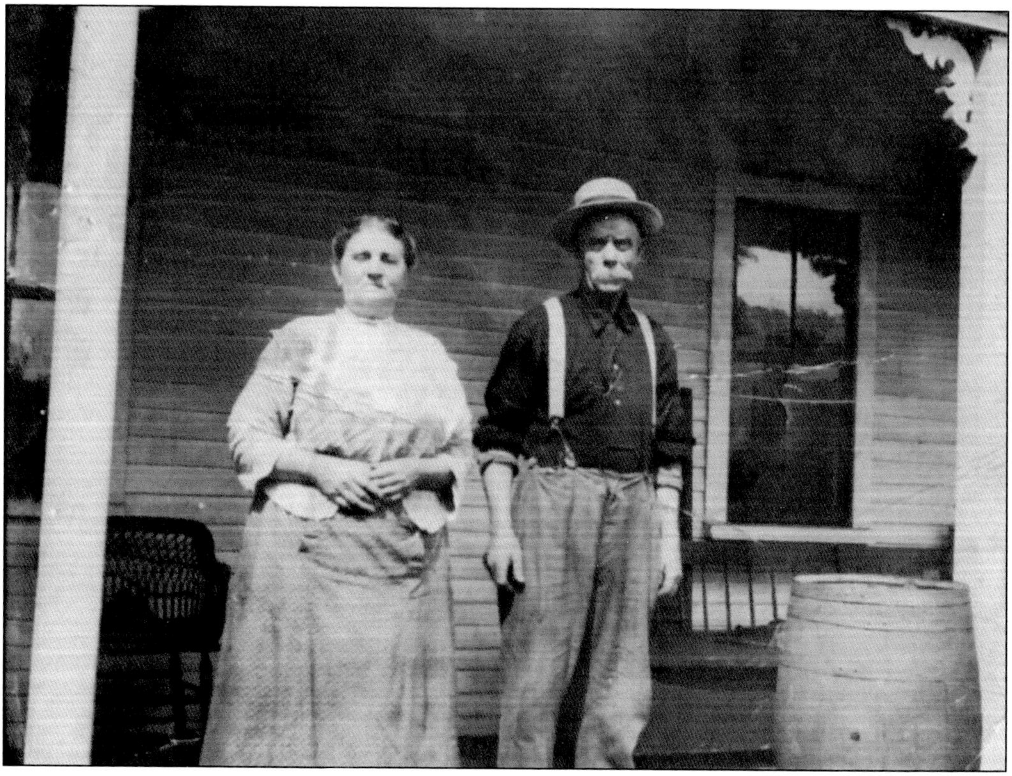

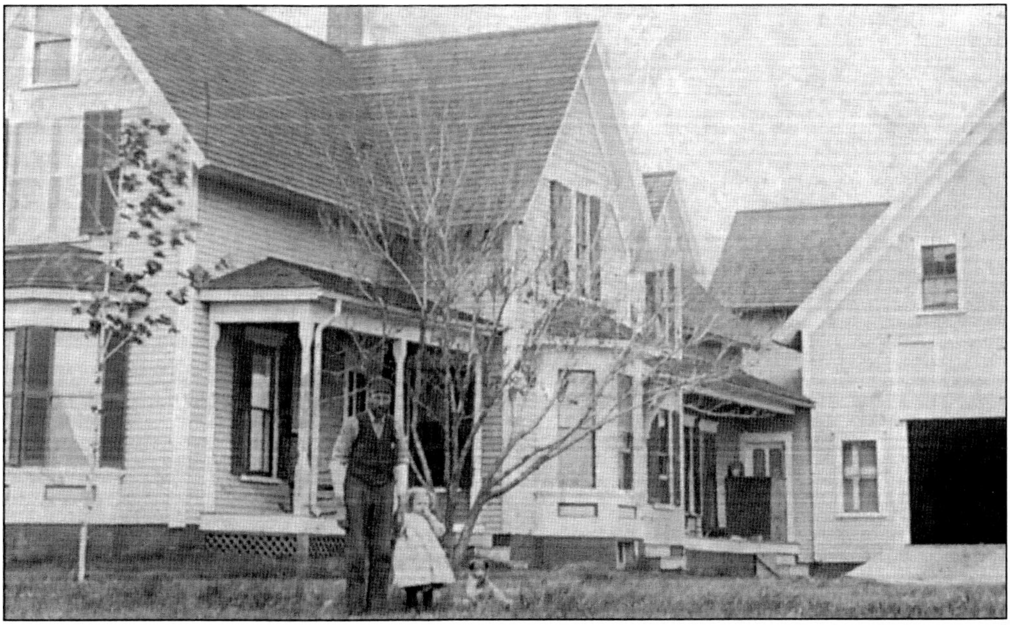

Laroy Rufus Thompson and his daughter Helen are standing in front of the family home and barn on School Street around 1898. Laroy delivered milk and eggs to customers in the Tilton area. Helen and her two brothers, along with their mother moved to "the house by the side of the road" after Laroy's death in 1917. (Courtesy of the Randall family.)

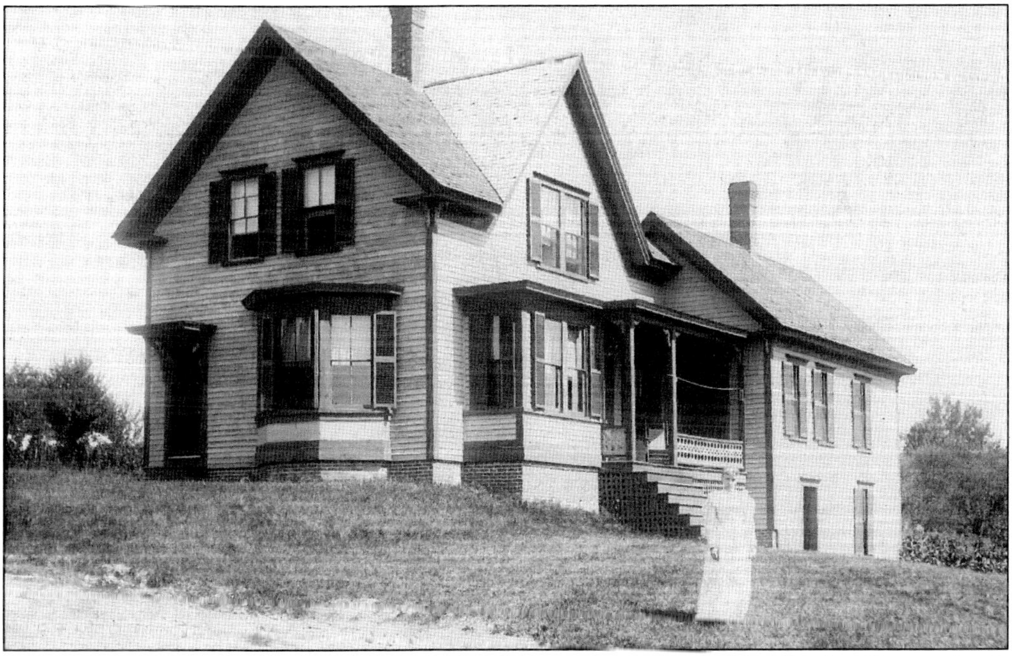

Eugenia Lupien Randall and her husband, Frank, owned this typical New England home. Frank was a supervisor at the G.H. Tilton Box Factory on East Main Street. Eugenia had immigrated to Lowell, Massachusetts, to work in the mills with many other young French–Canadian ladies. While there, she met and married Frank, and the young couple moved to Tilton to raise their family. (Courtesy of the Randall family.)

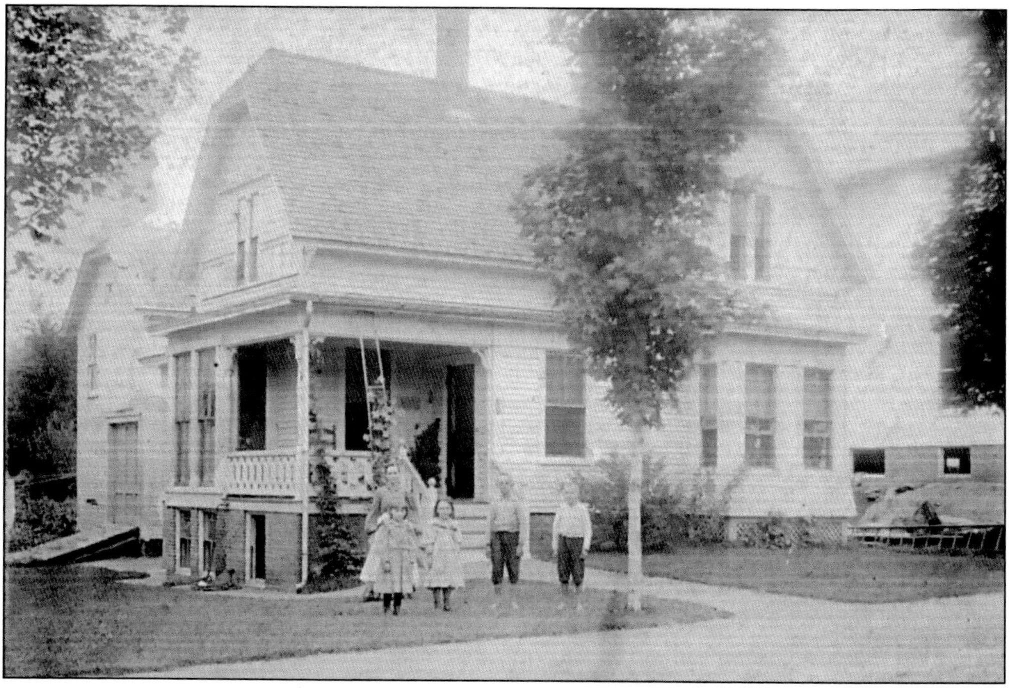

This typical New England home on Prospect Street (above) was built in 1915, and was the home of the Worthen family at that time. The woman in the photograph is Georgia Worthen Bailey with her two sons, Benjamin and George, and two unidentified young girls. The flower and vine enhanced stonewall (below), encloses this two-story, gambrel-roofed home on Lake Winnisquam that was built in 1907. This Lochmere home is situated on Route 3, which was unpaved at the time of this photograph. (Above, courtesy of Barbara Puffinberger; below, courtesy of the Karl Barnard family.)

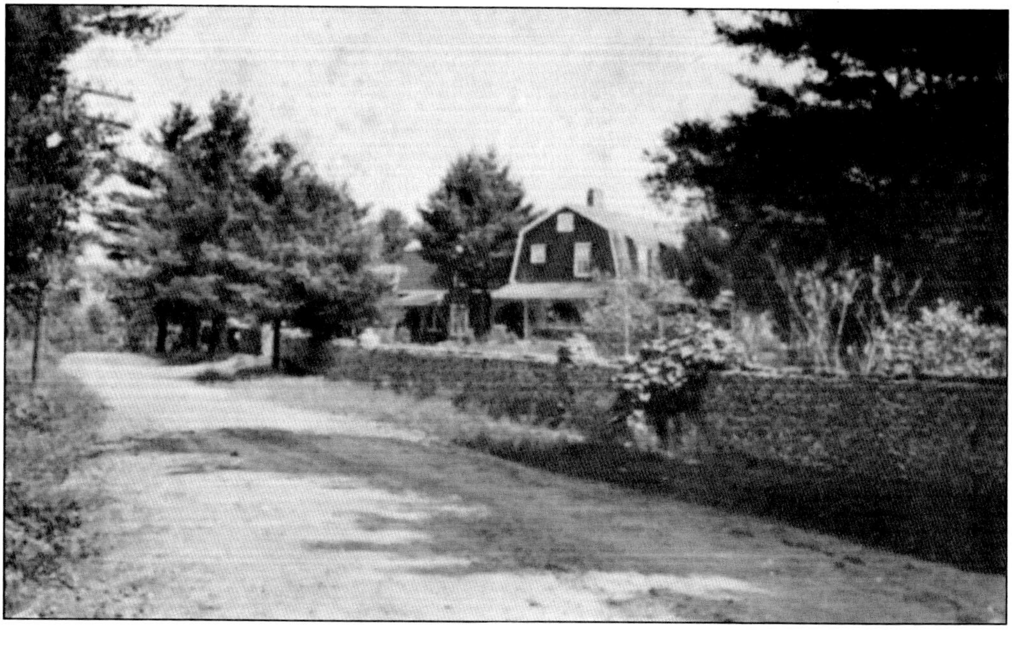

The William Fellows House was located across from the Tilton Island Park. This was the only house to survive a massive fire in the 1870s that destroyed almost everything on the north side of Main Street. (Courtesy of Louise and Bill Joscelyn.)

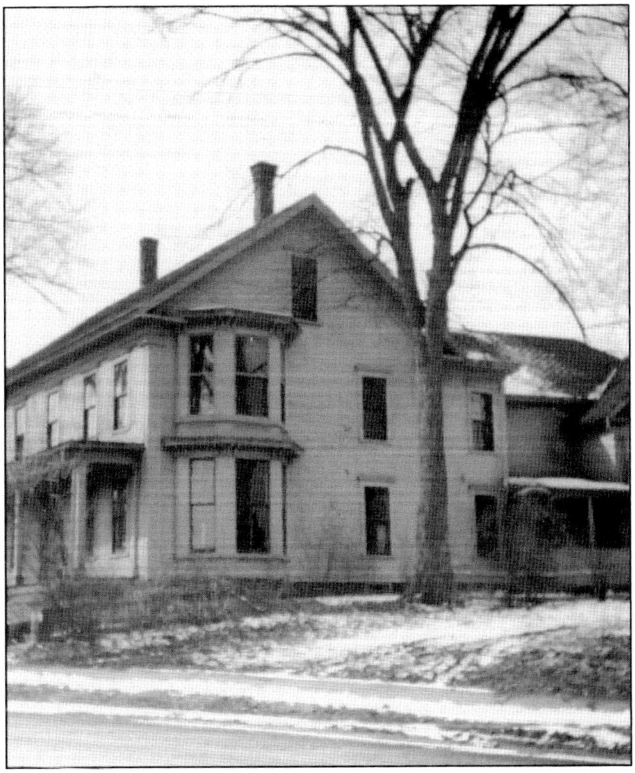

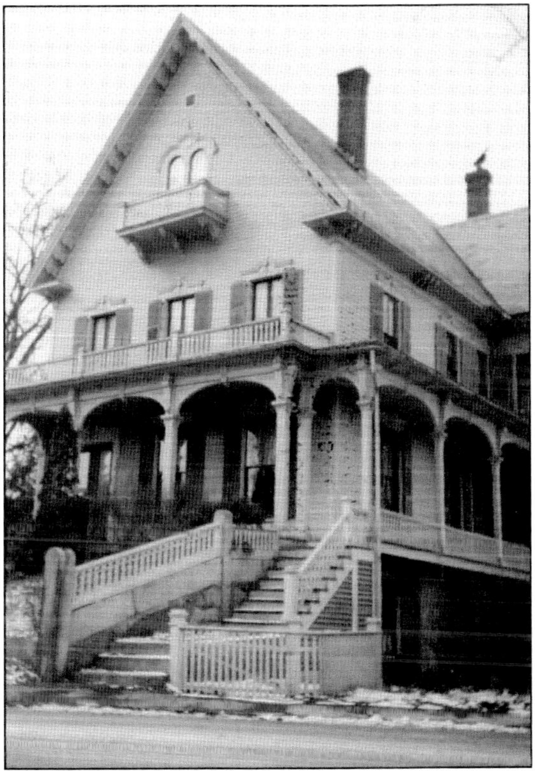

The Charles Curry Rogers house is a large, multilevel Victorian home next door to the Fellows House. It was built on the site of the Atkinson House, which was destroyed in the abovementioned fire. The small balcony on the third level appears more decorative than useful. The balcony on the second level would be more accommodating. The railed wraparound porch was very typical of homes built in that era. (Courtesy of Louise and Bill Joscelyn.)

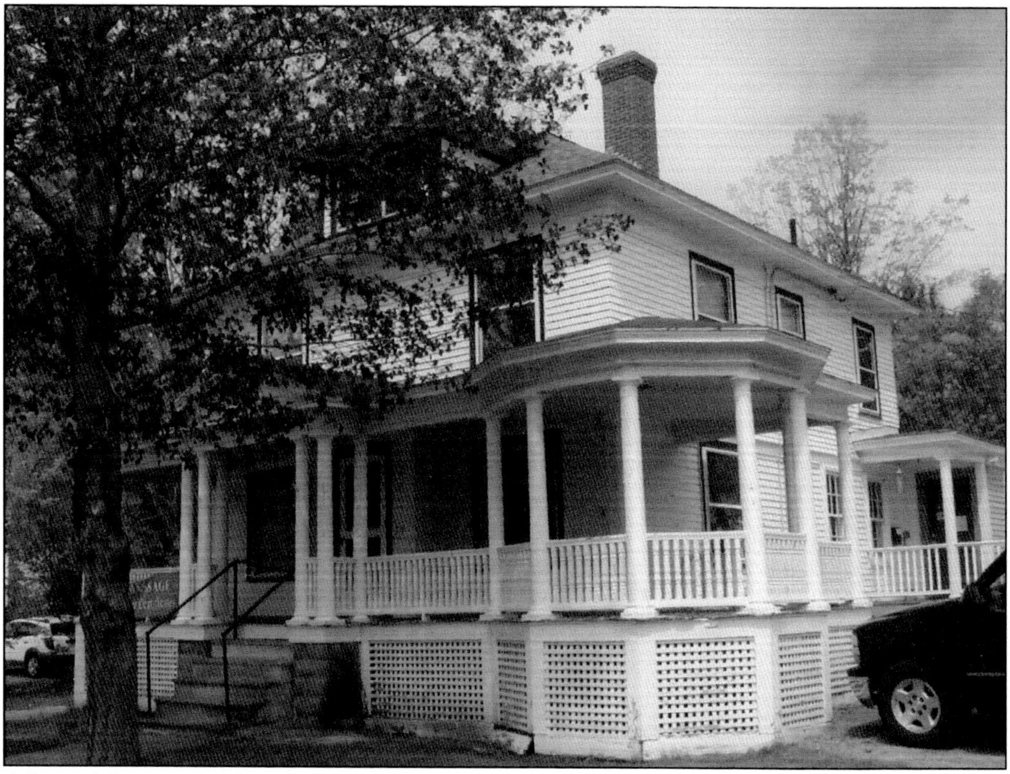

A beautiful wraparound porch, supported by numerous Romanesque columns, adorned this 2.5-story house on West Main Street. Built in 1924, this home was the parsonage for the Northfield–Tilton Congregational Church for a number of years. (Photograph by Dennis Evans.)

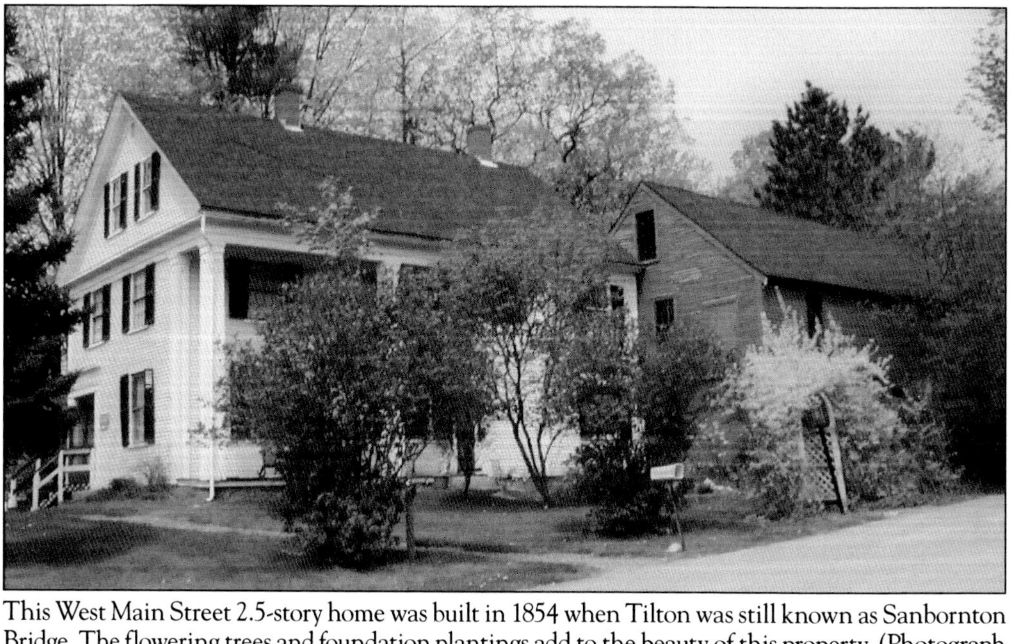

This West Main Street 2.5-story home was built in 1854 when Tilton was still known as Sanbornton Bridge. The flowering trees and foundation plantings add to the beauty of this property. (Photograph by Dennis Evans.)

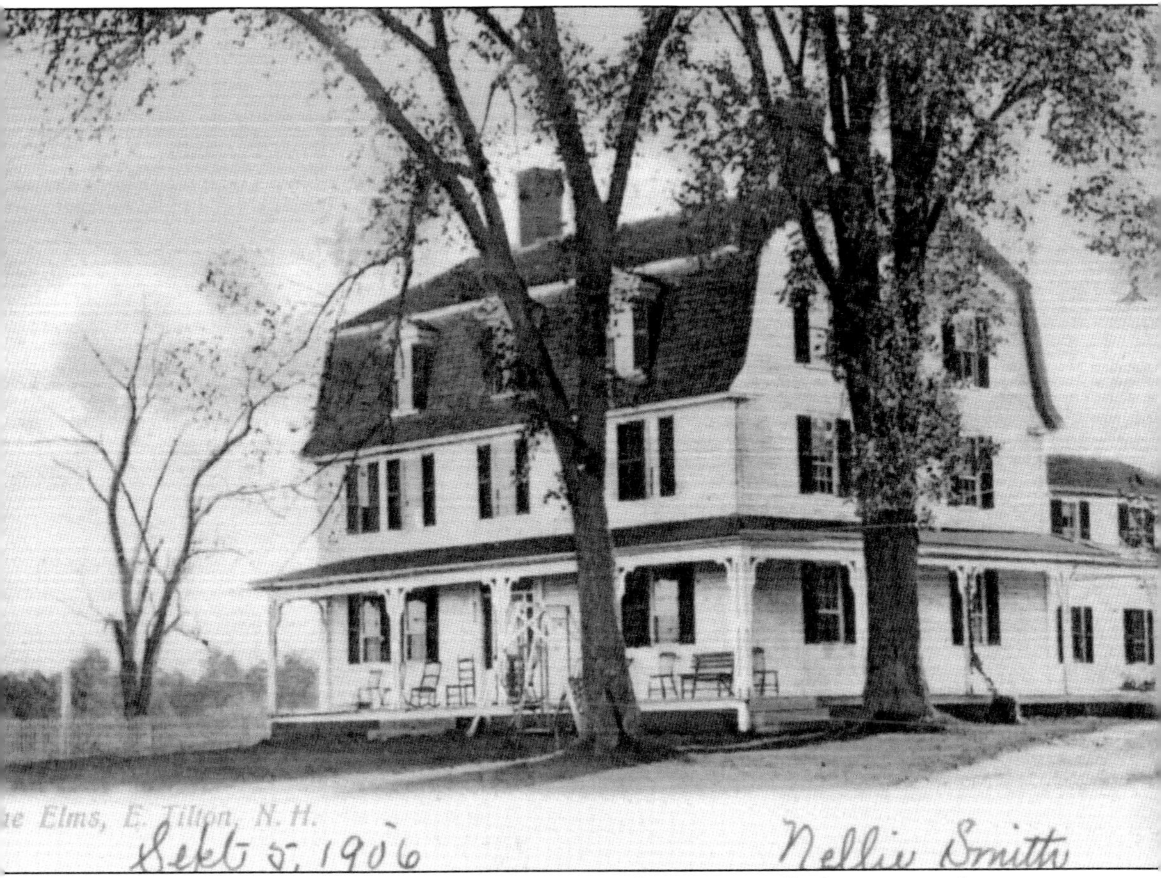

One of Lochmere's famous inns stood at the bottom of Lancaster Hill. Construction began on the three-story, gambrel-roofed inn around 1790. It had only two stories until 1880 when the third-story was added. The porch was added around 1860. At that time, the building changed from a private residence and dairy farm to an inn. The inn was known for the brick oven in the kitchen and the beautiful, reddish-brown, grained finish of the woodwork. The loom in the attic was used for weaving. The family patriarch was an Army officer who fought with Gen. George Washington. The elms, for which this inn was named, were about eight inches in diameter in the first photographs available. In later photographs, such as this one, the elms had become towering trees. This information came from *A History of Lochmere, New Hampshire*, by the Lochmere Woman's Club, 1974–1975. (Courtesy of the Moulton family.)

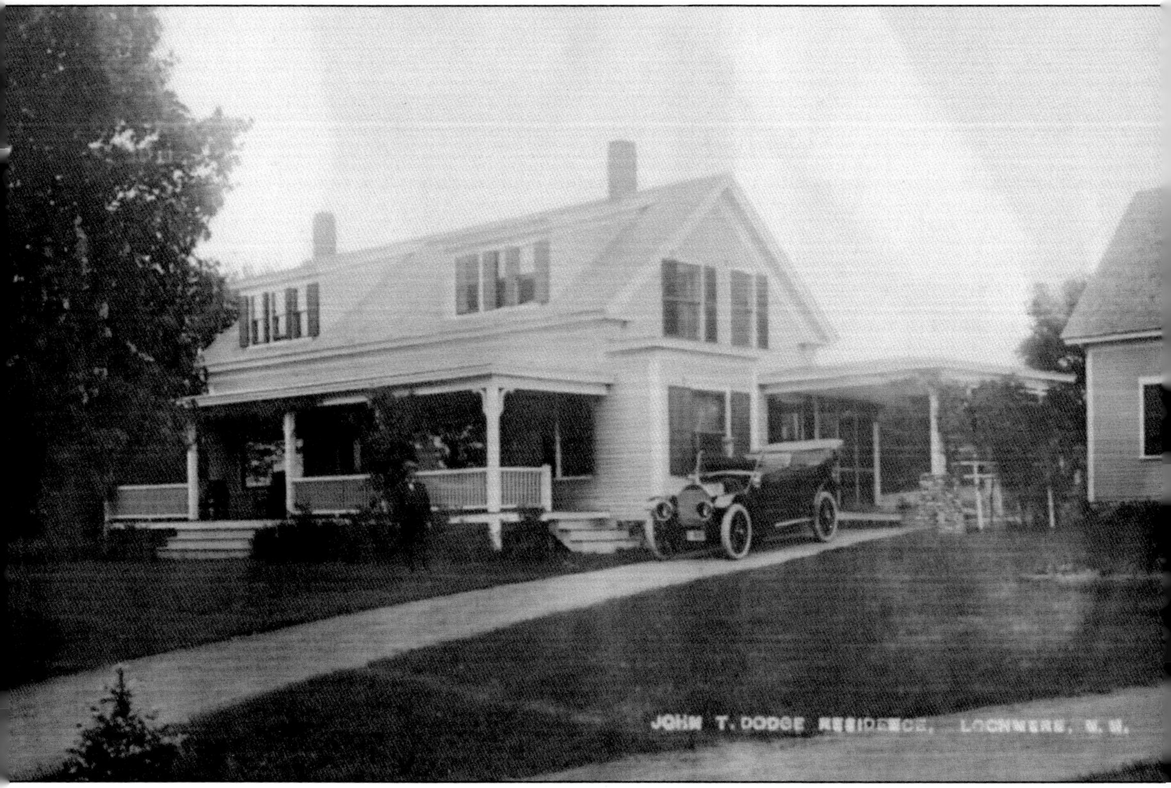

The Dodge family homestead stands on a hill overlooking Silver Lake. The home was built in the early 1800s as a summer home of John T. Dodge I—the gentleman standing on the front lawn. It is now the year-round home for the fifth generation of the Dodge family. The automobile in this photograph is a 1910, Model 48, Pierce Arrow, seven-passenger touring car. James B. Dodge, son of Dodge I, is the gentleman in the right side driver's seat. Dodge I was a lumberman and a member of the New Hampshire State Legislature. He sponsored a bill which, when passed, was known as the Dodge Stake Bill. This law required railroad flatcars carrying lumber to have staked sides. John T. Dodge II, son of James, was also a member of the New Hampshire Legislature, and his brother James W. Dodge had a long public career in Tilton. (Courtesy of the Dodge family.)

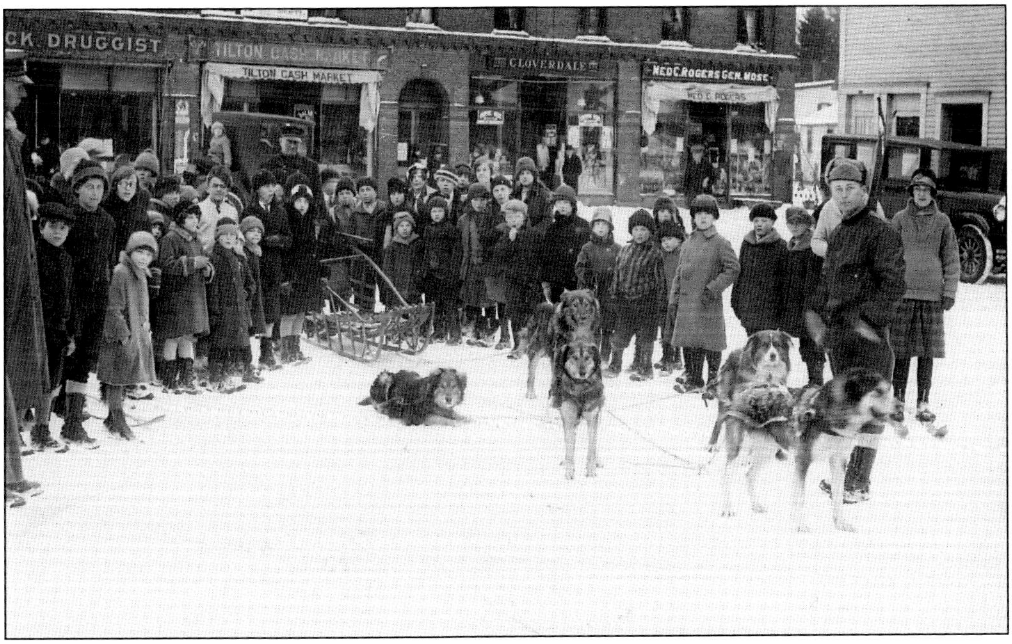

Sled dog racing has a long history in the Lakes Region. In the photograph above, people gather to see a team of dogs on the Main Street of Tilton during a winter carnival. The tall policeman on the left is Roy "Sliver" Sanborn, and the officer behind the sled is Chief Walt Bosworth. The stores in the background were in the Hill Block across from the town hall. Snowshoeing was another popular winter activity. In the 1920s, teachers and students participated in evening snowshoe hiking. In the photograph below, hikers pause by the snowcapped *World War I Monument* in Veterans Square. (Both photographs courtesy of the Randall family.)

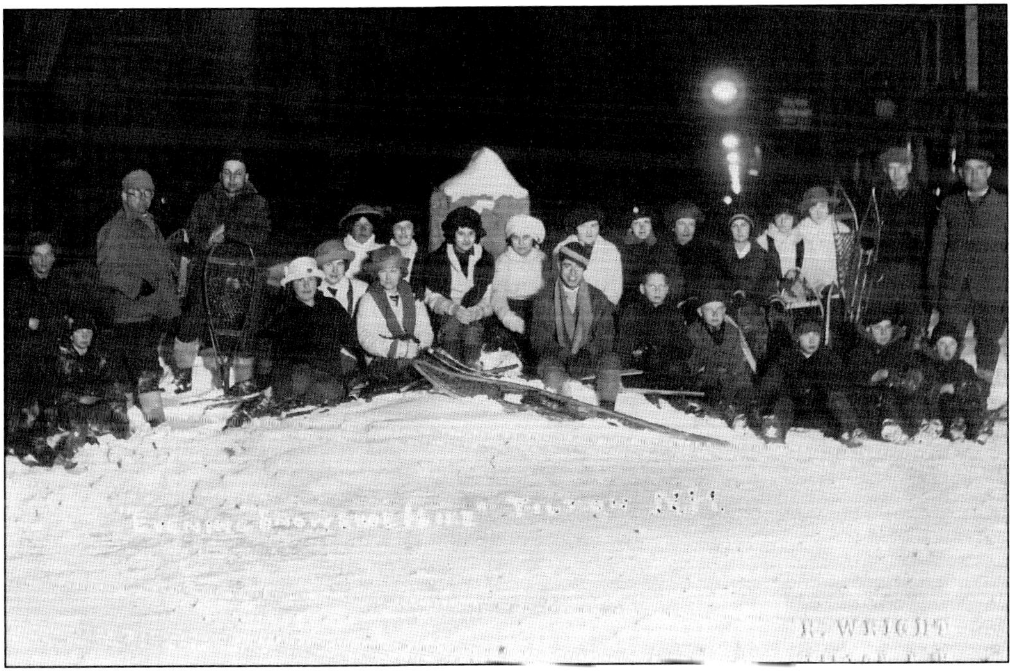

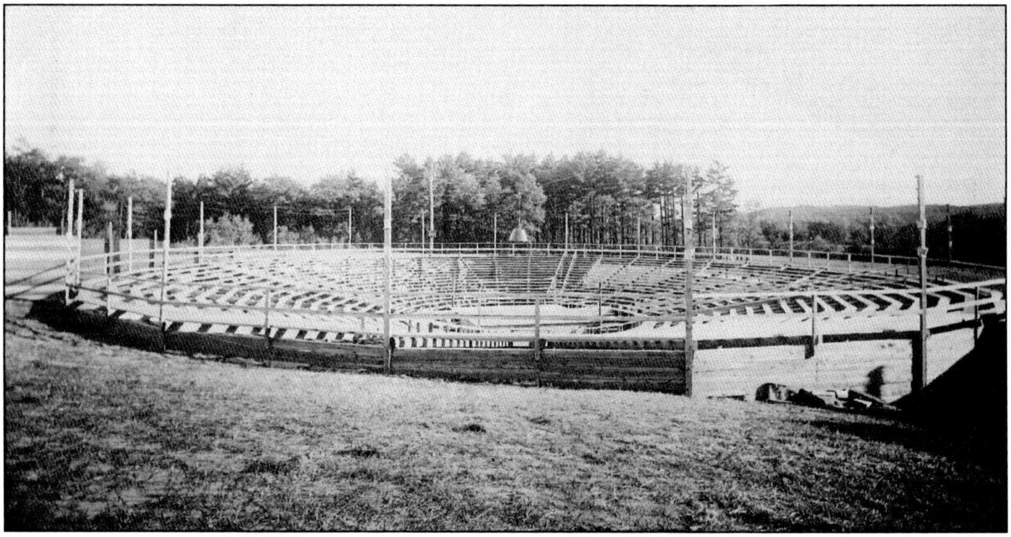

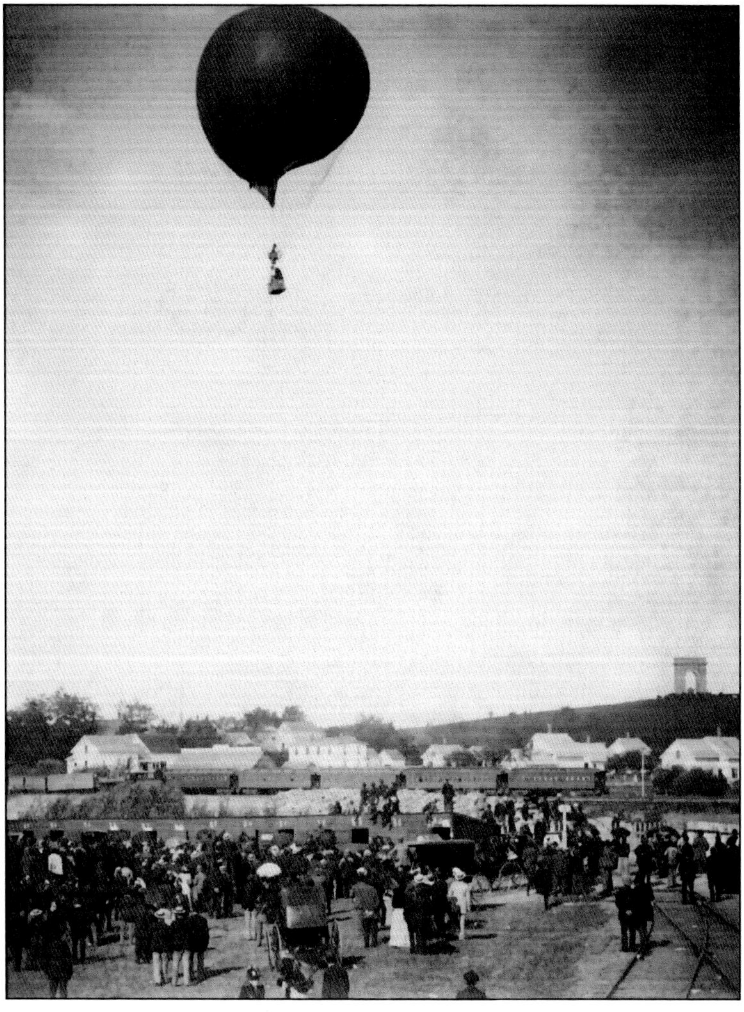

Recreational events were among the many things shared by Tilton and Northfield residents, and some of these were held at the Tilton Fairground on Sargent Street in Northfield. In 1891, Tilton Seminary held its first field day on those grounds. In 1918, Charles E. Tilton's son Maj. Charles E. Tilton gave the 25-acre field to Tilton School. The fairground was also the site of a boxing arena, as seen above. The hot air balloon, shown in the photograph below, was probably part of a summer fair celebration. The railroad and the *Memorial Arch* can be seen in the background. (Above, courtesy of Mike and Elaine Murphy; below, courtesy of Mariam Melendez.)

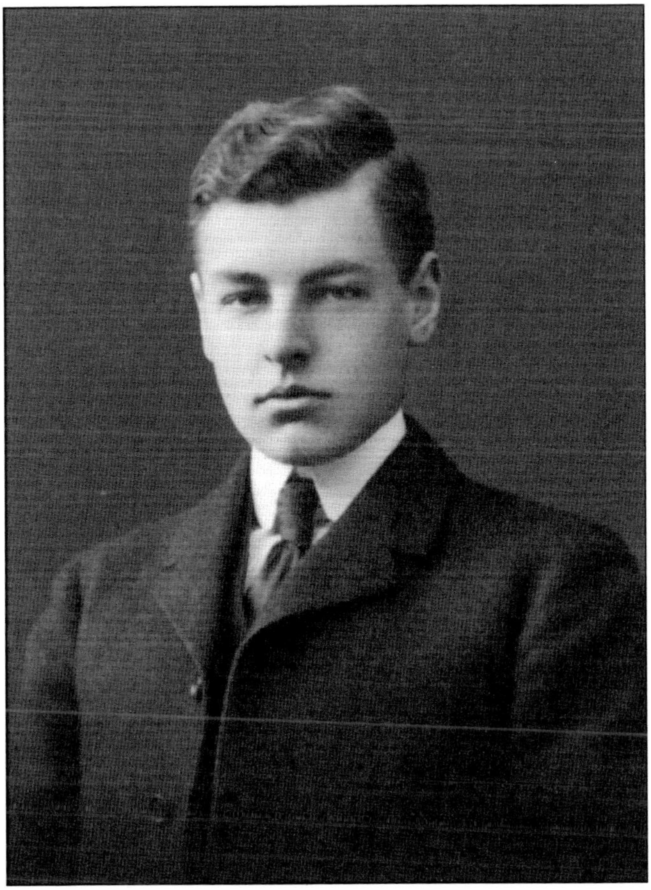

Charles E. Tilton II was born in 1887 in Tilton. Following his father's example, he built a block of commercial buildings on Main Street between the Congregational Church and the Loverin Block. Tilton was chosen as a representative to the General Court, and Governor Felker made him a member of his staff with the rank of major. (Courtesy of Joy Tilton.)

At the turn of the 20th century, country gentlemen chose the Bronson Wagon for a fast, relatively comfortable ride over bumpy roads. The four-passenger box had finished wood panels and luxuriant cushions upholstered with leather. Two pull-horses were custom-bred and trained to haul the wagon. The driver here is Harry Wyatt of Lochmere. (Courtesy of the Karl Barnard family.)

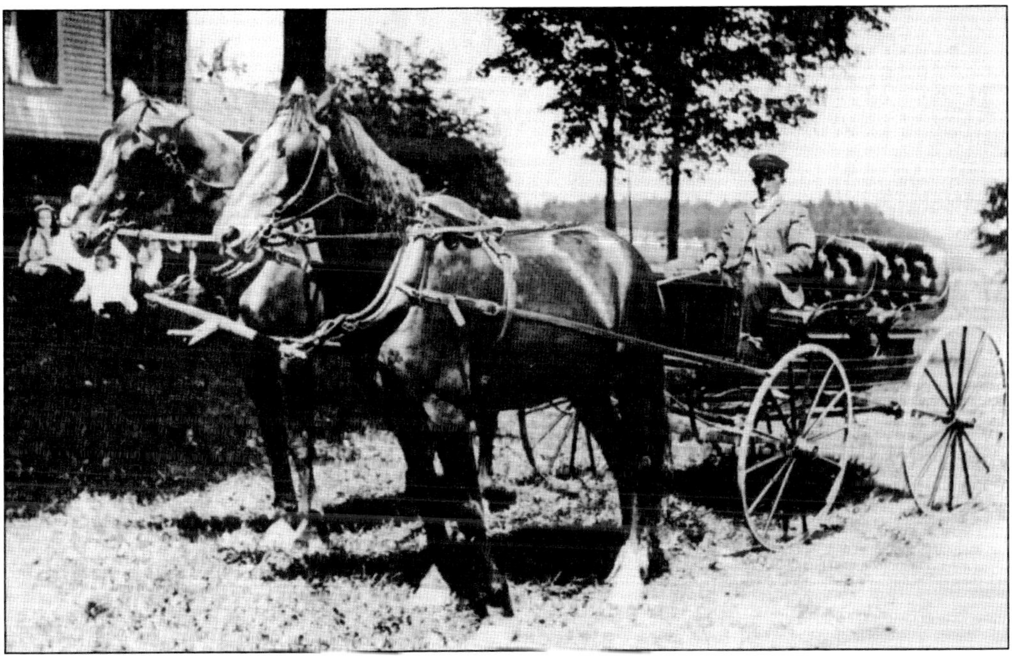

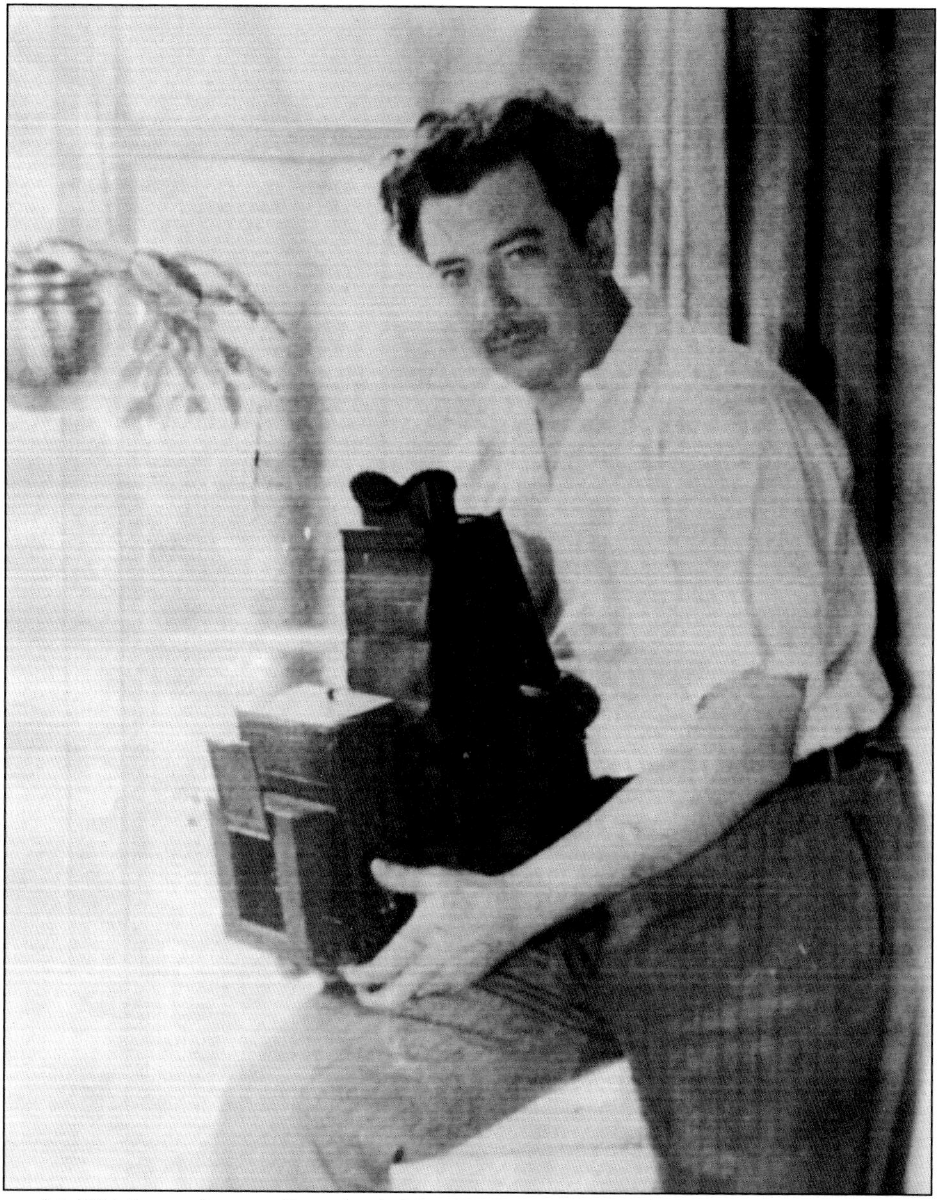

Roscoe M. Wright was born in Reinebeck, New York, in 1891. His father, Wallace Wright, moved the family to Tilton when Roscoe was still a boy. During Roscoe Wright's short life of 45 years, his only trade was that of a devoted photographer. Wright learned photography from his father. After high school, he joined his father's portrait business. When World War I started, Wright joined the Army to serve in France for one year as a photographer. Upon discharge, he worked as a photojournalist with the *Boston Post*. He moved on to the prestigious Bachrach portrait studios and managed the company's posing rooms in Boston and New York. Around 1925, Wright established several of his own studios in central New Hampshire, including one in Tilton. He worked as both a portrait artist and as an *Associated Press* photographer in the Tilton area. His journalistic photography was carried in many local and national newspapers. Tilton is privileged to have had Wright chronicle life in Tilton during the 1920s, and many of those images are featured in *Around Tilton*. (Courtesy of Tilton Town Hall.)

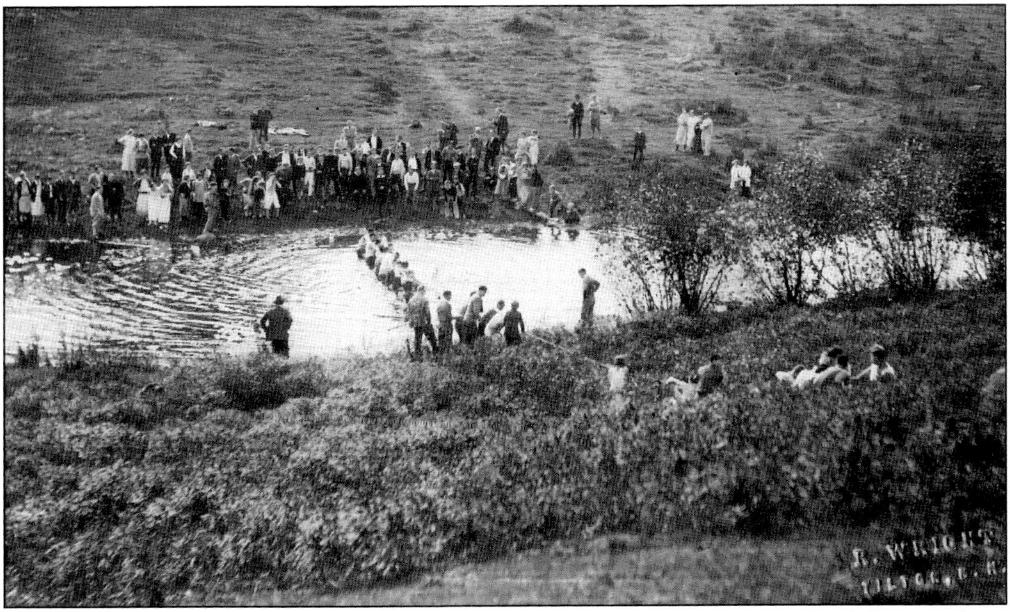

These postcards reveal the storyteller in Roscoe Wright. The 1924 photograph of this tug-of-war tells of struggle and conquest. The perspective was carefully chosen to emphasize the strain of the students pulling uphill, while below, others are mired in the muddy water. Spectators of all ages cheer on their teams. Some casually observe with folded arms. For the sled dog race (below), Wright is on the second floor of the Hill Block building where his studio was located. The woman standing on the fence rail by *America* mirrors the lofty vantage point of the photographer. Several people in the crowd are looking up at the photographer. The fact that there is rain instead of snow appears to deter neither dogs nor people. (Courtesy of the Hall Memorial Library.)

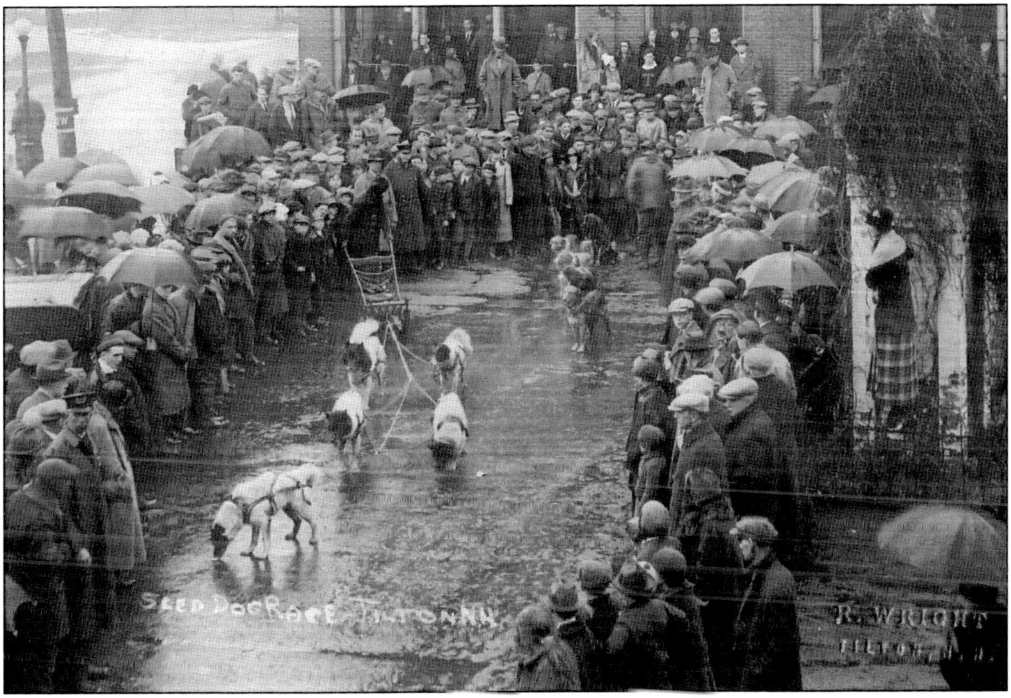

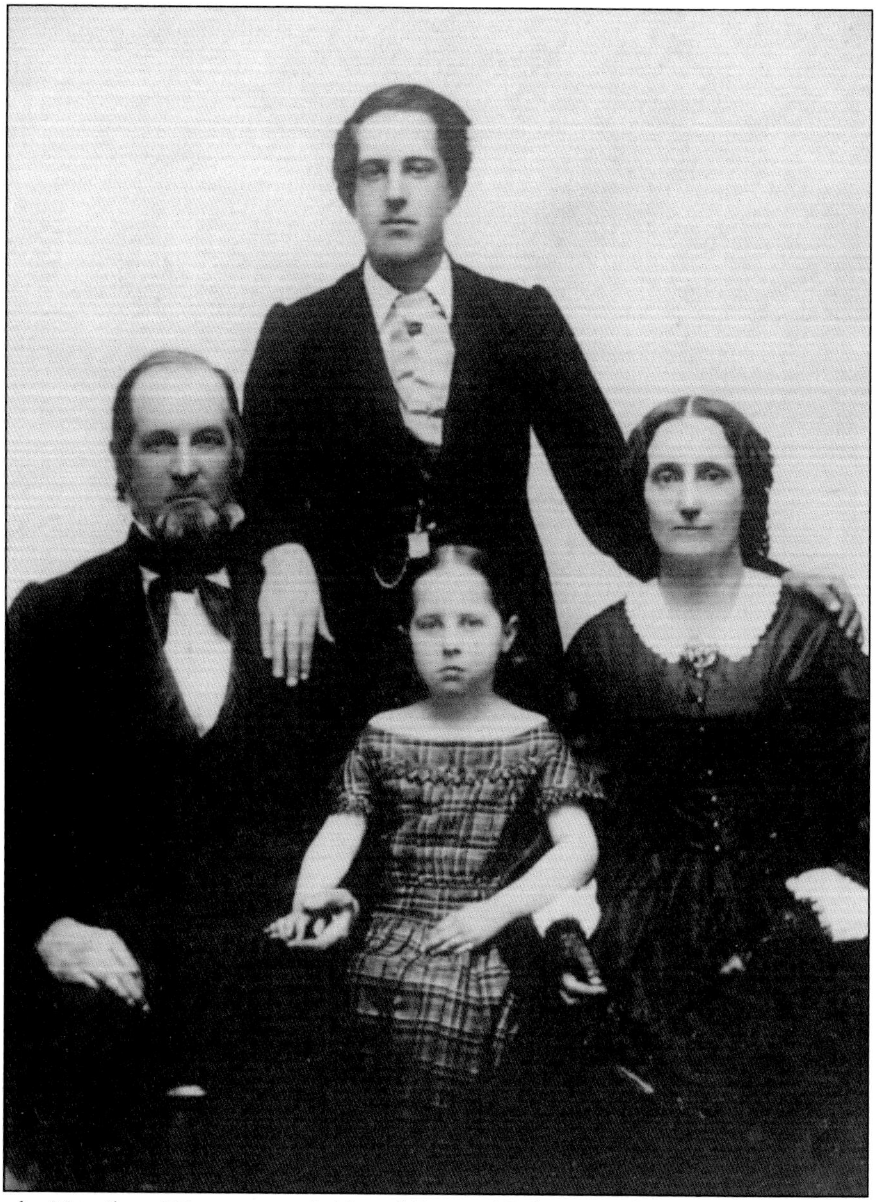

Alexander Hamilton Tilton married Abigail Barnard Baker on July 27, 1837. This 1862 family portrait shows them with their children, Albert and Evelyn. Abigail was the eldest daughter of Mark and Abigail Ambrose Baker. Abigail's younger sister, Mary Morse Baker, would become Mary Baker Eddy. At the age of 16, Alexander Hamilton began working for an older brother Jeremiah Tilton Jr., who operated a textile mill in Northfield. In 1859, the A.H. Tilton Mill began operations at a dam downriver in Sanbornton Bridge. After her husband's death in 1878, Abigail continued to operate the mill in partnership with Selwyn B. Peabody. The mill produced unique cloths invented by Tilton called "Tilton Tweeds." Tilton was considered a pillar of his community. He was respected for his civic service as a justice of the peace, as a philanthropist, and as the director of the Boston, Concord, and Montreal Railroads. One of his gifts to the town was a large receiving tomb for the Park Cemetery. (Courtesy of the Longyear Museum, Chestnut Hill, Massachusetts.)

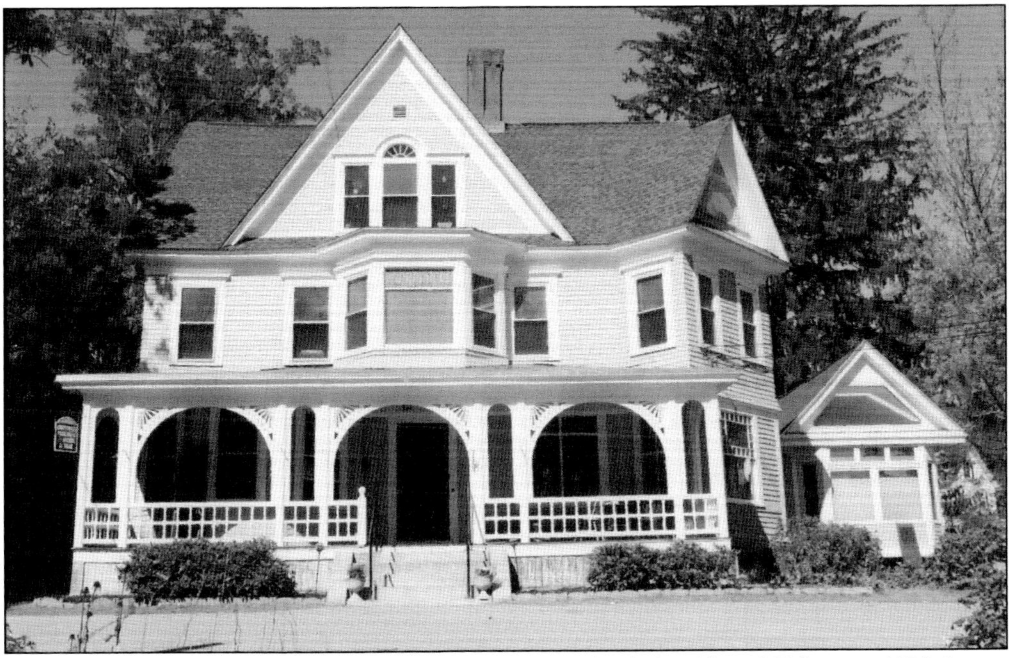

This lovely Victorian home on West Main Street was built for Abigail Tilton in 1886. It was directly across the road from the Peabody–Brown estate. The sidewalk opposite, provided by Abigail, went from the Peabody–Brown estate to Park Cemetery. The sidewalk was her gift to the town, but it also provided her easy access to the family plot. Around 1895, Frank Hill built the house that is pictured below on the corner of West Main and Peabody Streets. Charles Lane purchased the home from the Hills and operated a printing press on the property. In 1945, Harold and Alice Thompson bought the home. Thompson operated a fuel-oil business in the area. (Above, photograph by Dennis Evans; below, courtesy of the Harold Thompson family.)

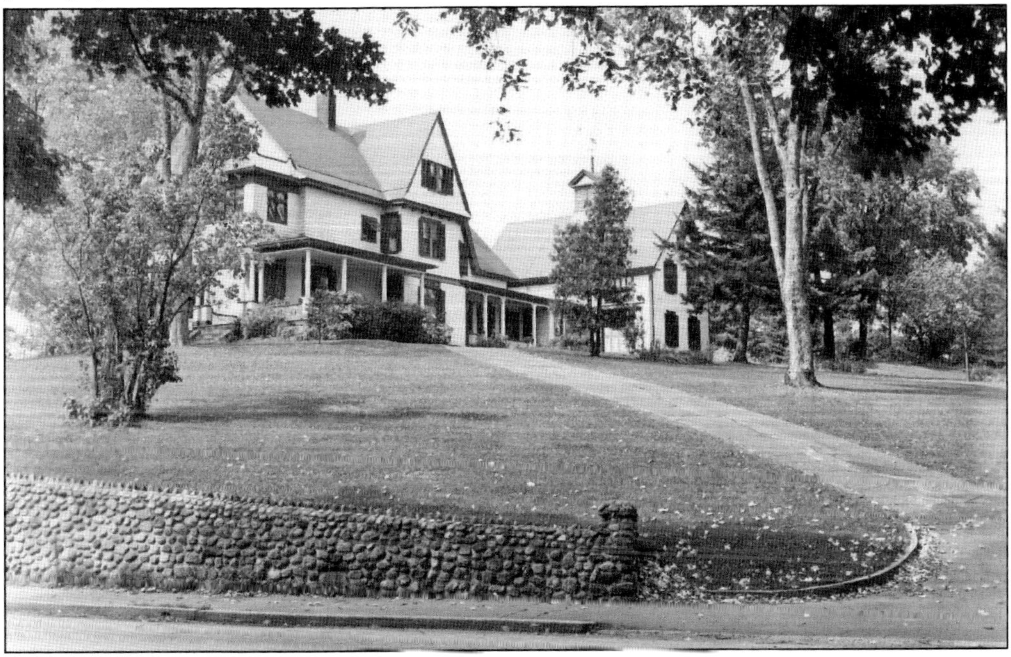

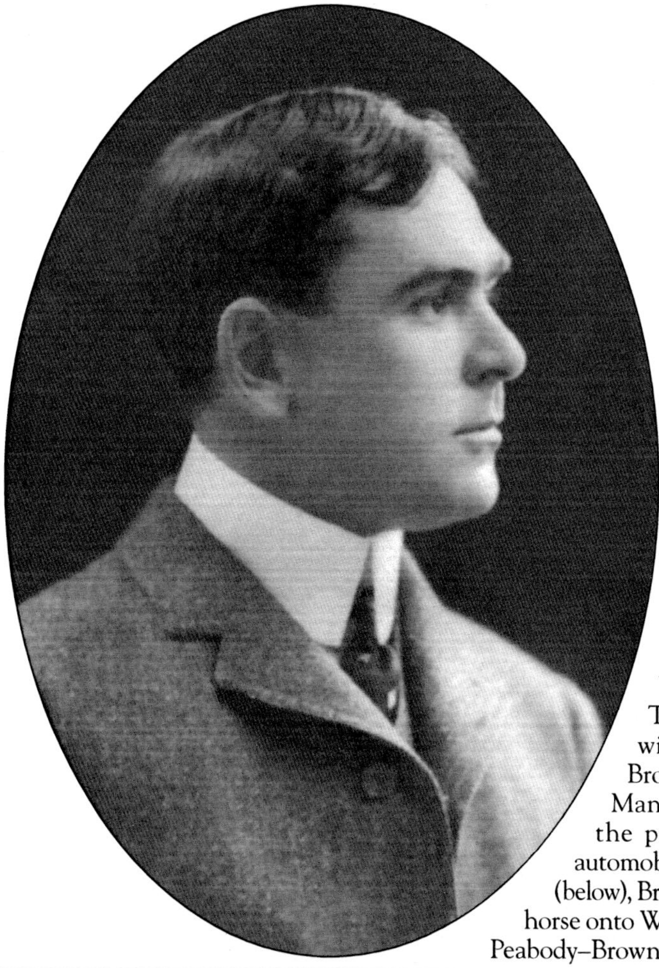

Arthur S. Brown was a telegrapher for the Boston and Maine Railroads when he came to Tilton before the turn of the century. He married Isabella Peabody in 1898 and became associated with the Tilton Woolen mill through his wife's family connections. In 1912, Brown started the Arthur S. Brown Manufacturing Company and began the production of endless belts for automobiles. In the driveway of his home (below), Brown drives an extremely handsome horse onto West Main Street. (Courtesy of the Peabody–Brown estate.)

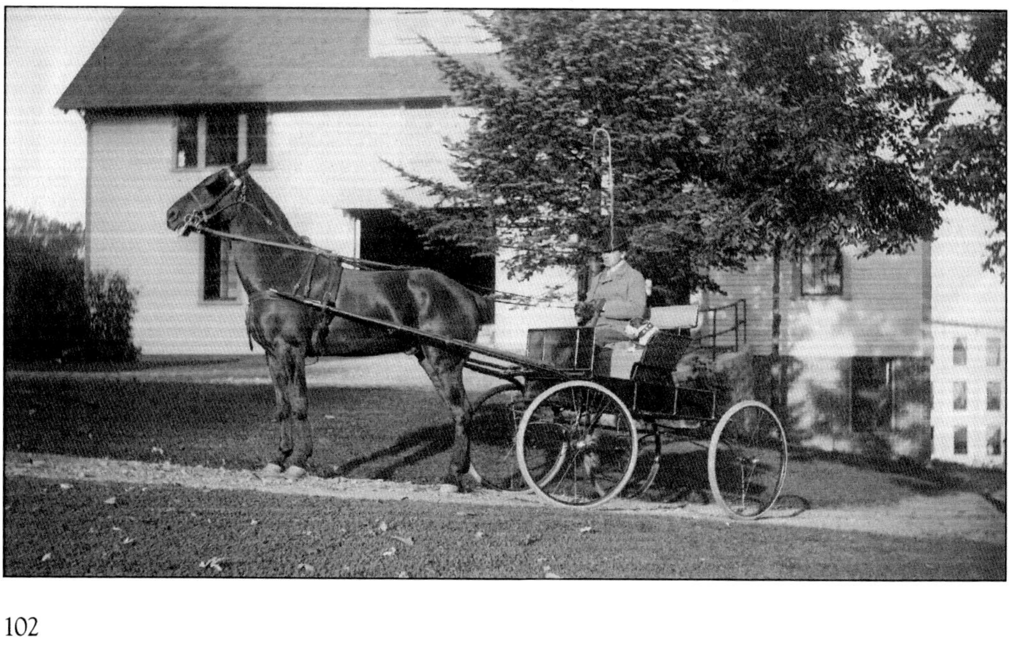

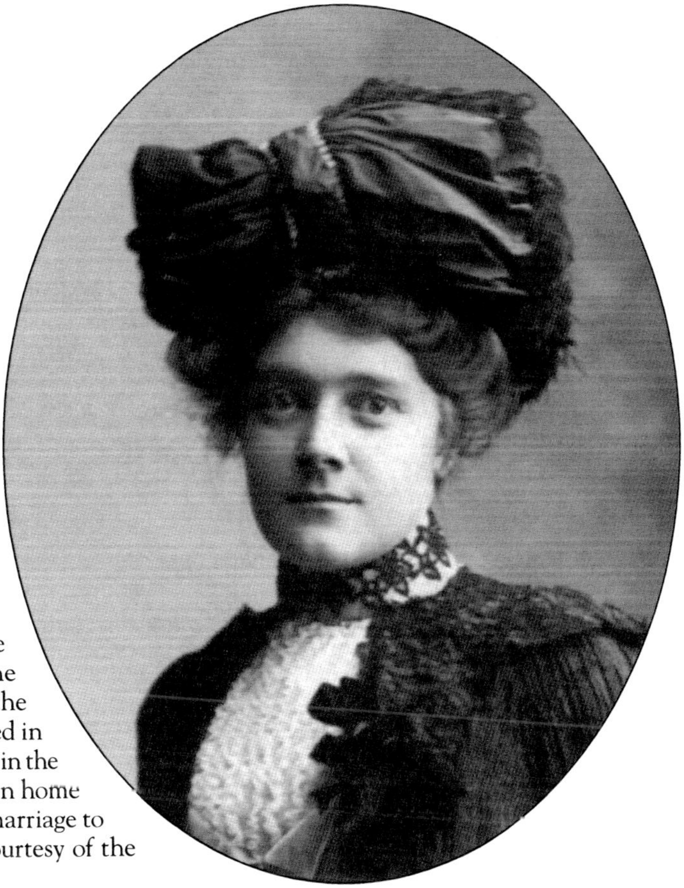

Isabella Weston Peabody was the lovely daughter of Elizabeth Richards and Selwin Bancroft Peabody. Born December 18, 1871, she was known as Belle by her friends and family. In 1880, Belle's father built a fine residence for his family on East Main Street, on the slope of land between the Winnipesaukee River and the home of Charles E. Tilton. In the photograph below, Belle is posed in her elegant horse-drawn carriage in the driveway of the Peabody–Brown home where she lived following her marriage to Arthur S. Brown in 1898. (Courtesy of the Peabody-Brown estate.)

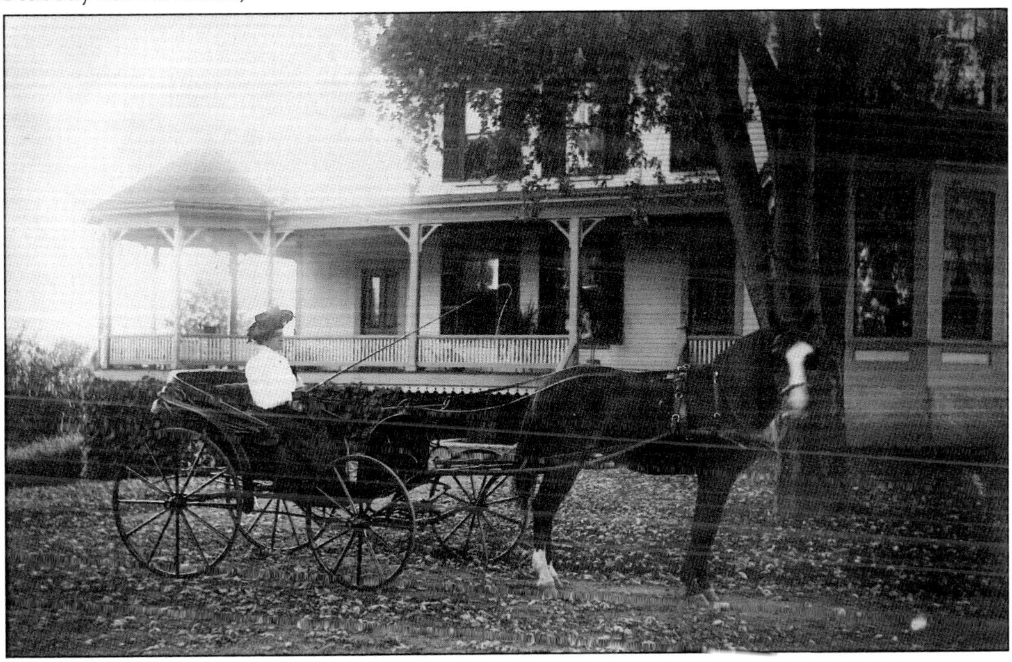

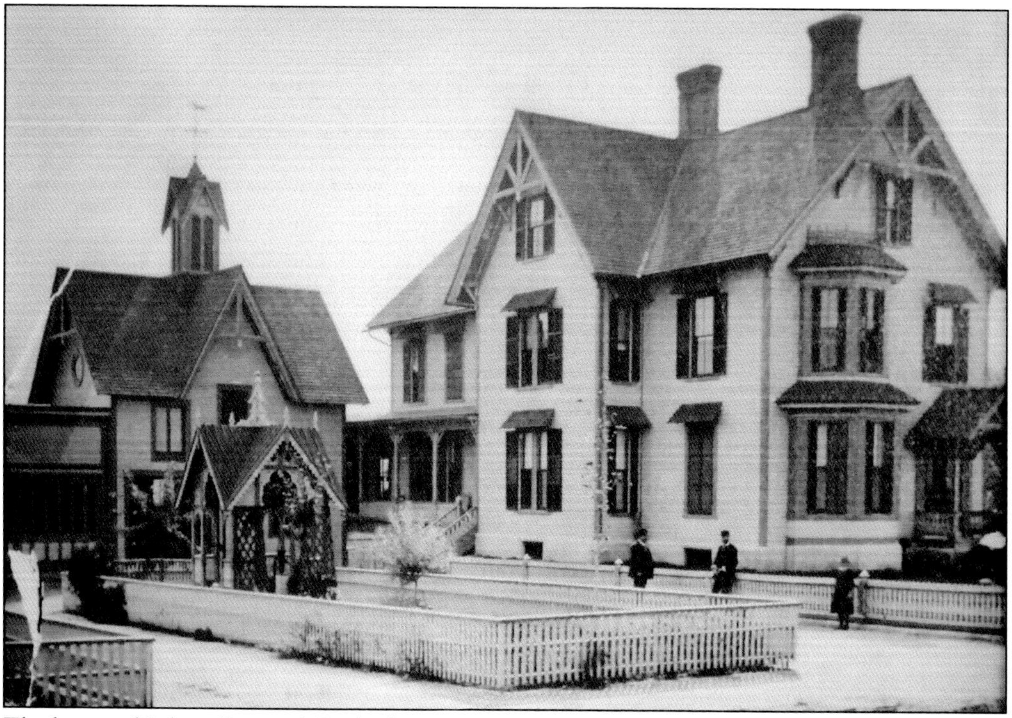

The home of Selwin Bancroft Peabody appears in the photograph above. Born in 1839, Peabody was three years old when his family moved to Sanbornton Bridge. He attended Tilton Seminary in preparation for entrance to Dartmouth College. He married and had three children. The first two died in early infancy. The third child was Isabella Weston (see page 103). Built in 1880, the 2.5-story Victorian home on West Main Street is seen in the photograph above. The carriage house is visible just beyond the main building. Note that the small, fenced-in structure in the foreground most likely housed a water pump. Enclosures such as these protected persons from the elements as they drew water. The photograph below presents new additions and updates to the Peabody home. The two-story alcove with the partially stained-glass windows gives elegance and dimension to the home. (Courtesy of the Peabody-Brown estate.)

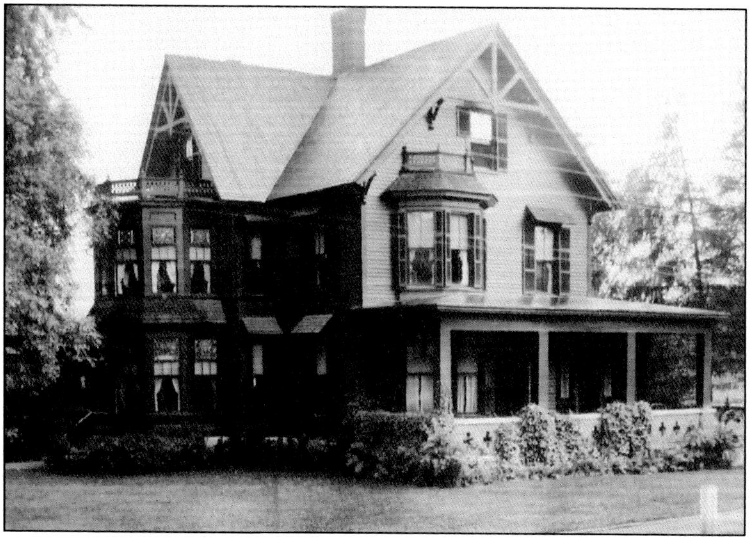

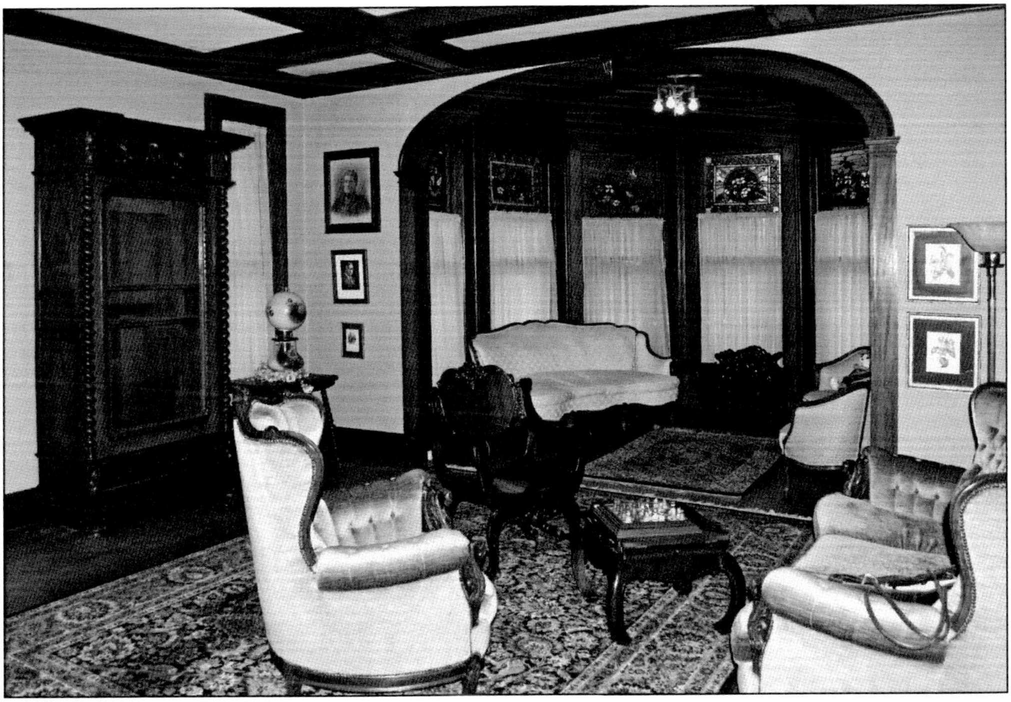

The receiving room of the Peabody–Brown Estate on West Main Street is a warm and welcome introduction to the home of the Selwin Peabody family. In later years, it became the home of Arthur S. Brown and his wife Isabella "Belle" Peabody Brown. The alcove with the full-length windows faces the main street. The stained glass panels that top the windows are comprised of delicate birds and floral patterns that catch and refract the rising sun, spraying colorful light throughout the receiving room. The alcove ceiling is a masterpiece of inlayed wood sections that fan outward. (Photographs by Rob Brown of OBEO.)

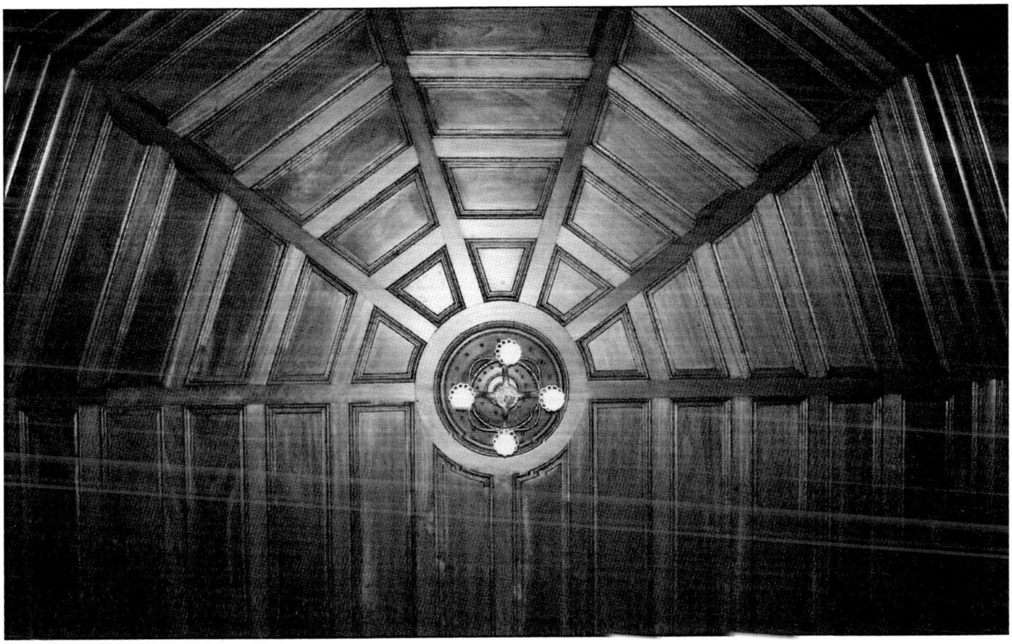

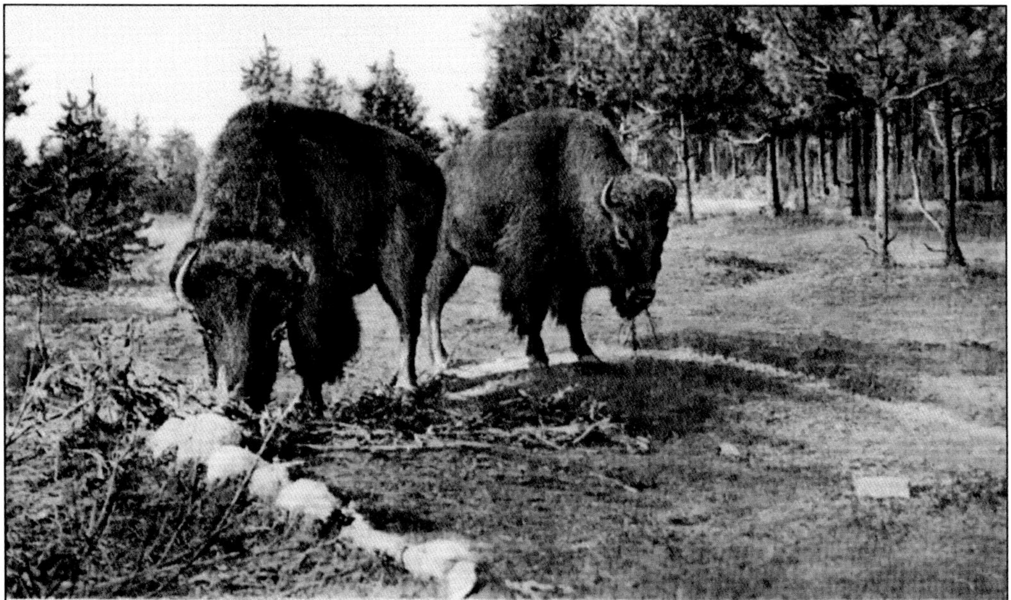

BUFFALO, MOSES PARK, TILTON, N. H.

Yes, there were buffalo in Buffalo Park! This was a 55-acre, private game preserve that reached from the Soldiers' Home to School Street. It belonged to William and Mabel Pillsbury Moses, ancestors of the William Lawrence family. The Moseses were avid game hunters who traveled extensively to add to their collection of stuffed game for the trophy room on the second floor of their carriage house. Their Victorian home was located at the top of Prospect Street. The building shown below was next to the carriage house and was the home of Moses family employees. Pictured with the chauffeur, the car was a 1911 Locomobile seven-passenger touring car. (Above, courtesy of the Hall Memorial Library; below, courtesy of Barbara Puffinberger.)

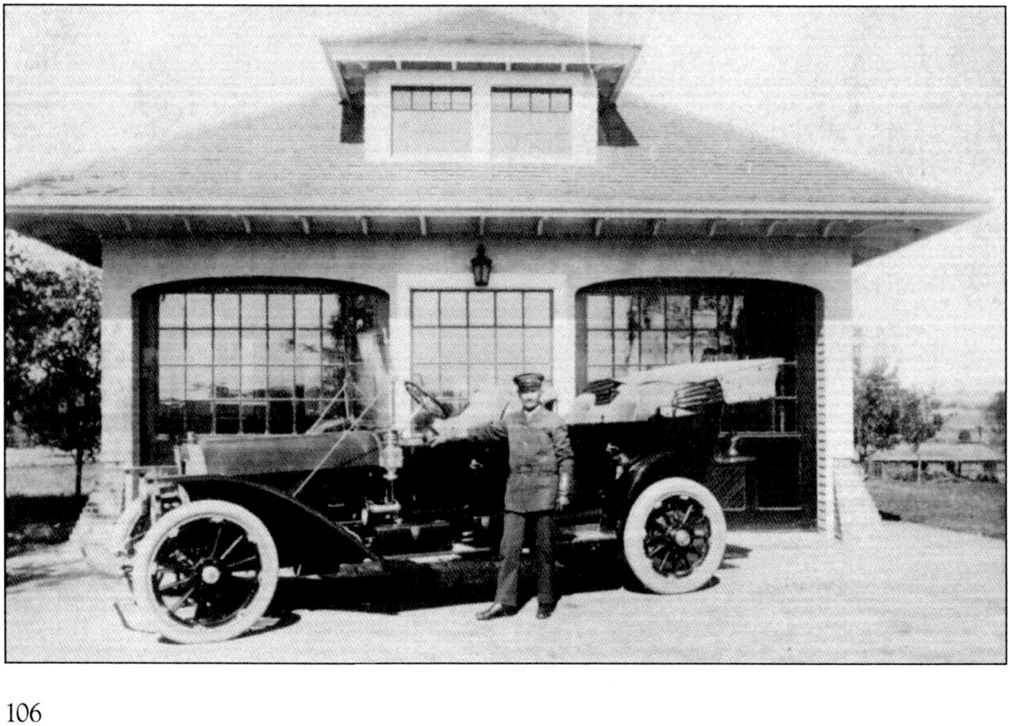

Five

LEARNING AND FAITH

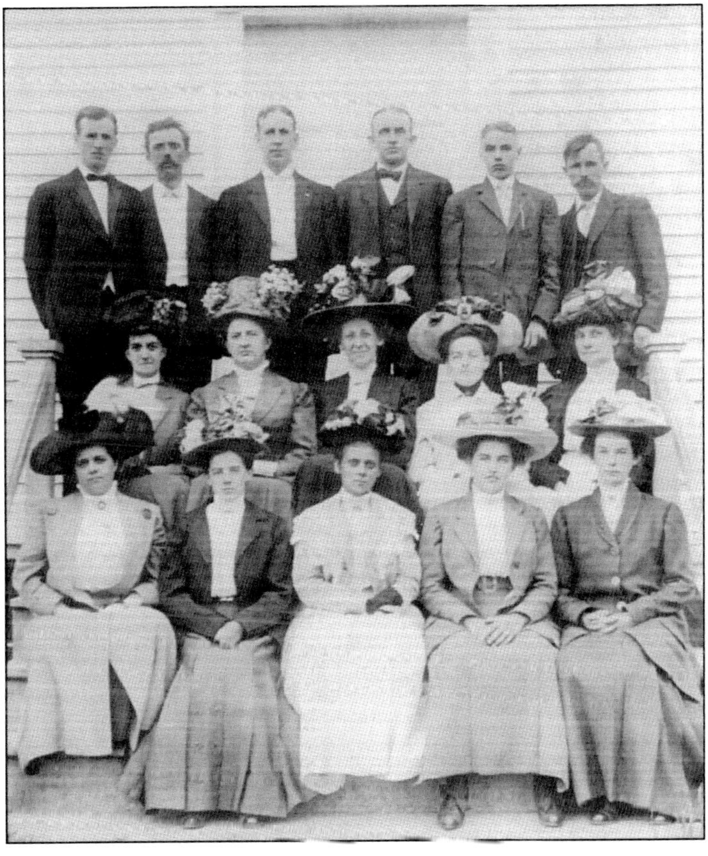

The adult Sunday school class gathered for this formal portrait in front of the Lochmere Baptist Church. The display of glorious hats is a milliner's talent showcase. These women may have been customers of E.R. Jackson, a milliner on Main Street in the Thompson Block who advertised up-to-date millinery fashions around 1908. (Courtesy of the Karl Barnard family.)

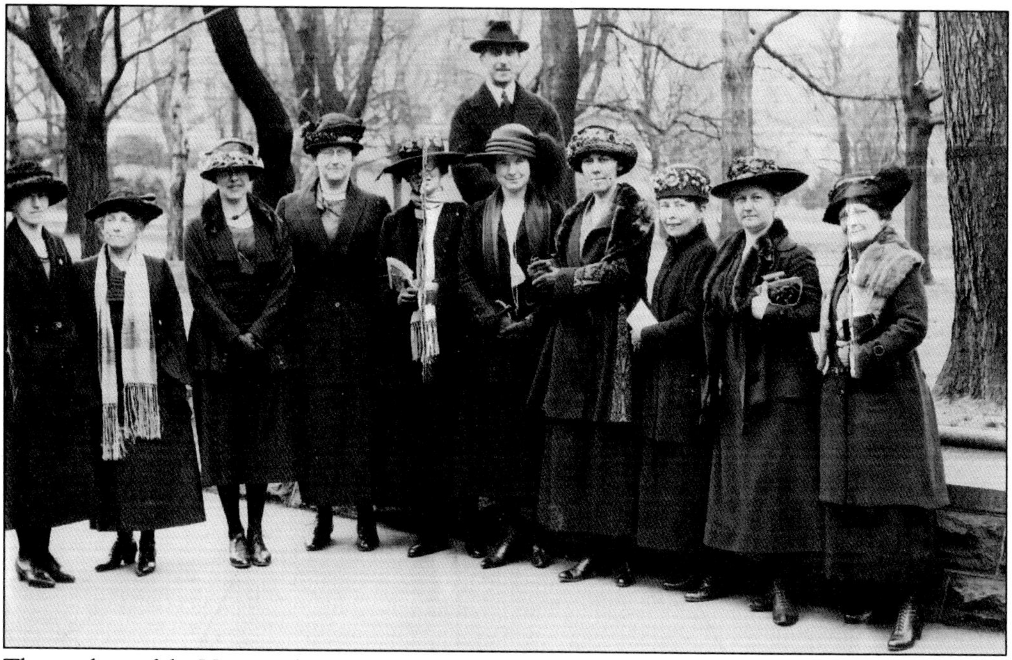

The teachers of the Union School District gathered for this photograph around 1922. The gentleman seen behind the ladies is superintendent of schools Channing T. Sanborn. Third from the left is Helen Thompson—the only identified teacher. Fourth from the left is Lulu J. Meserve, who was the principal of the Union School at that time. (Courtesy of the Meserve family.)

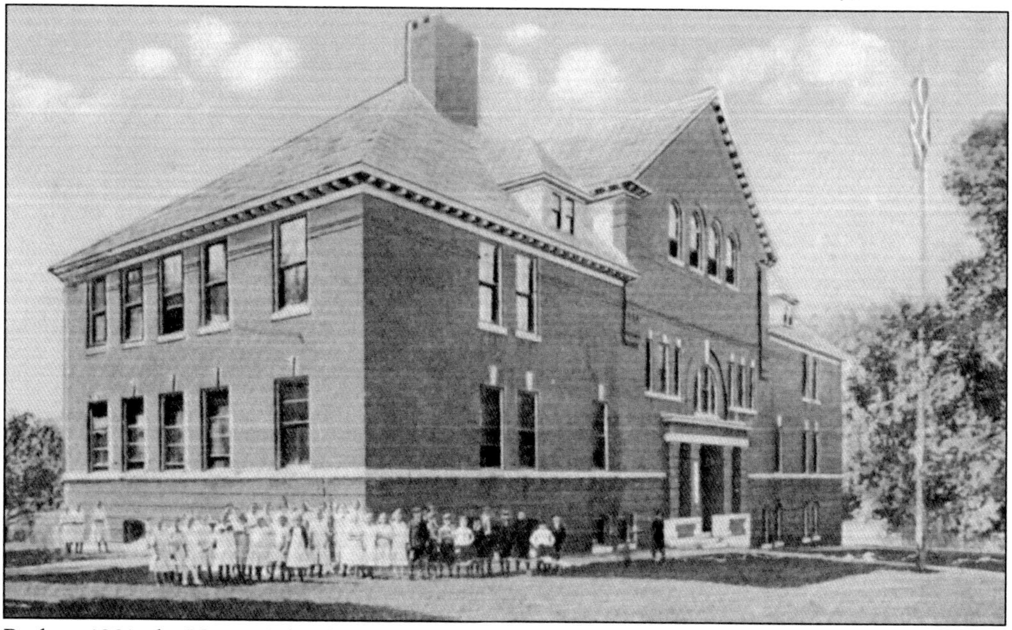

Built in 1901, the Union School was as a combination of four of the seven schools in the district: the Tin Corner School located at the top of Winter Street, the Sanborn Road School, the Union Bridge School, and the No. 4 School on East Main Street. Lochmere was the location of the Rollins Corner School, the District No. 16 or Keniston School, and Bamford School. (Courtesy of the Randall family.)

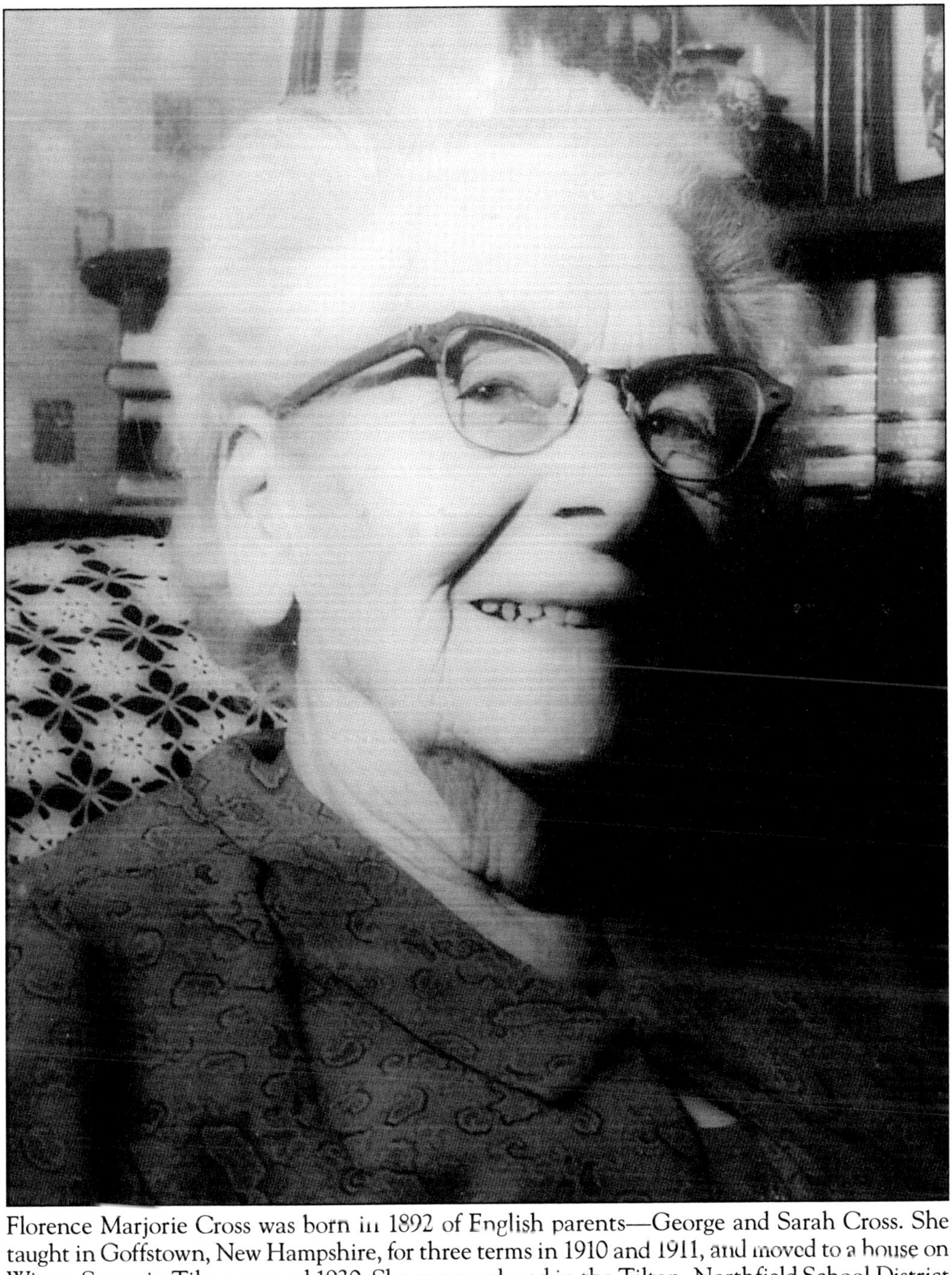

Florence Marjorie Cross was born in 1892 of English parents—George and Sarah Cross. She taught in Goffstown, New Hampshire, for three terms in 1910 and 1911, and moved to a house on Winter Street in Tilton around 1930. She was employed in the Tilton–Northfield School District teaching junior high school English, and had a library in her classroom before school libraries were required. According to many of Cross's former students, she was a wonderful educator, a great disciplinarian, and a thoughtful neighbor. What she taught and how she taught it served as lifelong lessons to her students, as well as everyone with whom she came in contact. Although diminutive in size and nature, she is remembered and respected by all those who knew her. (Courtesy of the F. Marjorie Cross Library, Winnisquam Regional Middle School.)

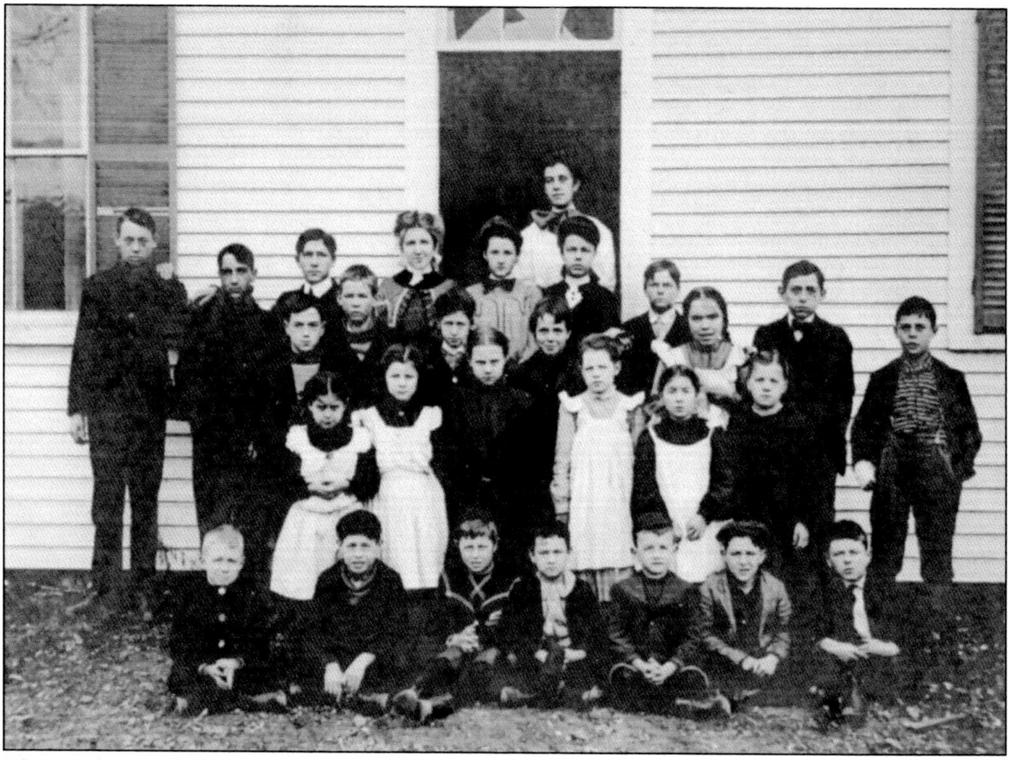

The teacher and students at the No. 4 School on East Main Street appear in this photograph around 1905. Composed of grades one through eight, it is almost certain that some of the older ones taught some of the younger. In the front row are the three Randall brothers: William (far left), Arthur (third from the right), and Earle (far right). (Courtesy of the Randall family.)

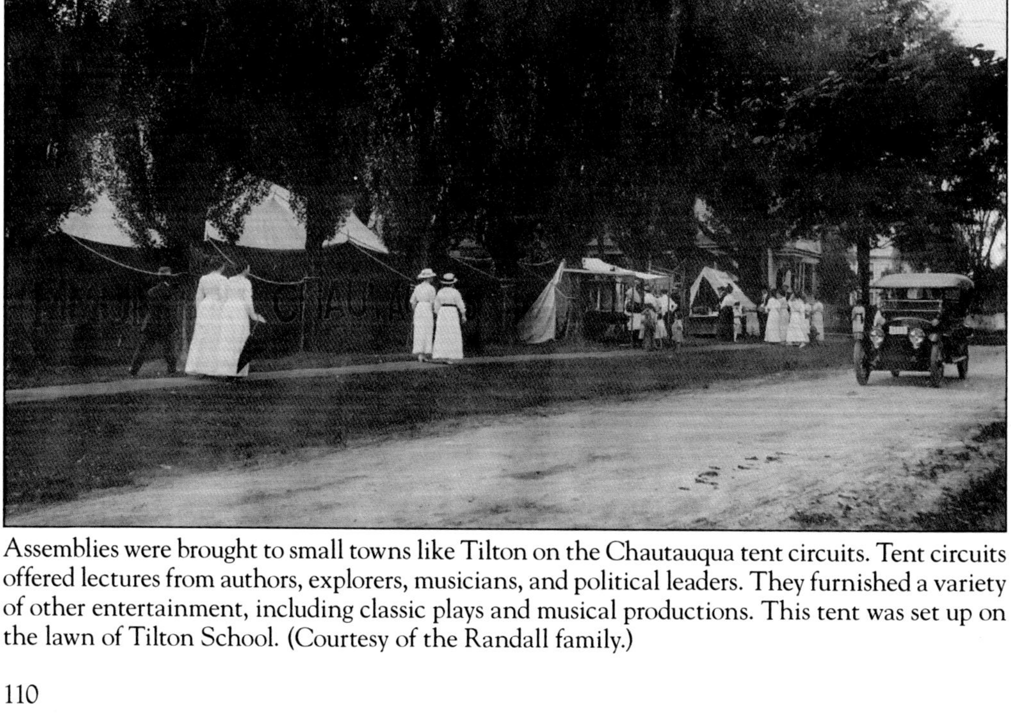

Assemblies were brought to small towns like Tilton on the Chautauqua tent circuits. Tent circuits offered lectures from authors, explorers, musicians, and political leaders. They furnished a variety of other entertainment, including classic plays and musical productions. This tent was set up on the lawn of Tilton School. (Courtesy of the Randall family.)

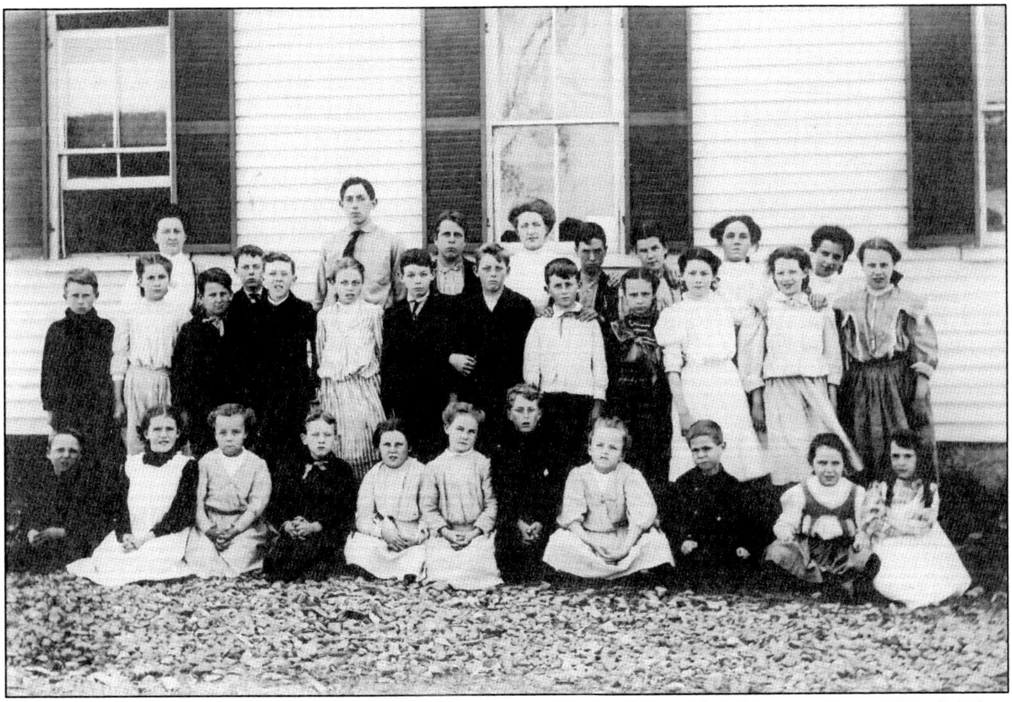

Children of varying ages pose with their teacher outside their school on Sanborn Road. This schoolhouse was at the intersection of Lancaster Hill and Sanborn Road. The tallest boy in the back row may be Arthur Wyatt. Upon graduation, the students would attend a two-year high school program at Tilton Seminary through an agreement made in 1897 between the town and the school. (Courtesy of the Randall family.)

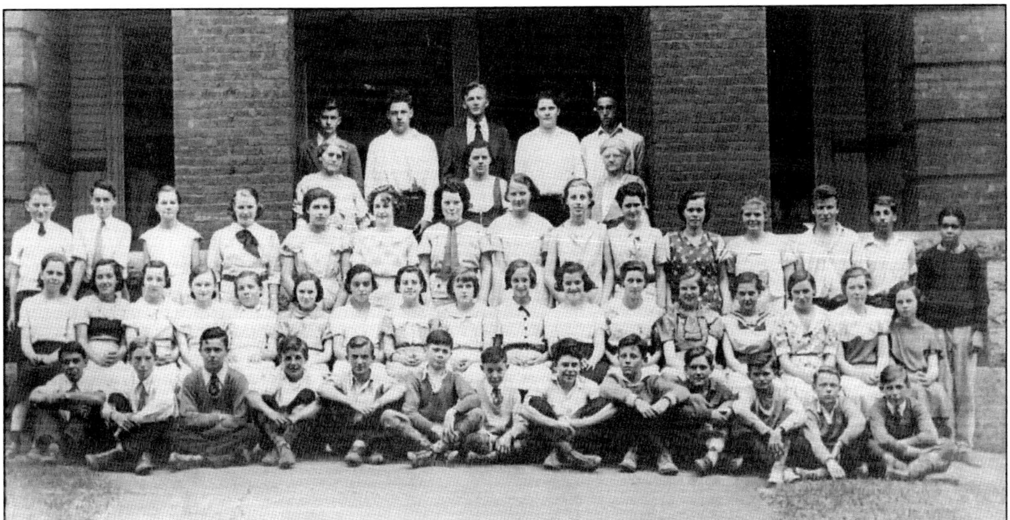

The seventh- and eighth-grade classes gather for a picture at the Union School in the early 1930s. Of note are two women in the fourth row between the columns: teacher Florence Marjorie Cross (left) and teaching principal Lulu Meserve (right). Helen Hollister, niece of Maude Bickford (see page 49), is the second from the left in the second row. (Courtesy of Helen Hollister Holbrook.)

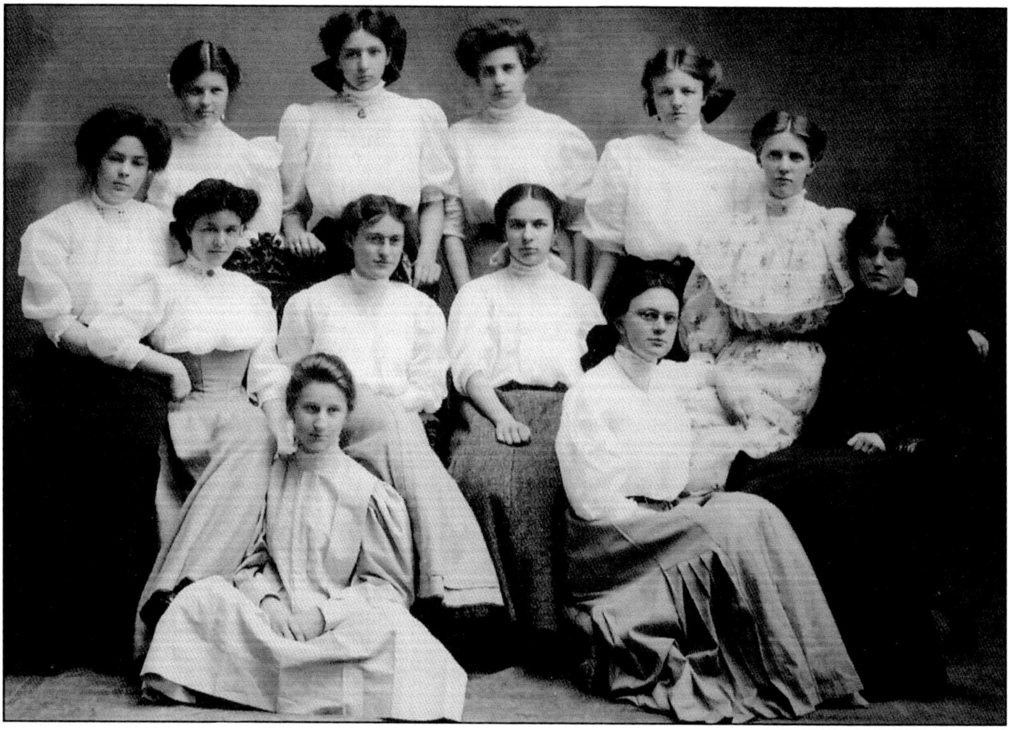

These young ladies were seniors at Tilton Seminary in the early 1900s. Martha Herrick is seated in the second row with a white shirtwaist and her hand in her lap. She is the daughter of Charles P. and Emma J. Herrick—owners of Herrick's Drug Store in Tilton. (Courtesy of Mariam Melendez.)

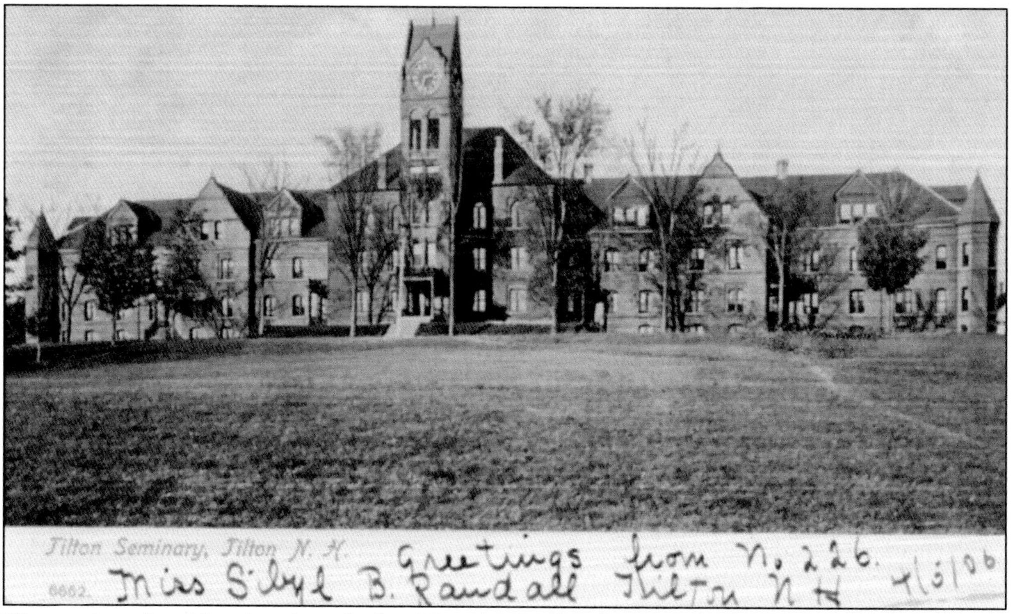

The entire school lived and worked at Knowles Hall—the main building at Tilton Seminary. Built in 1888, Knowles Hall contained student rooms, classrooms, an infirmary, a chapel, and faculty apartments. The clock and the bell in the central tower were gifts of Charles E. Tilton. (Courtesy of the Randall family.)

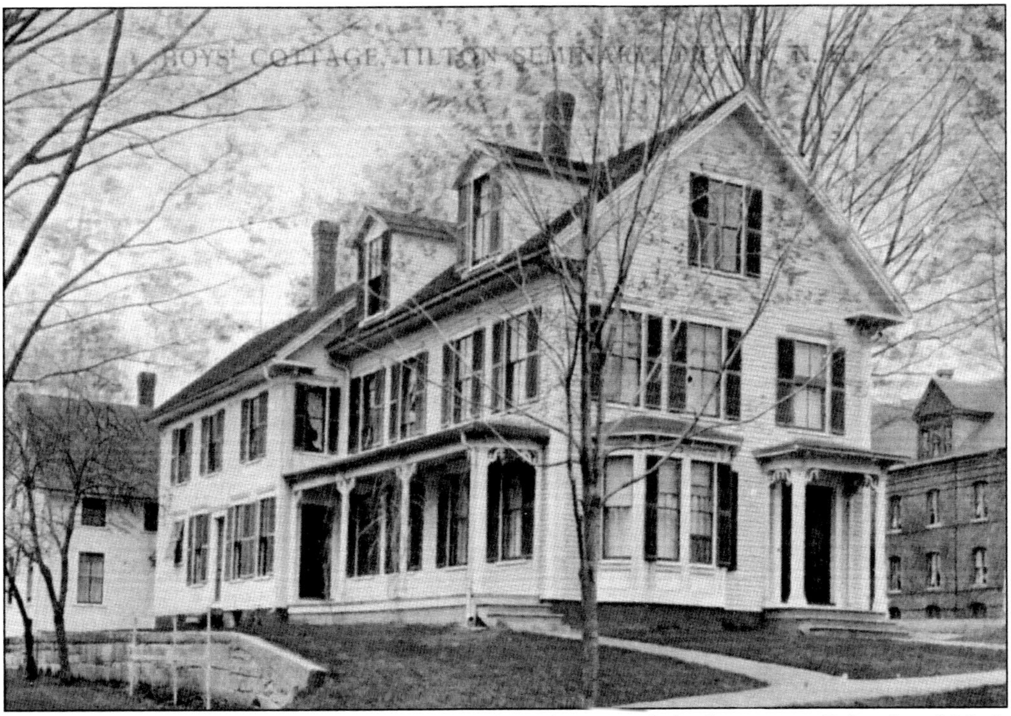

From 1904 until 1920, Tilton Seminary purchased many of the homes on School and High Streets for faculty housing and dormitory space. The Crockett House (above) was purchased in 1904. First used as the principal's house, it became a dormitory housing 40 boys and two teachers. The Phelps House (below) was acquired in 1907 and was converted into a girls' dormitory for 15 students and two teachers. It later became a boys' lower school dorm. In 1919, the trustees decided to rename the Crockett House and the Phelps House, and they became Barrows Cottage and Chase Cottage. (Courtesy of the Meserve family.)

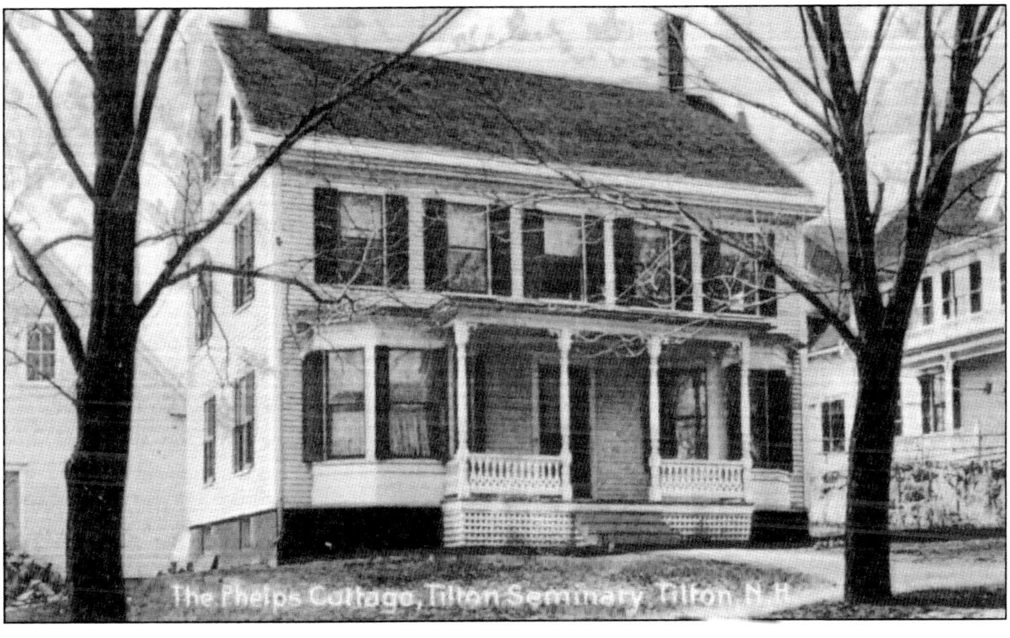

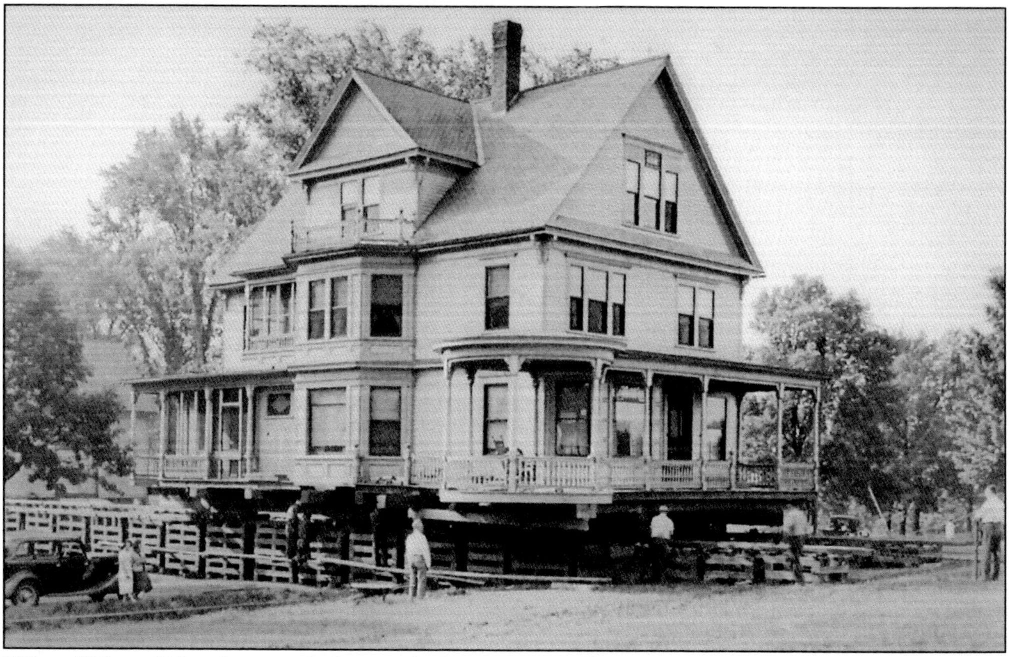

When Tilton School expanded to include a junior college in 1936, a new dormitory became a priority. W.B. Hill and Sons of Northfield moved the headmaster's residence across School Street to One School Lane to make room for Pfeiffer Hall. The ropes attached to the house were pulled by a horse turning a capstan. When in place, the house was pivoted 90 degrees on rollers. (Courtesy of the Tilton School.)

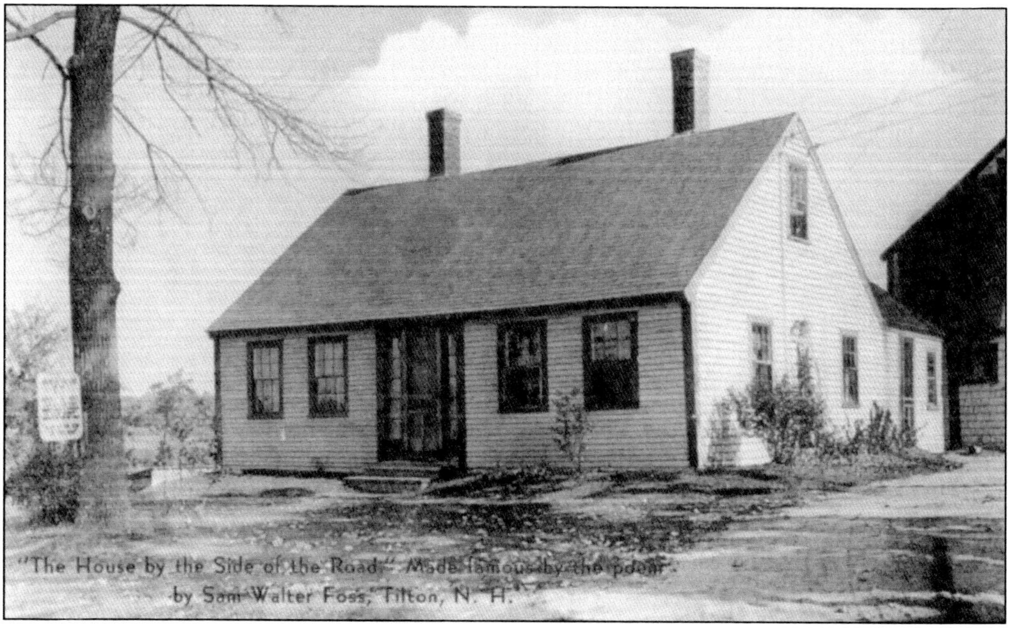

This house on School Street stands near the Tilton School. In 1877, Sam Foss attended the school for one year. The sign on the tree reads, "House by the side of the Road / where the poet Sam Walter Foss / roomed while a student / at Tilton Seminary / Inspiration for his poem / 'House by the Side of the Road.' " (Courtesy of the Hall Memorial Library.)

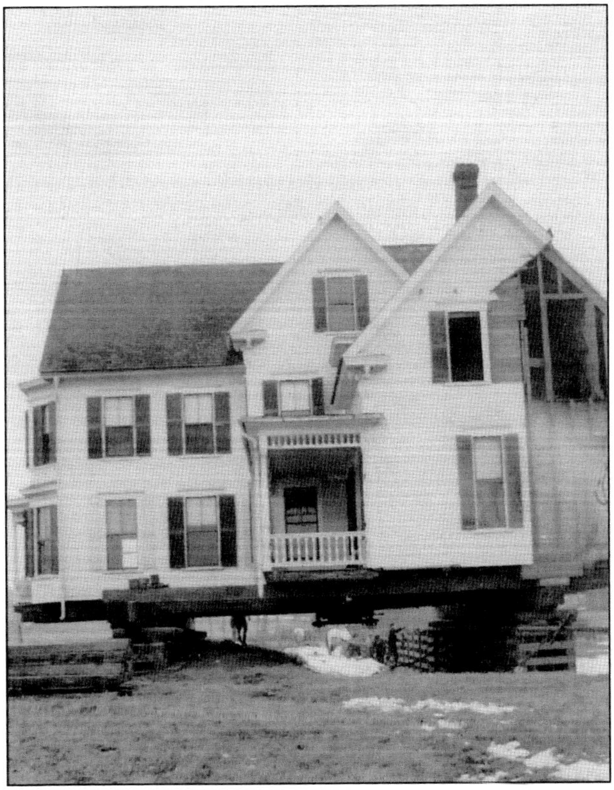

The house pictured above was located at 362 West Main Street until 1938, when construction of the Tilton–Northfield High School was about to begin. It was moved to a site on Winter Street by the W.H. Hill Moving Company. Both the Tilton School and the Tilton–Northfield School District used the services of this moving company. Printed in January 24, 1940, the program for the dedication of the new Tilton–Northfield High School is pictured below. School board members present for the dedication were Dr. Joel E. Nordholm, dentist; Judge John W. Crawford, an attorney and judge; Dr. Archie Grevior, physician; Winnifred F. Walker, town clerk of Northfield; Helen T. Randall, former teacher at the Union School; and Charles W. Colby, agricultural businessman. (Courtesy of the Meserve family.)

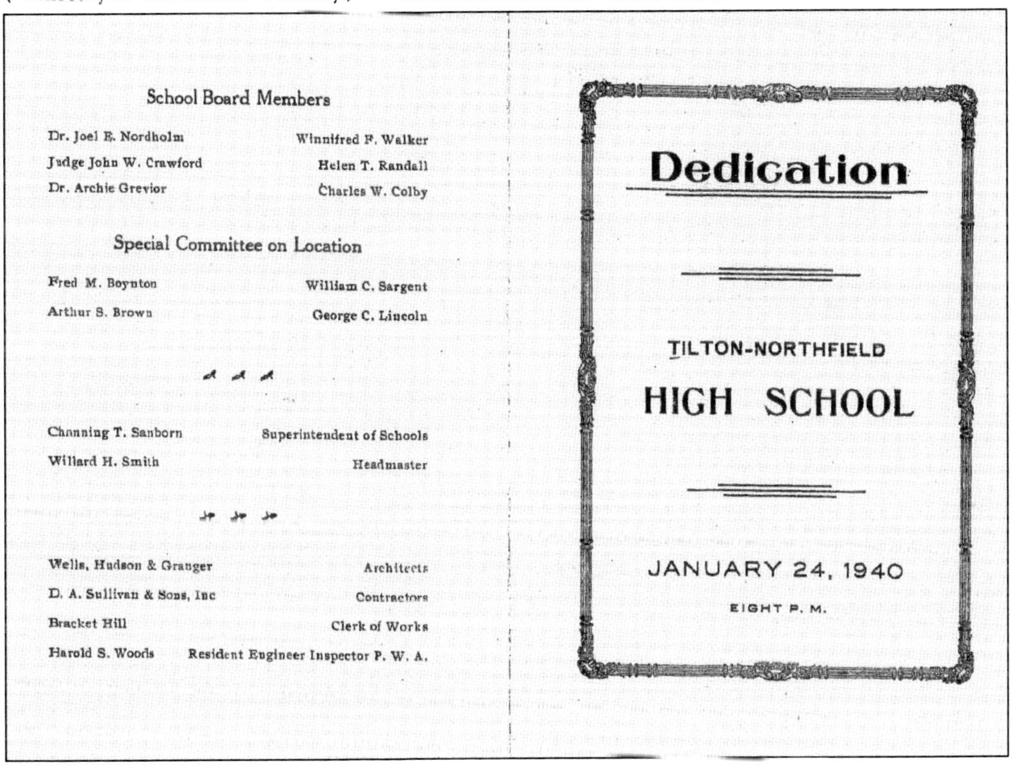

School Board Members

Dr. Joel E. Nordholm	Winnifred F. Walker
Judge John W. Crawford	Helen T. Randall
Dr. Archie Grevior	Charles W. Colby

Special Committee on Location

Fred M. Boynton	William C. Sargent
Arthur S. Brown	George C. Lincoln

Channing T. Sanborn	Superintendent of Schools
Willard H. Smith	Headmaster

Wells, Hudson & Granger	Architects
D. A. Sullivan & Sons, Inc	Contractors
Bracket Hill	Clerk of Works
Harold S. Woods	Resident Engineer Inspector P. W. A.

Dedication

TILTON-NORTHFIELD

HIGH SCHOOL

JANUARY 24, 1940

EIGHT P. M.

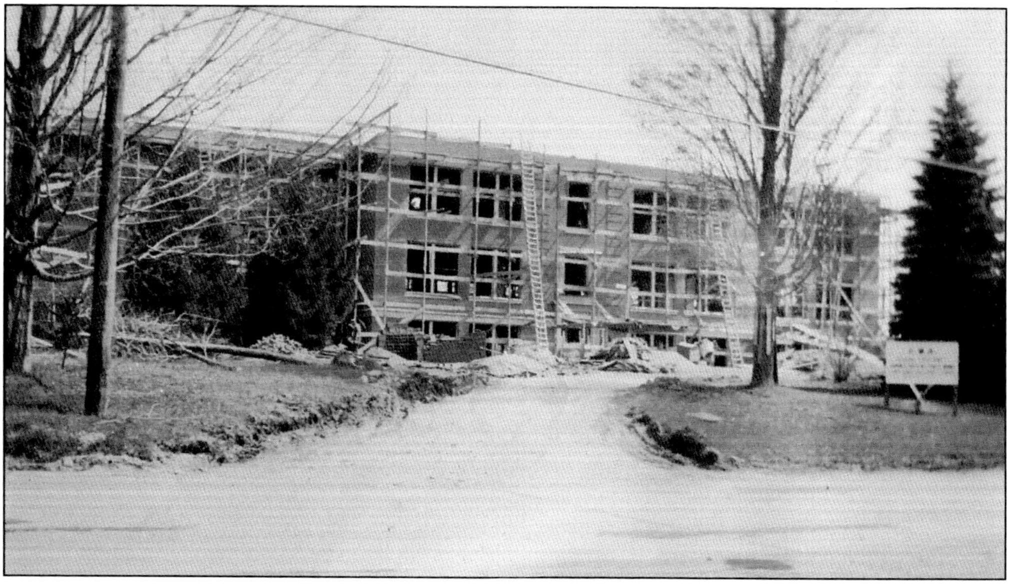

Tilton–Northfield High School, shown above during the construction, was dedicated on January 24, 1940. This was the first public high school building of the Tilton and Northfield Union School District. Prior to 1927, there were three separate school districts. Each succeeding year, a warrant article had been brought before the residents at an annual school district meeting asking for action on a new high school. The warrant article was not adopted until 1938. The photograph below shows the completed building. The administration for the new high school consisted of a principal, an assistant principal, and 12 teachers. There were 310 students—180 in the senior high school and 130 in the junior high school. The senior class consisted of 23 students. (Both photographs courtesy of the Meserve family.)

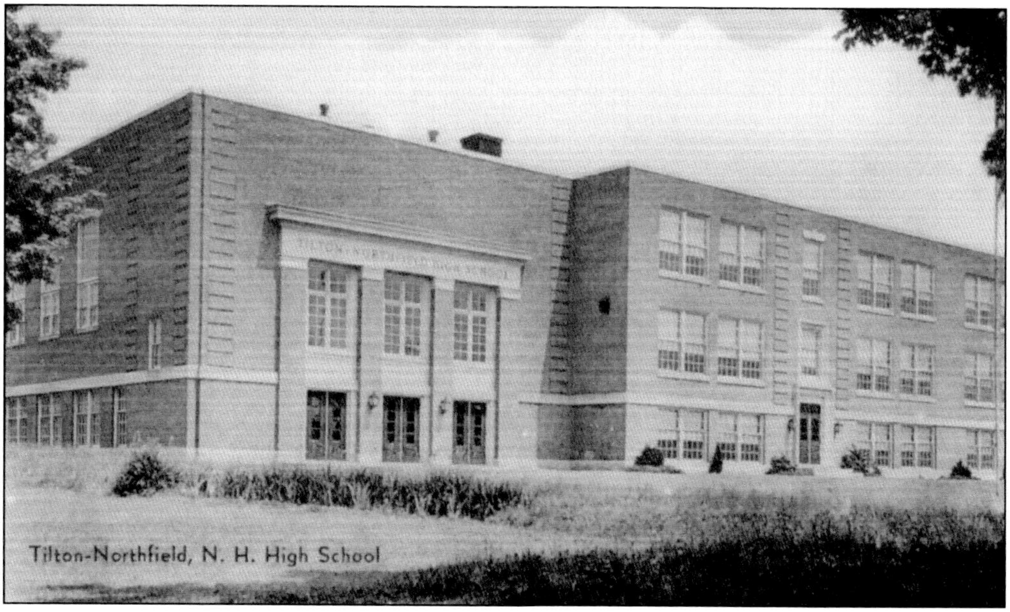

THE TATTLER

VOL. I, NO. 10 TILTON-NORTHFIELD HIGH SCHOOL, TILTON, N. H. 10c Per Copy

FIRST GRADUATING CLASS OF T.N.H.S.

CLASS MOTTO

By Hilda Pickering and Amos Bryenton

"In Ourselves Our Future Lies"

All of us have particular dreams, desires, and ambitions that we hope to see fulfilled. In their achievement, success or failure depends upon ourselves.

There is no excuse for those who evade their responsibilities. No matter what the obstacle, it can be overcome by courage and determination. The only real danger lies in saying "I can't" instead of "I will."

Many people have a false notion that ill health is justification for giving up hope. Among the most important people in our history are many who were physically handicapped. One of our very popular Presidents

(continued on page four)

CLASS POEM

By John Nichols

Farewell dear Tilton-Northfield High
We've reach our goal at last
Goodbye to teachers, students, friends
Our days with you are past.

Gay times we've had in pleasures free
Four years of work and play
We'll e'er remember days gone by
When we are far away.

Forever loyal will we be
We wish you true success
As we go out to face the world
And seek our happiness.

CLASS HISTORY

By George Loranger

On September 6, 1927, thirty-nine timid, optimistic children entered the first grade at Tilton-Northfield Union School. The twenty-two boys and seventeen girls gave the patient Miss Hobbs many troubled moments; for example, one child placed his lunch box under the slide. When an exceptionally heavy pupil came gliding down, he landed squarely on the box. The student who went wailing to Miss Hobbs over his lost lunch was none other than George Loranger. Another little boy who tried the patience of his teacher was Roy Jordan. Every night after school he stuck his head in the door and cheerfully said, "Good-night Miss Hogs!"

By the eighth year, the membership of the class reached forty-nine.

(continued on page four)

FIRST TILTON-NORTHFIELD GRADUATING CLASS

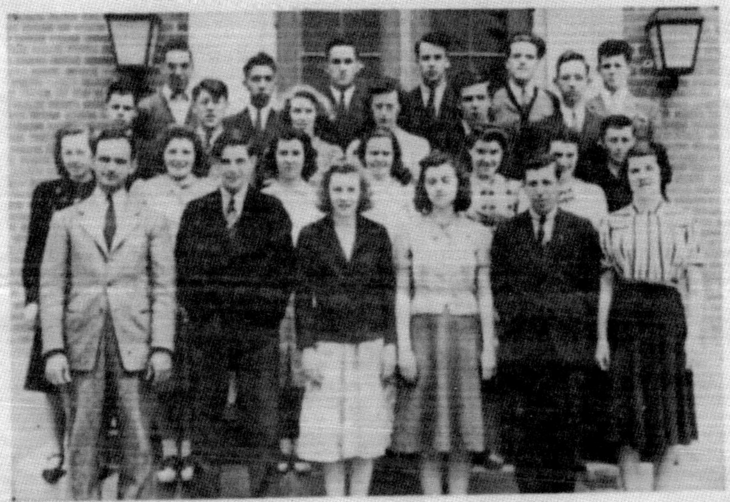

Tilton-Northfield High school's first graduating class, 23 in number, pictured on the school steps. In the front row, left to right, are: S. Gordon Smith, faculty advisor; George Loranger, president; Pearl Chapman, secretary Barbara Howe, vice president; Roland Boudreau, treasurer; Miss Alice Solana, faculty advisor.

The school newspaper for the new Tilton–Northfield High School had this photograph in their final issue of the year showing the 23 members of the graduating class. This Vol. 1, No. 10 issue of the *Tattler* cost 10¢ per copy. These students had entered first grade on September 6, 1927, at the Tilton–Northfield Union School with an additional 16 students in their class. The class motto was "In ourselves our future lies." Only the front row of students in the photograph could be identified. The following are, from left to right, S. Gordon Smith, faculty advisor; George Loranger, president; Pearl Chapman, secretary; Barbara Howe, vice president; Roland Boudreau, treasurer; and Miss Alice Solana, faculty advisor. One of the students in the class was Roy Jordan Jr. (see page 20). (Courtesy of the Harold Thompson family.)

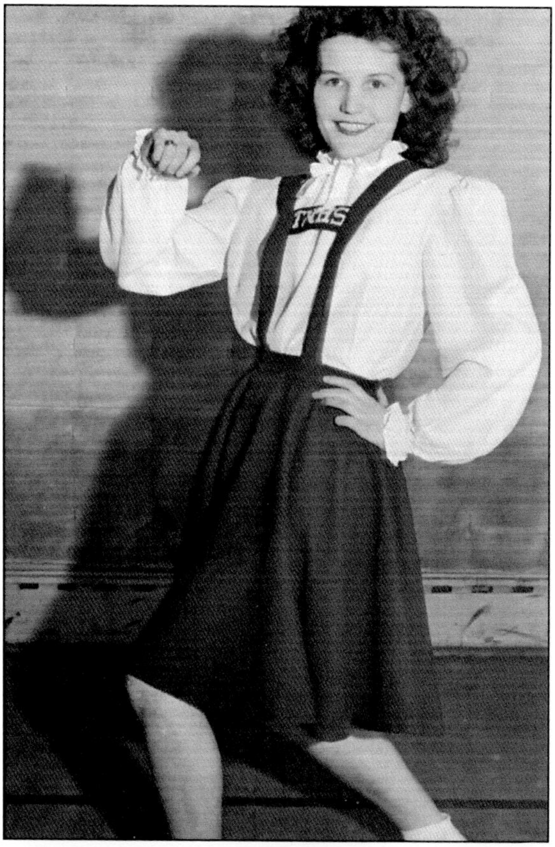

Louise Watson and her family lived in the former Sanborn Road School. She graduated from Tilton–Northfield High School in 1947. She was very active in sports until her senior year when basketball was no longer available, so cheerleading became her senior activity. (Courtesy of the Karl Barnard family.)

In 1943, the varsity girls' basketball team of Tilton–Northfield High School enjoyed a good season. Team members are, from left to right, (first row) Ethel Thompson, Anne Crawford, co-captain Madalene Murphy, co-captain Millie Dunlop, Phyllis Barnes, and Anne Sheldon; (second row) manager Lorraine Ketchum, Suzanne Vassamillet, Elaine Nordholm, Joyce Jordan, June Rollins, and coach Vivian Fox. (Courtesy of Madalene Murphy Dunlop.)

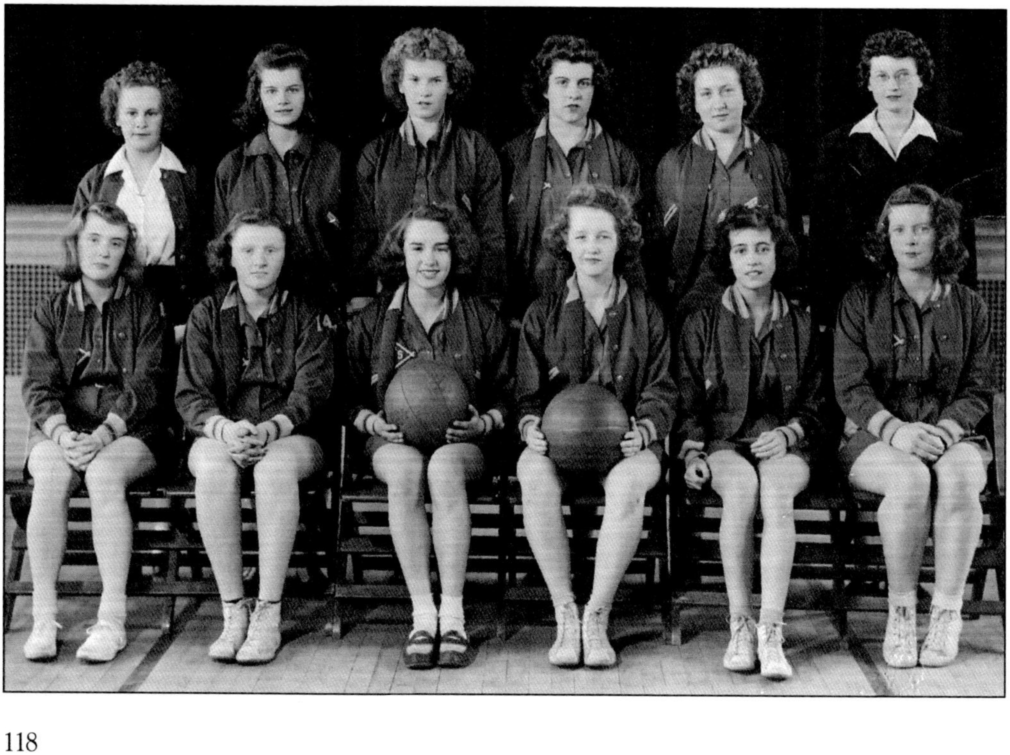

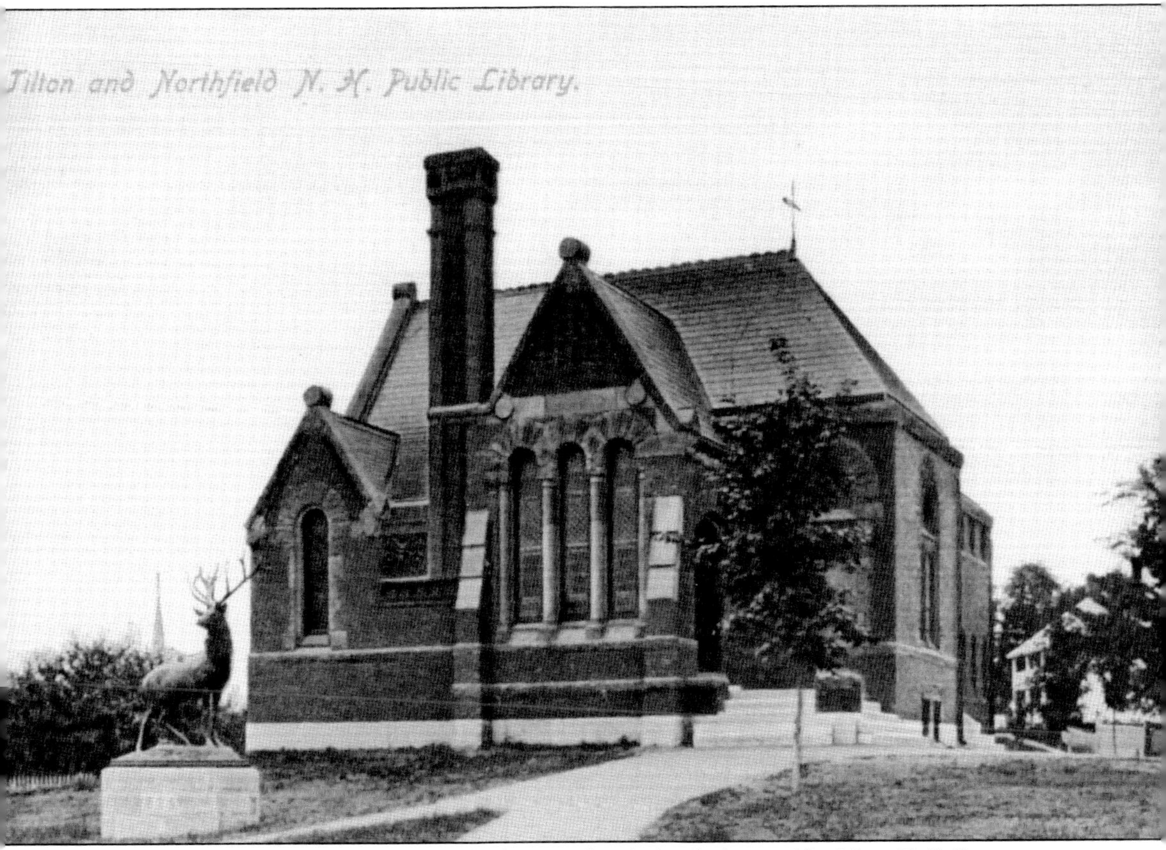

The Hall Memorial Library was established in 1885 with funds donated by Mary Hall Cummings to the towns of Tilton and Northfield. The library was a memorial to Cummings late husband, Adino Brackett Hall, MD. Genevieve Eastman Tilton donated the land. The architectural style of the library is Queen Anne. According to Lucy Cross in *History of Northfield, New Hampshire, 1780–1905*, the building is fine brick, with ample sandstone trimmings and terra-cotta ornamentations. The outside walls have many buttresses with windows of stained glass. A graduate of Tilton Seminary and Simmons College in Boston, Massachusetts, Mary Ellen Osgood was the librarian of Hall Memorial Library for many years. Her professional expertise in cataloging and classifying books was exemplary, setting the standard for years to come. (Courtesy of the Hall Memorial Library.)

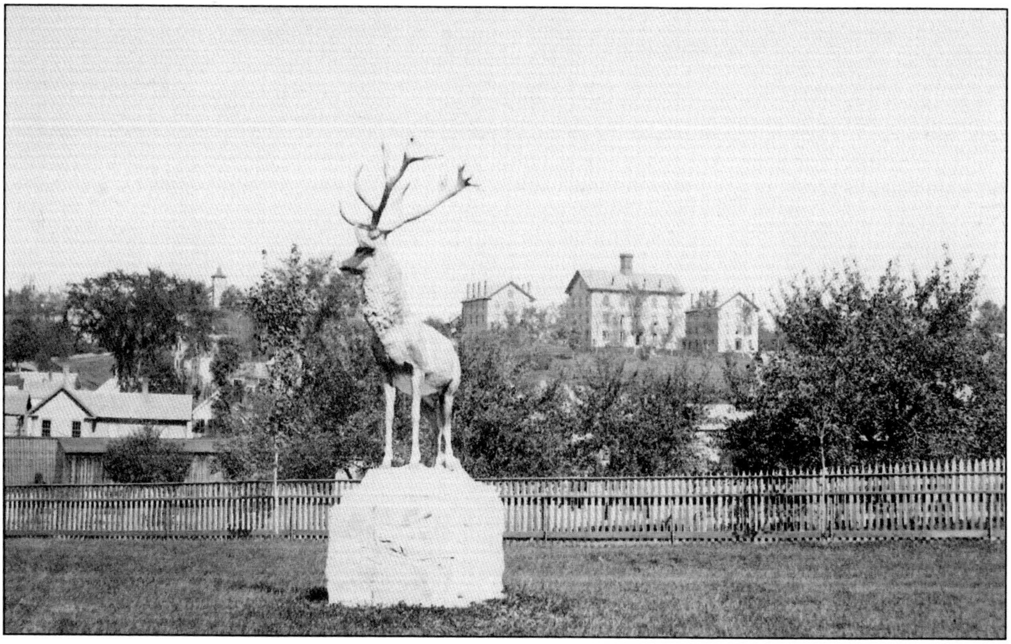

This rare photograph shows the elk statue that stood in Deer Park prior to the construction of the Hall Memorial Library. The three structures in the background are part of the New Hampshire Conference Seminary and Female College, later Tilton School. The original seminary was in Northfield and was destroyed by fire on November 7, 1862, in the midst of a snowstorm. The New Hampshire Conference made the decision to rebuild the school in what was then Sanbornton Bridge. In the photograph below, taken before 1885 by photographer F.J. Moulton, the elk statue can be seen. The mill directly beyond the statue is the Pillsbury Mill, later known as the Tilton Tannery. The wagon track at the left became the space between the Union School and the library. (Above, courtesy of the Hall Memorial Library; below, courtesy of the Dodge family.)

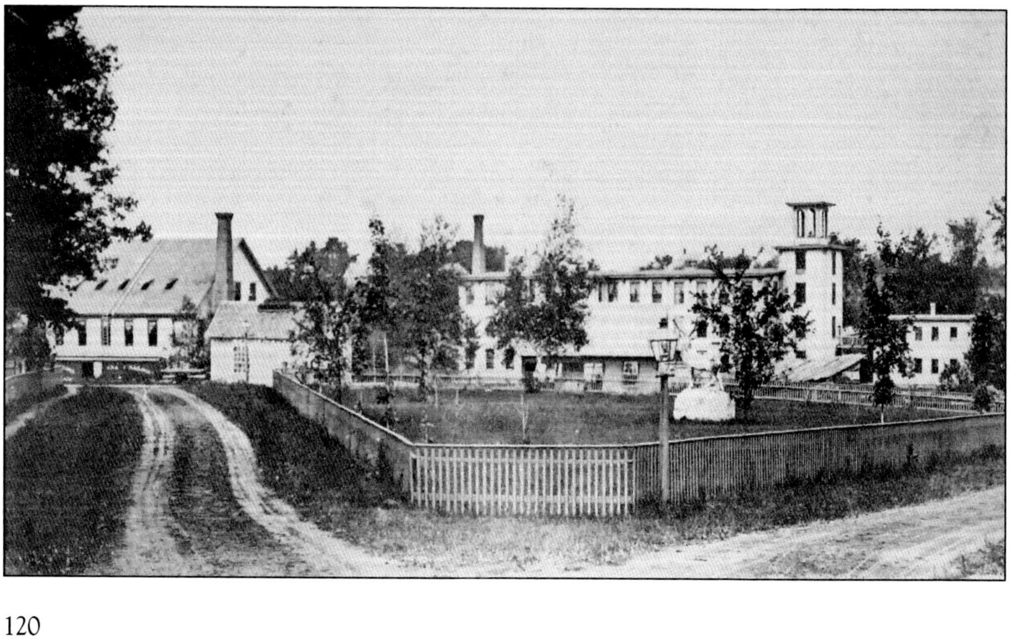

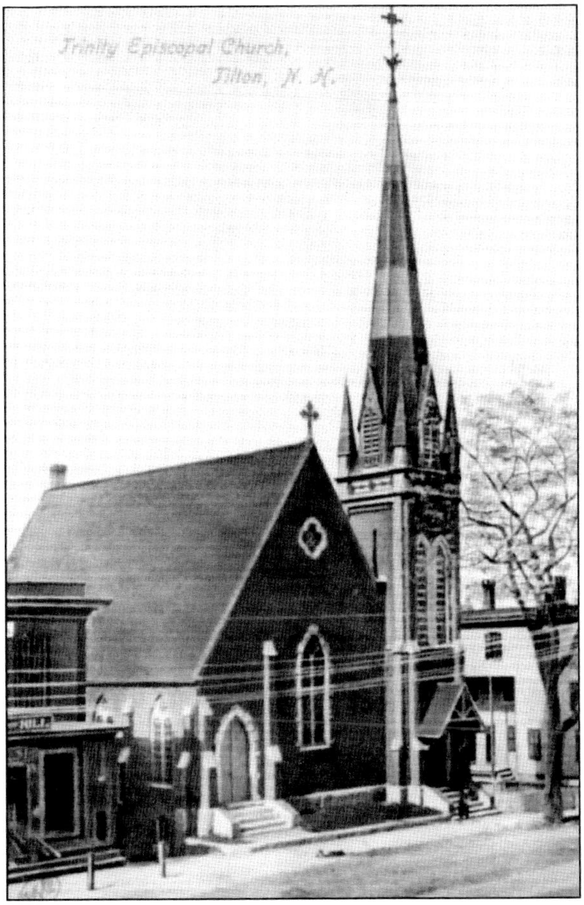

The Trinity Episcopal Church, like several Tilton churches, started in Northfield and then moved into Tilton. In 1861, the Episcopalian parish organized in Northfield as the Parish of Trinity Church, Sanbornton Bridge. In 1872, the parish bought land on the Tilton side of the river and erected a brick building on Main Street, which was opened on Easter Sunday 1873. A house lot next to the church was offered to and accepted by the parish in 1881. The spire was added as a gift from Abigail B. Tilton in 1883. This is considered by some to be the best surviving nineteenth century Gothic Revival church in Belknap County. The automobile accident below occurred on the house noted above. It involved a 1918 Nash Model 681 touring car (on the left) and a 1917 Model T Ford. (Above, courtesy of the Hall Memorial Library; below, courtesy of James and Elaine Lamanuzzi.)

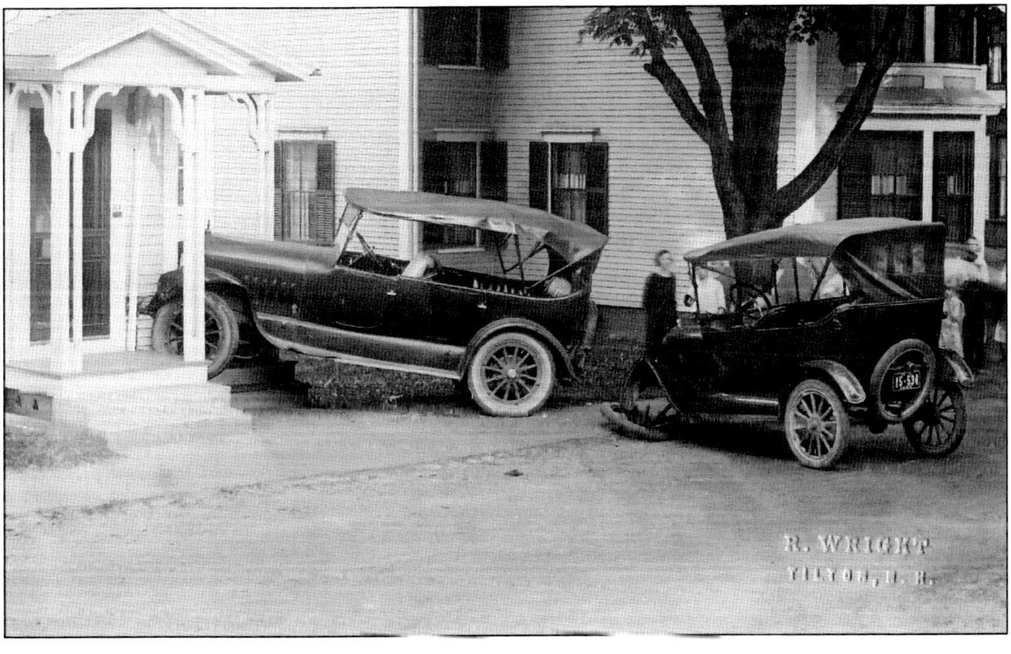

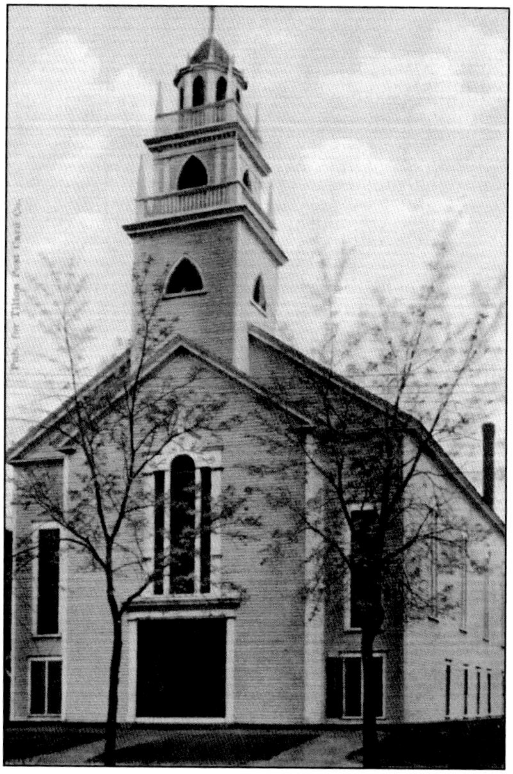

The history of the Northfield–Tilton Congregational Church in Tilton began in 1793 with the building of the first meetinghouse in Northfield. The church was formally organized in 1822. The first pastor, Reverend Liba Conant, was ordained the following year. In 1838, the congregation built its first house of worship in Sanbornton Bridge with the generous assistance of unidentified benefactors. (Courtesy of the Hall Memorial Library.)

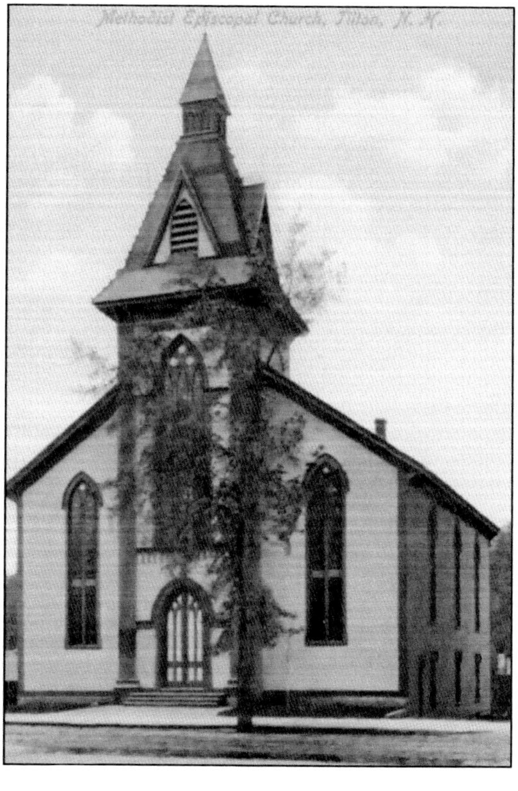

The Methodist Episcopal Church of Northfield and Tilton is the oldest religious congregation in our community. The church was formed on the Northfield side of the river in 1806 and remained there until 1857 when this new building was constructed on Main Street in Tilton. In 1880, during extensive repairs, the old tower was removed, and a new one was erected. (Courtesy of the Randall family.)

There were three Catholic families in Tilton when, in 1854, Reverend John Daly celebrated Mass in the home of Michael Ennis. In 1879, Reverend John Shackers offered monthly Mass at William Twombly's home. The first resident pastor, Reverend John Finen, began services in 1891 in the home of Joseph Twombly. On Christmas Day, 1894, Father Finen held the first Mass in the new Church of the Assumption. (Courtesy of the Hall Memorial Library.)

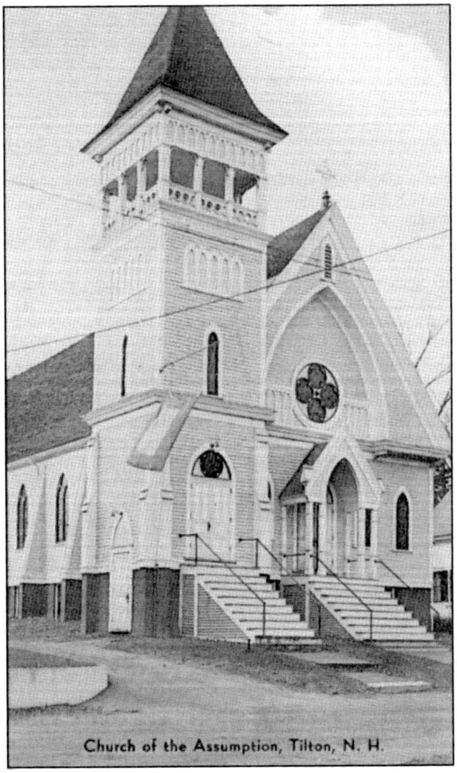
Church of the Assumption, Tilton, N. H.

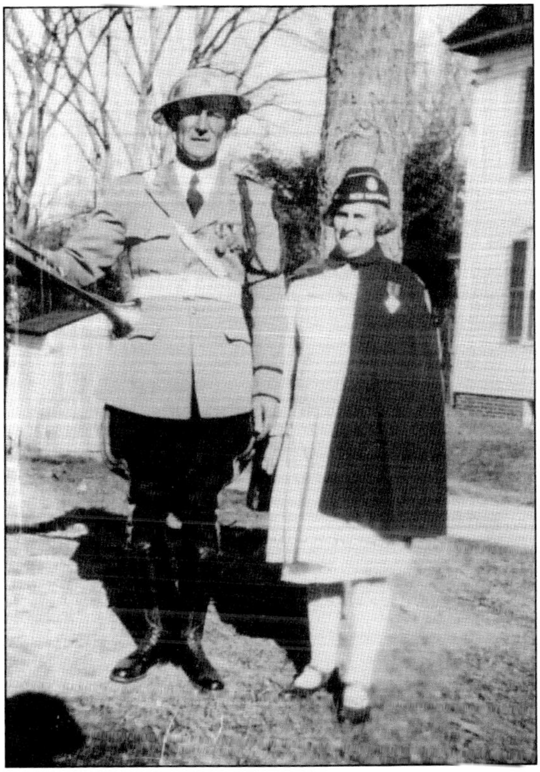

Henry and Eva Ketchum, seen here, were longtime members of the Whiteman–Davidson Post No. 49 of the American Legion and Auxiliary, as well as the Assumption Church Parish. They were very involved in charitable activities for these organizations. They raised a family of six in their home on High Street. Henry worked for the railroad and Eva was known for her cooking skills. (Courtesy of Sandra Gorman D'Amico.)

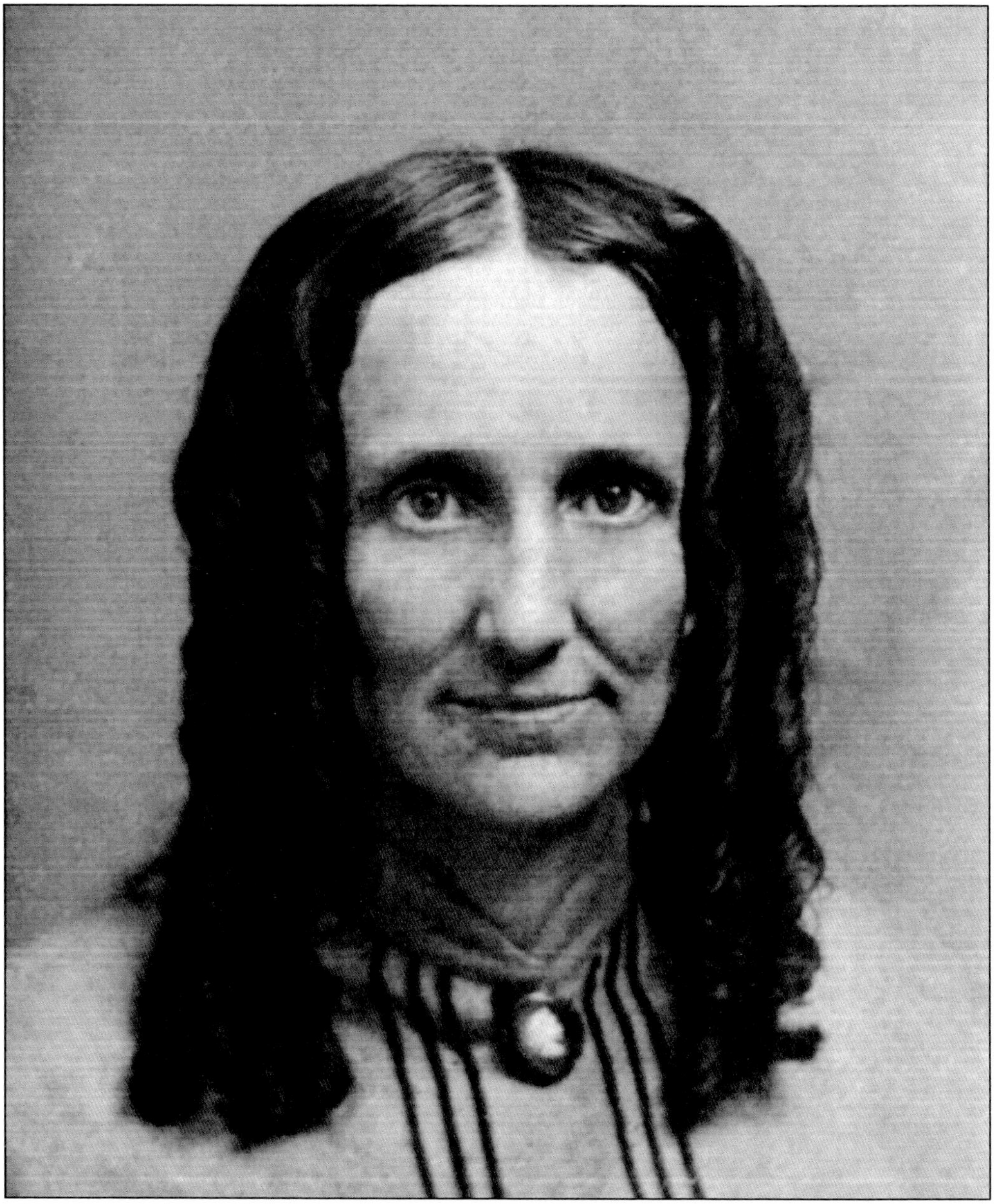

Mary Morse Baker was born in 1821 on a farm in Bow, New Hampshire. Her parents were Mark and Abigail Ambrose Baker. In 1836, her father moved the family to a farm in Sanbornton Bridge. Mary Baker has come to be known by the name of her third husband—Asa Gilbert Eddy. Mary Baker Eddy's first marriage was to George Washington Glover in 1843. Sadly, her husband died of yellow fever just six months after the marriage. She then moved back to her parents' farm, where her son, George W. Glover II, was born. In 1849, when Eddy's mother died, she and her father moved to the center of Sanbornton Bridge. When her father remarried a year later, Eddy's older sister, Abigail Tilton, offered her home as a place to stay. To help with her many trials and fragile health, Eddy relied on her study of the Bible and prayer for comfort and healing. She would go on to become the discoverer and founder of Christian Science. (Courtesy of the Longyear Museum, Chestnut Hill, Massachusetts.)

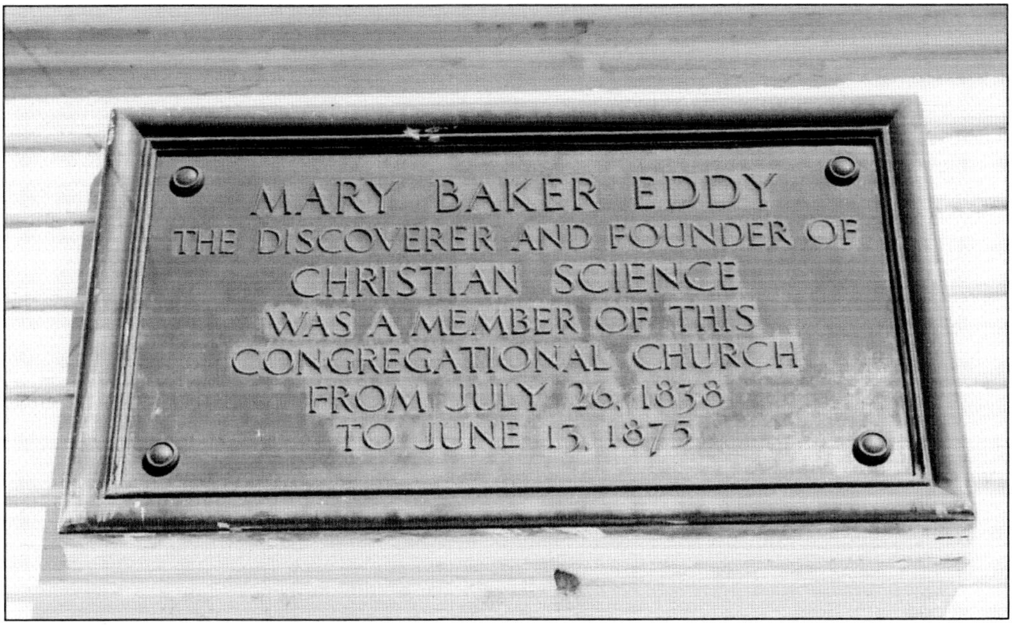

Mary Baker Eddy's parents were devout Congregationalists, and in 1838, the Bakers joined the Northfield and Sanbornton Bridge Congregational Church. In time, Eddy became a Sunday school teacher. The plaque on the front of the Northfield–Tilton Congregational Church states that Eddy was a member until 1875. By 1875, however, Eddy had become a Christian Scientist, and she made a formal withdrawal from the Congregational Church in that year. The home shown below was Eddy's last residence in Tilton. It was the home of Eddy's sister and brother-in-law, Abigail Tilton and Alexander Tilton (see page 100). Eddy lived there from 1851 to 1853, when she married Daniel Patterson and moved to Franklin, New Hampshire. (Above, photograph by Dennis Evans; below, courtesy of the Randall family.)

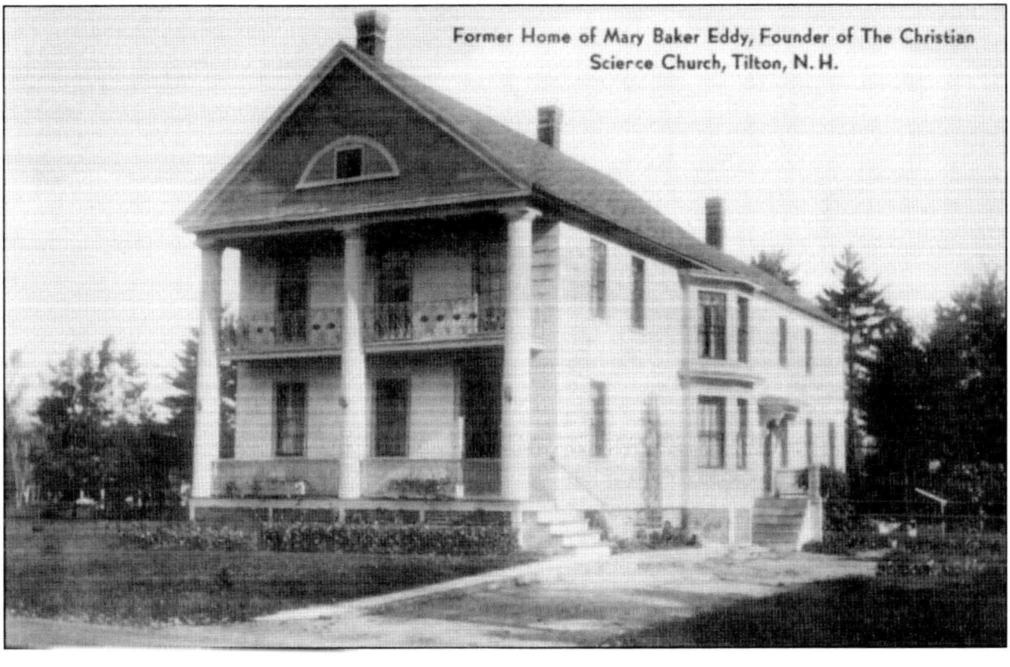

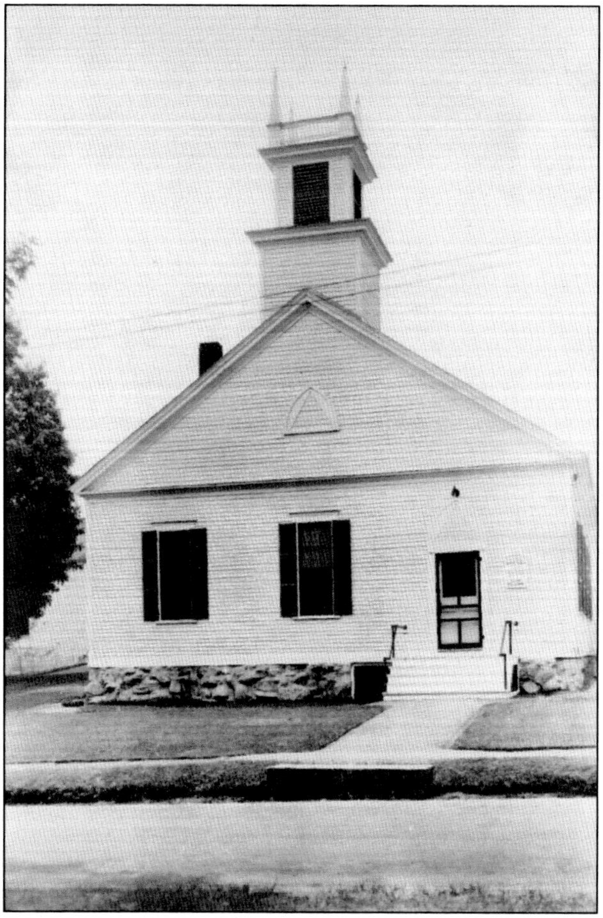

Originally organized in 1827, the Lochmere Baptist Church had a congregation of 11 men and 4 women. In subsequent years, the church was known as the Free United Brethren, the First Free Will Baptist Church of Sanbornton, and Union Bridge Free Will Baptist Church. The building shown here was constructed in the spring of 1834 and was turned to face the road in 1861, with a slight remodeling 15 years later. The chapel at the Soldiers' Home is shown below. This was an interdenominational house of worship for the residents, staff, and visitors. (Above, courtesy of Marjorie Rudolph; below, courtesy of the Randall family.)

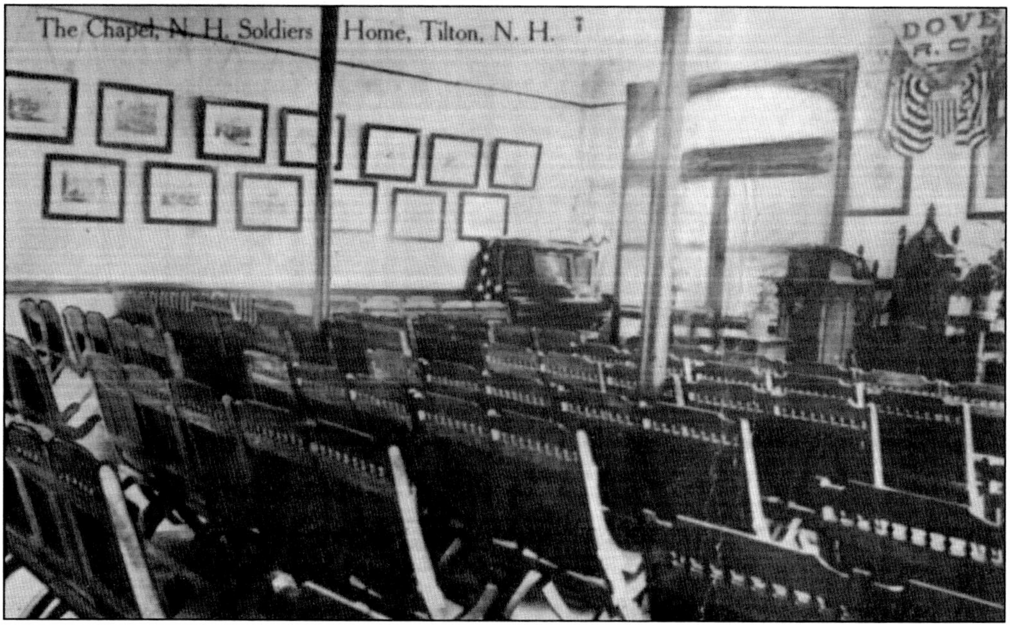

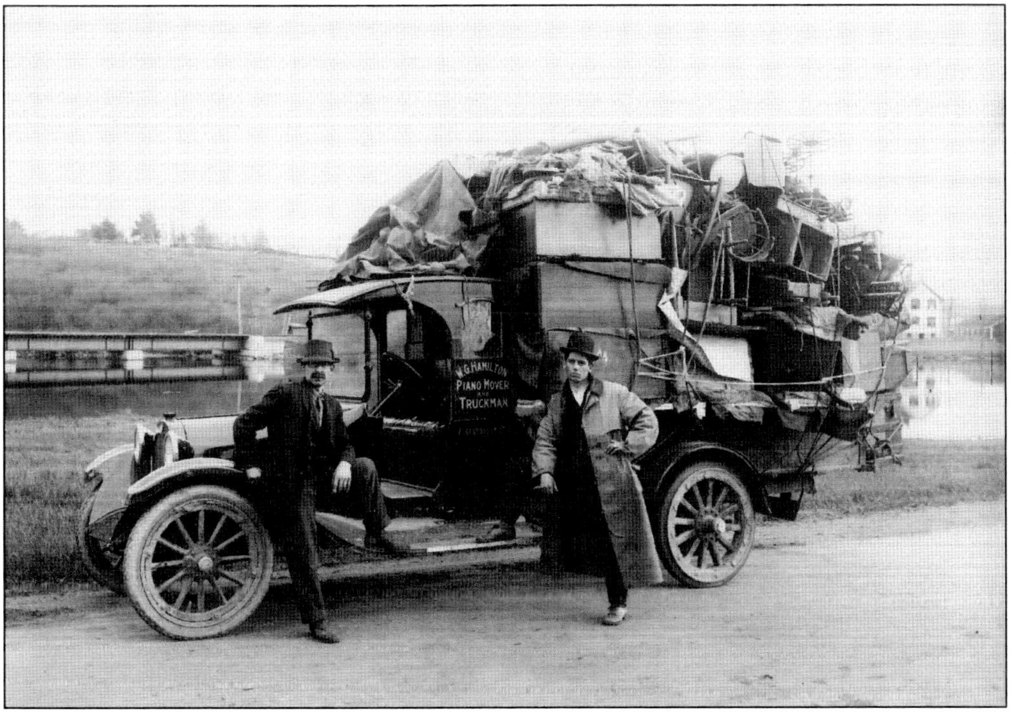

W.G. Hamilton Piano Movers and Trucking workers (above) from Laconia, New Hampshire, posed for this photograph of their packing prowess. It appears that the entire contents of a home are expertly balanced on this Dodge Brothers truck, which was manufactured between 1917 and 1920. Another form of transportation during this period was the 1918 Buick Express Wagon, shown below. These were being used as taxis between Franklin, Franklin Falls, and Tilton. Two men in the taxi on the right appear to be wearing World War I uniforms. (Above, courtesy of Tilton Town Hall; below, courtesy of the Randall family.)

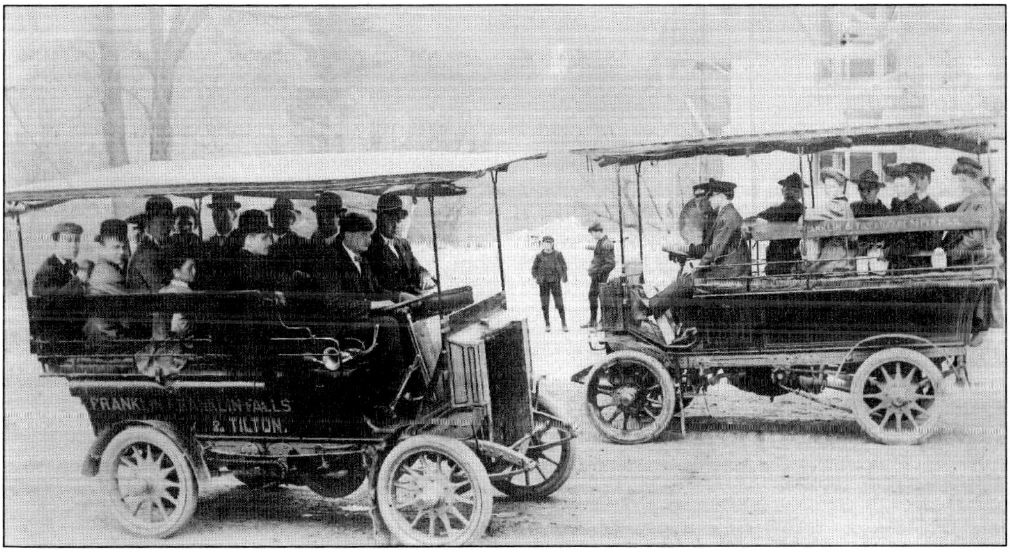